MAKING MIDDLE-CLASS MULTICULTURALISM
Immigration Bureaucrats and Policymaking
in Postwar Canada

‖‖‖‖‖‖‖‖‖‖‖‖‖‖‖‖‖‖‖‖
I0222984

In the 1950s and 1960s, immigration bureaucrats in the Department of Citizenship and Immigration played an important yet unacknowledged role in transforming Canada's immigration policy. In response to external economic and political pressures for change, high-level bureaucrats developed new admissions criteria gradually and experimentally while personally processing thousands of individual immigration cases per year.

Making Middle-Class Multiculturalism shows how bureaucrats' perceptions and judgments about the admissibility of individuals – in socioeconomic, racial, and moral terms – influenced the creation of formal admissions criteria for skilled workers and family immigrants that continue to shape immigration to Canada. A qualitative content analysis of archival documents, conducted through the theoretical lens of a cultural sociology of immigration policy, reveals that bureaucrats' interpretations of immigration files generated selection criteria emphasizing not just economic utility, but also middle-class traits and values such as wealth accumulation, educational attainment, entrepreneurial spirit, resourcefulness, and a strong work ethic. By making "middle-class multiculturalism" a demographic reality and basis of nation-building in Canada, these state actors created a much-admired approach to managing racial diversity that has nevertheless generated significant social inequalities.

JENNIFER ELRICK is an assistant professor in the Department of Sociology at McGill University.

MAKING MIDDLE-CLASS
MULTICULTURALISM

Immigration Bureaucrats and Policymaking in Postwar Canada

JENNIFER ELRICK

UNIVERSITY OF TORONTO PRESS
Toronto Buffalo London

© University of Toronto Press 2021
Toronto Buffalo London
utorontopress.com

ISBN 978-1-4875-2777-8 (cloth)   ISBN 978-1-4875-2780-8 (EPUB)
ISBN 978-1-4875-2778-5 (paper)   ISBN 978-1-4875-2779-2 (PDF)

Library and Archives Canada Cataloguing in Publication

Title: Making middle-class multiculturalism : immigration
bureaucrats and policymaking in postwar Canada / Jennifer Elrick.
Names: Elrick, Jennifer (Jennifer Margaret), author.
Identifiers: Canadiana (print) 20210303239 | Canadiana
(ebook) 20210303859 | ISBN 9781487527778 (hardcover) |
ISBN 9781487527785 (softcover) | ISBN 9781487527808 (EPUB) |
ISBN 9781487527792 (PDF)
Subjects: LCSH: Canada – Emigration and immigration – Government
policy – History – 20th century. | LCSH: Canada – Emigration and
immigration – History – 20th century. | LCSH: Canada – Emigration
and immigration – Social aspects – 20th century. |
LCSH: Multiculturalism – Canada – History – 20th century. |
LCSH: Middle class – Canada – History – 20th century.
Classification: LCC JV7233.E47 2021 | DDC 325.71–dc23

This book has been published with the help of a grant from the Federation
for the Humanities and Social Sciences, through the Awards to Scholarly
Publications Program, using funds provided by the Social Sciences and
Humanities Research Council of Canada.

University of Toronto Press acknowledges the financial assistance to its
publishing program of the Canada Council for the Arts and the Ontario Arts
Council, an agency of the Government of Ontario.

Canada Council   Conseil des Arts
for the Arts   du Canada

ONTARIO ARTS COUNCIL
CONSEIL DES ARTS DE L'ONTARIO
an Ontario government agency
un organisme du gouvernement de l'Ontario

Funded by the   Financé par le
Government   gouvernement
of Canada   du Canada

Canadä

For my parents, Robert and Sharon Elrick

Contents

Acknowledgments

Academia is a team sport, and I have had the good fortune to be a member of a very large and talented team. This team comprises a range of institutions and individuals, each of which has contributed in one way or another to the publication of this book.

Starting with the publication process, I would like to thank my editor at the University of Toronto Press (UTP), Daniel Quinlan, as well as his colleague Christine Robertson, for guiding me through the process of publishing a book for the first time. They were very patient and diligent in addressing my questions and concerns. The two anonymous external reviewers and a designated reader on the UTP academic board provided invaluable feedback that improved the manuscript immensely. Kristina Brousalis did an excellent job of reviewing the final proofs. Any remaining errors or omissions are, however, solely my responsibility.

At different stages of writing, Robert Elrick and Lisa Schincariol McMurtry read, and suggested substantial edits to, the manuscript. They improved its clarity and readability, with a view to making the final product more accessible to a general readership outside my academic field. If this book is relatively easy and enjoyable to read, it is in no small part due to them. Tim Elrick, a master of all software, recreated figures 2.1 and 5.1 from photos of archival records. Michelle Hopgood provided the excellent data visualizations in figures 2.2 and 2.3.

The evolving manuscript has benefited immeasurably from feedback from colleagues near and far. I am especially grateful to the following people for taking the time to engage with my work: Christopher Anderson, Saskia Bonjour, Irene Bloemraad, Antje Ellermann, Sunmin Kim, Anna Korteweg, Patricia Landolt, Mike Molloy, Merin Oleschuk, Mireille Paquet, Jeffrey Reitz, Vic Satzewich, Erik Schneiderhan,

Brendan Shanahan, Phil Triadafilopoulos, Roger Waldinger, and Elke Winter. Excellent research assistance was provided by Weeam Ben Rejeb, Maeanna Merrill, and Ayal Bark Cohen.

I wish to acknowledge and express my gratitude for research funding from the Social Sciences and Humanities Research Council of Canada (SSHRC), which has supported me at every stage of research and writing, through a CGS Doctoral Scholarship and an Insight Development Grant. This book has been published with the help of a grant from the Federation for the Humanities and Social Sciences, through the Awards to Scholarly Publications Program, using funds provided by SSHRC.

Finally, I would like to thank the following family members and friends for the love, support, and patience that made writing a book possible: Robert, Sharon, Tim, and Kieran Elrick; Gundel Fallenbacher and Lothar Almaschan; Nina and Norbert Kellner; Stephanie Natzer and Oliver Krause; Denica and Johannes Arendt; Salina Abji; Jup Bhasin and his mother, Mrs. Nicket Bhasin; Emily Laxer; Paulina Garcia Del Moral; Dave Hicks; Jennifer and Alec Delorme; Dina Brandt; Julia Clarke; and Marcella McIndoe.

Some material that appears in chapters 2 and 4 was published in the *Journal of Ethnic and Migration Studies* (Elrick 2020) and is used here with permission of the publisher.

MAKING MIDDLE-CLASS MULTICULTURALISM
Immigration Bureaucrats and Policymaking
in Postwar Canada

Chapter One

Introduction

In 1967, Canada introduced new criteria and procedures for selecting skilled immigrant workers and family members as permanent residents and future members of the Canadian nation. Until then, immigrant admissibility had been defined mainly in reference to national origins, and only individuals from European and Western Hemisphere countries were welcomed with open arms. From 1967 onwards, admissibility was defined in terms of individual traits, including human capital (e.g., education, occupational experience, and language ability) and social ties within Canada (primarily to family).[1] This kind of policy has become known as "universal" or "merit-based," because it is widely considered to be non-discriminatory, that is, open to anyone regardless of race, nationality, gender, or other ascribed group memberships.

Coupled with a new commitment to large annual immigrant quotas – equivalent to roughly 1 per cent of the Canadian population – this new policy markedly changed the demographic composition of Canada's immigrant population in the proceeding decades. Statistics Canada data on the distribution of the foreign-born population by region of birth show that, in 1971, almost 80 per cent of all immigrants to Canada had been born in the British Isles or Europe, while only 5 per cent and 1.4 per cent had been born in Asia[2] and Africa, respectively. In 2016, only 27.7 per cent of all immigrants reported being born in the British Isles or Europe, while 48.1 per cent were born in Asia and 8.5 per cent were born in Africa (Statistics Canada 2017a). Canada's "merit-based" immigration policy thus made multiculturalism a demographic fact in a country that had, for the previous hundred years, used racist[3] immigration policies to build a White settler state.

Canada was not the only settler colonial state to adopt this kind of merit-based immigrant selection policy in the postwar era. However, it did so relatively early, in a series of regulatory changes in 1962 and

1967 (when the "points system" was introduced), which were later anchored in law in the 1976 Immigration Act. By comparison, the move away from nationality-based selection in the United States and Australia – settler colonial states with similarly large-scale immigration programs – occurred slightly later and (in the case of the United States) was less far-reaching. Australia only abandoned its White Australia policy formally in 1973, although the entry of non-European immigrants was eased somewhat beginning in 1966 (Hawkins 1991). The Hart-Celler Act of 1965 officially ended racist national preferences in the United States, but this reform is considered to be more limited in scope than Canada's, given its focus on family reunification and legislators' beliefs that this focus would ultimately limit, rather than foster, inflows of non-European immigrants (Lee 2015; Wolgin 2013).

The relatively comprehensive nature of Canada's postwar merit-based immigration policy, and its comparatively early adoption, have made Canada an important case in a body of scholarship in political science and sociology that seeks to understand why countries in the Global North jettisoned their explicitly racist immigration policies when they did. The most widely accepted explanations point to a combination of macro-level (cultural, political) and meso-level (organizational) pressures (see, e.g., FitzGerald and Cook-Martín 2014; Joppke 2005b; Triadafilopoulos 2012). On the macro level, the horrors of the Holocaust, processes of decolonialization, and the adoption of human rights norms made political legitimacy on the world stage contingent on states' formal commitments to non-discrimination in immigration and other policy areas. These factors led to isomorphism in immigration policies across countries with otherwise dissimilar histories of immigration and immigration management. Building on this macro-level explanation, some scholars see meso-level institutional responses by different branches of the state as key to explaining Canada's postwar policy change. For example, FitzGerald and Cook-Martín (2014) highlight the Canadian government's overarching foreign policy ambitions within the international relations context that emerged after the Second World War. From this point of view, Canada's drive to become a middle power among Western liberal-democratic states could not be realized without demonstrating moral legitimacy by abandoning its racially discriminatory immigration policy.

In contrast, micro-level factors, like the actions of high-level immigration bureaucrats, have generally been depicted as a barrier to policy change. Using archival records of policy discussions within Canada's Department of Citizenship and Immigration (commonly referred to as the Department), scholars document how these state actors resisted and delayed formal policy changes and attempted to maintain racially exclusionary selection practices by moving them "behind the scenes" to policy implementation (e.g., FitzGerald and Cook-Martín 2014; Triadafilopoulos 2012). Indeed, many scholars assert that the merit-based admissions policy established in Canada in 1967 has continued to facilitate racist exclusion, covertly, through discretionary implementation practices (see, e.g., Aiken 2007; Sharma 2006).

Given the potential implications of this depiction of bureaucratic implementation practices for racialized inequality under Canadian immigration policy, it is noteworthy that these practices themselves have not featured prominently in empirical analyses of the postwar emergence of merit-based immigration policies (Fox 2015; Motomura 2015). This absence persists despite the demonstrated effect of immigration policy implementation on shaping immigrant inclusion and exclusion along the lines of race, gender, and social class (see, e.g., Wray 2009; Eggebø 2013). Additionally, in the historical Canadian case, scholars like Hawkins (1988) have documented how important the actions of high-level immigration bureaucrats were, not just in formulating policy but also in their discretionary adjudication of large numbers of immigration cases. There is thus reason to believe that inattention to micro-level implementation practices has left the historiography of the postwar adoption of universal immigration policies, in Canada and elsewhere, incomplete.

This book takes the novel step of centring the interpretive practices of high-level immigration bureaucrats in the historiography of postwar immigration policy change in Canada. The following case helps to illustrate why this undertaking is necessary.

A Case in Point

In 1959, a Chinese-Canadian couple in Victoria, British Columbia, wrote to the Department of Citizenship and Immigration to seek admission to Canada for two Chinese children residing in China, whom they wished to adopt. On 9 February of that year, Director of Immigration C.E.S. Smith wrote a memo to Deputy Minister of Citizenship and Immigration Laval Fortier outlining the case and recommending it be approved.[4] Clearly, this couple was in need of help and worthy of the Department's consideration. In the eyes of the Department, Chinese people were known to place great importance on family life. This Chinese-Canadian woman was medically certified as unable to bear children, and, although the province's Department of Welfare had declared the couple to be suitable adoptive parents, adoption authorities could not locate any "pure Chinese children" in the province for the couple to adopt. The couple were of more than sufficient means to support a family: the man was not only a partner in a wholesale produce business but also had substantial financial assets. Moreover, as Smith pointed out, a nearly identical case had already been approved by the Department in late 1958 and an order-in-council was subsequently issued for the admission of two Chinese children for adoption. (Orders-in-council are legislative instruments that are devised and put into effect by cabinet without parliamentary or judiciary control.) The deputy minister followed his colleague's recommendation, approving the application two days later and adding the following hand-written comment in the margin of the original memo: "We should note this type of case. It is already two cases in six months."

For those familiar with Canadian immigration policy, three elements make this exchange appear exceptional at first glance. The first is the date. Provisions for the admission of adopted children and children to be adopted would not enter the immigration regulations until 1967, but this application for admission, and its approval, took place almost ten years in advance of that formal policy change.

The second unusual aspect is the racial group membership of the persons involved. Historically, Chinese people have faced among the strongest levels of direct and indirect racial discrimination aimed at any immigrant group under Canadian immigration policy. From 1923 to 1947, the Chinese Immigration Act had made entry to Canada so restrictive for that group that only fifteen Chinese immigrants were admitted during that period (Kelley and Trebilcock 2010, 204). The order-in-council admission of Chinese children for adoption by Chinese-origin parents in Canada is remarkably accommodating towards an historically excluded group, given the strong history of racist exclusion and the documented reluctance within the Department to abandon the racist status quo.

The third element that stands out is the people deciding the case and the admissions procedure they used. Typically, in Canada and elsewhere, the processing of applications for admission under immigration laws falls to lower-level civil servants. These are the people Lipsky ([1980] 2010) calls "street-level bureaucrats," due to their direct interactions with members of the general public. Formally, there is a division of labour between higher-level bureaucrats, who are involved in developing policies and their accompanying implementation instructions, and street-level bureaucrats, who interpret and apply such instructions to those designated as their clients. But in the case of the Chinese-origin couple in Victoria, it is the deputy minister and director of immigration – two of the highest-level actors in the Department – who are adjudicating an immigration case. Moreover, they are not applying existing laws but using a legislative instrument (an order-in-council) to override them altogether. Furthermore, the memo suggests that this is not an isolated occurrence.

The three seemingly anomalous aspects of this case represent an empirical puzzle that challenges the established historiography of postwar immigration policy change in Canada. According to this historiography, immigration bureaucrats resisted external pressures to make immigration policy more racially inclusive, ultimately delaying policy change. Yet, in this case, these state actors are moving ahead of policy, admitting Chinese-origin immigrants that they were under no obligation to even consider.

This book addresses the empirical puzzle presented by the 1959 case and others like it. In doing so, it offers answers to the following research questions. What was the scope of the implementation (case processing) practices engaged in by high-level immigration bureaucrats? What role did these practices play in the process of devising Canada's new merit-based immigration policy? Finally, what did these practices mean for the substance of the new policy, particularly the evolution of the role of race in defining immigrant admissibility?

Canadian Immigration Bureaucrats and the Making of Middle-Class Multiculturalism

The answers to the three questions posed above foreshadow the arguments put forward in this book. First, the scope of case-processing activities engaged in by high-level immigration bureaucrats (i.e., the deputy minister and high-ranking civil servants) in the Department of Citizenship and Immigration was broad and significant in legal, numeric, and substantive terms. Legally, the 1952 Immigration Act (like others that preceded it) gave the Minister of Citizenship and Immigration the power to use orders-in-council to admit or exclude any group or individual notwithstanding the Immigration Act and regulations. They could do this in reference to individual cases and by creating immigration regulations that institutionalized immigrant selection principles more broadly, without parliamentary oversight. In terms of volume, the minister, with the aid of the deputy minister, the head of the Immigration Branch of the Department of Citizenship and Immigration, and others adjudicated thousands of individual cases a year from the early 1950s onward. These were forwarded to the deputy minister's office by lawyers, community organizations, or lower-level bureaucrats who were unclear on how to interpret some of the vague language of Canadian immigration policy. Assessing these individual cases required interpreting who the individual applicants in question were – in reference to individual traits and ascribed membership in racial and other social groups – and whether or not they should be considered admissible. Since immigration policies are an aspect of nation-building (Zolberg 2006), the case-processing activities of immigration bureaucrats contributed, cumulatively, to a rearticulation of Canadian national identity. Because the high-level immigration bureaucrats adjudicating these cases could also formulate policy, the interpretations of admissibility they generated subsequently became institutionalized in the 1967 immigration regulations, amplifying their effect over time.

Second, high-level immigration bureaucrats were admitting individuals for whom there were no provisions in immigration law, via order-in-council, as a form of low-risk policy experimentation that would subsequently open the door to a more systemic policy shift. Beyond adopted children, they experimented with admitting a range of skilled workers and family members from non-European, non-Western Hemisphere origin countries. It was clear to them that domestic and international pressures to universalize immigrant admissions would eventually lead to the legal inclusion of "undesirable" racial groups like the Chinese in the 1959 adoption case. Since policy change was inevitable, high-level bureaucrats became primarily concerned about *who precisely* to admit and *how* to manage change in the nation's racial composition.

Third, by experimenting with admitting individuals of diverse origins, immigration bureaucrats gradually recognized the potential to create multicultural social cohesion on the basis of a new and shared middle-class national identity. In characterizing this emergent identity as "middle class," I draw on Lamont's (1992) description of the term as denoting membership in a group defined in socio-economic terms (e.g., wealth, occupational prestige); cultural terms (e.g., education, manners); and especially moral terms. While the range of moral distinctions employed by social actors to classify themselves and others as middle class varies over time and across national contexts, Lamont (1992, 34–5) highlights a range of relatively stable moral distinctions identified by social theorists, going as far back as the mid-Victorian era, including the following: ambition, dependability, self-reliance, discipline, being a patriotic and responsible citizen, perseverance, audacity, self-mastery, long-term planning, and community-mindedness. Hence the focus, in the adjudication of the Chinese-origin couple's case, on their wealth, entrepreneurship, and community standing can be read as immigration bureaucrats' attentiveness to traits denoting middle-class membership. Lamont (1992, 11) and other cultural sociologists are careful to note that the distinctions people use to draw boundaries between groups are not created "from scratch" by social actors but are rooted in pre-existing repertoires that actors can draw on creatively. As this book shows, this holds true for the case adjudication practices of Canadian immigration bureaucrats, whose moral terminology for identifying admissible immigrants from non-European and non-Western Hemisphere countries mirrored that used to describe the qualities that made European-origin groups desirable and admissible. Over the course of the postwar era, immigration bureaucrats came to see the management of multicultural demographics along middle-class lines as a means of avoiding the racialized poverty and strife that they perceived as resulting from immigration mismanagement in the United States and the United Kingdom. While immigration bureaucrats may have recognized its potential to make Canada a multicultural trailblazer, a "striking example to the world,"[5] this middle-class multicultural vision of nation-building has not been without consequences for social stratification.

In sum, taking the micro-level practices of immigration bureaucrats – particularly case processing – into account changes our understanding of how these state actors shaped not only Canada's universal immigration policy but also the multiculturalism that emerged in its wake. Canada's new postwar selection criteria for skilled immigrants and their family members did not *replace* selection based on race, as the standard argument goes. Instead, the selection criteria evolved in the course of efforts to *manage* racial diversity at the intersection of social class. Postwar immigration bureaucrats created a policy that was not "universal," that is, accessible to anyone regardless of his/her social group memberships, but *intersectional*. The term "intersectional" refers here to "the critical insight that race, class, gender, sexuality, ethnicity, nation, ability, and age operate not as unitary, mutually exclusive entities, but as reciprocally constructing phenomena that in turn shape complex social inequalities" (Collins 2015, 2). The implication of intersectionality for immigration policy is that it, like other legal and administrative constructs that purport to be neutral and non-discriminatory, is actually a means of defining the nation state in reference to multiple, overlapping social group ascriptions, including race, class, and gender (Spade 2013). Canada's multiculturalism is a middle-class multiculturalism, and it was made that way by the state actors tasked with revising immigration policy in the mid-twentieth century. By overlooking the micro-level, interpretive practices of immigration policymakers, we have missed an opportunity to give due consideration to what the middle-class character of Canadian multiculturalism means for debates about the kinds of social inequalities associated with this "Canadian model."

Immigration Bureaucrats, Implementation, and Policymaking: Towards a Cultural Sociology of Immigration Policy

Looking beyond the Canadian historical case, this book advances state-centric approaches to understanding immigration policymaking, specifically ones that theorize the role of immigration bureaucrats in shaping policymaking processes and their substantive outcomes. It does so by combining insights from scholarship on what are often seen as two separate areas of concern: immigration policy formulation and implementation.

The first line of investigation that this book builds on considers how immigration bureaucrats act as policymakers, that is, how individuals in public administration formulate policies in response to directives from elected lawmakers. Following broader developments in public administration (e.g., Kaufman 2001; Page and Jenkins 2005), scholarly debates in this area tend to look at how mid- and high-level individuals within the civil service carry out the work of *policy formulation*. Policy formulation refers to the stage of the policymaking process in which important decisions about policy design, monitoring activities, the use of expert knowledge, writing, consultations and other aspects of the process are performed (Paquet 2019, 168).

Recent contributions to this literature emphasize how immigration bureaucrats at different levels of the organizational hierarchy influence policy formulation. Some scholars show how higher-level immigration bureaucrats – "state managers" in federal agencies like the Immigration and Naturalization Service (INS) in the United States (Calavita 2010) or "policy entrepreneurs" in provincial governments in Canada (Paquet 2015) – shape policies in line with their own career and organizational interests. Other scholars have shown that high-level bureaucrats shape policy formulation by containing political pressures in their policymaking venues (Boucher 2013) or assert moral obligations and norms (Bonjour 2011). Moving down the organizational hierarchy, scholars point to a range of interpretive practices that occur within immigration bureaucracies and thereby shape policy formulation. These include problem definition and consensus building (Paquet 2019); the generation and use of research and expert knowledge to legitimize claims to resources, jurisdictions, and authority, and to substantiate organizational interests (Boswell 2009); and interpretive and cognitive work aimed at balancing ideas and beliefs about appropriate policy interventions with mandates from elected officials and public expectations (Slaven and Boswell 2019). In sum, this line of scholarship shows that high- and mid-level immigration bureaucrats are responsible for a lot of "what happens after an election and before policy implementation" (Paquet 2019, 168). One conclusion to be drawn from this is that it is impossible to understand the policy formulation process and its outcomes (e.g., laws, regulations, policy statements) fully without examining the actions of immigration bureaucrats.

The second line of investigation this book builds on examines how lower-level immigration bureaucrats shape the substantive content of immigration policies *after these have been formulated*, through implementation practices in areas like deportation, border control, and family/marriage migration. Legal scholars of immigration policy note that the "gap between law on the books and law in action is filled by countless government decisions that reflect the exercise of discretion" (Motomura 2014, 4). Building on Lipsky's ([1980] 2010) influential study of "street-level" bureaucrats, scholarship on immigration policy implementation shows how these discretionary decisions shape the effects of immigration laws and regulations. The vague language and discretion built into government policies mean that implementing bureaucrats must develop cognitive routines (i.e., techniques for applying schematically structured information) to interpreting the meaning of complex concepts in an efficient manner. They do so in the context of organizational constraints such as high caseloads and processing targets. In turn, these cognitive routines come to define the very content of policy itself. For example, frontline immigration bureaucrats are given the task of interpreting, and ultimately defining, key concepts such as "family," "marriage," and "highly skilled" in the relational context of interactions with applicants (see, e.g., Bhabha 2006; Bouchard and Carroll 2002; Kim 2011; Eggebø 2013; Friedman 2010; Gilboy 1991; Pellander 2015; Pratt 2005; Satzewich 2015; Scheel and Gutekunst 2019).

This book brings together these two strands of scholarship – on immigration policy formulation and implementation – by illustrating how *implementation can be part of policy formulation*. Kang (2017) has taken a step towards documenting this kind of "bottom up" dynamic in the United States, focusing on the formulation of internal regulations. However, she does not address the role of case processing, which immigration policy implementation scholarship has shown to be important for shaping the substance of immigration policies. In contrast, this book foregrounds case processing as a theoretically and empirically important aspect of immigration bureaucrats' contribution to policy formulation from the bottom up.

A unique feature of the historical Canadian case that facilitates this book's theoretical and empirical contribution to immigration policy scholarship is the dual function of high-level immigration bureaucrats.[6] Canadian immigration acts have historically given the minister and those advising him/her vast discretionary powers to admit/exclude individuals and groups, and to change the immigration regulations that define admissions criteria, using the order-in-council instrument. As Knowles (1997, 138) describes it, orders-in-council have not just been a means of flexibly interpreting immigration policy (in individual cases); rather, they have allowed immigration bureaucrats to make "fundamental changes" to that policy. Both the 1962 and 1967 immigration regulations that introduced universal skilled worker and family admissions, respectively, were passed by order-in-council, without parliamentary oversight. The fact that implementation and policy formulation were legally part of the job descriptions of high-ranking bureaucrats throughout the period under consideration means that the case can illustrate even more explicitly the link between these two bureaucratic activities.

The insight that immigration policy implementation can inform immigration policy formulation is important not just for understanding the role of immigration bureaucrats in policymaking *processes* but also for understanding the *substance* of the policies they help create. This is particularly important when the substance is not explicitly articulated in written laws and regulations but relegated to vague terminology that is further subject to interpretive practices at the implementation stage. Merit-based immigration policies like the one developed by Canada in the postwar era are widely understood to be neutral selection frameworks that apply to individuals irrespective of ascribed social group memberships like race, class, and gender (Joppke 2005a). For example, in the case of skilled workers, "merit" is considered to be a term that denotes economic utility, which can be achieved by anyone with the appropriate qualifications. However, the present study shows that the interpretive practices of immigration bureaucrats, which generated selection criteria later institutionalized in formal policies, were about managing race along class lines: not just in terms of economic position and utility but also in terms of moral assessments of traits that cultural sociologists like Lamont (1992) see as denoting middle-class status. This middle-class valence is suggested in the wording "personal assessment" criterion under the 1967 "points system," which officially comprises middle-class attributes like "adaptability, motivation, initiative, resourcefulness and other similar qualities" as determined by a visa officer's "judgment of the personal suitability of the applicant and his family." However, as chapters 4 and 5 show, this valence is clearly visible in the cumulative assessments of individual cases of skilled workers and family members, which generated these and other selection criteria that were subsequently institutionalized in the immigration regulations.

The argument that economic and cultural assessments are at the heart of nation-building instruments like immigration policies is not new. Zolberg (1999) was among the first to theorize the existence of economic and cultural "axes" in immigration policymaking. This book builds on work by Elrick and Winter (2018), Ellermann (2019), Bonjour and Duyvendak (2018), and others in highlighting how economic, cultural, and moral assessments overlap in immigration policy to define admissibility in facially neutral ways that can have differential outcomes for immigrants along the lines of race, gender, and class. It also builds on studies of immigration policy implementation that show how notions of moral deservingness influence case decisions in ways that can negate legal definitions of immigrant admissibility (see, e.g., Chauvin and Garcés-Mascareñas 2014; Ellermann 2009). The book's contribution here is twofold. It shows how these overlapping economic, cultural, and moral assessments can emerge during the policy formulation process and become institutionalized in immigration policies. It also shows how interpretive practices in the context of policy formulation can serve as a means of experimenting with – and paving the way for – paradigmatic changes in how immigrant admissibility is defined.

Theoretically, this book proposes a new framework for uniting insights from the literatures on state-centred theories of immigration policy formulation and immigration policy implementation. This framework is designed to account for how culturally informed interpretive practices and meaning-making in immigration case processing affect policy formulation. This "cultural sociology of immigration policy" draws on scholarship in the areas of cultural sociology and discursive intuitionism (e.g., Carstensen 2015; Schmidt 2010; Steensland 2006) that foregrounds the role of culture and meaning-making in producing public policies outside the domain of immigration. This work posits that culturally informed notions of who people are influence how state actors conceptualize both the policies they create and how those policies are applied – or not – to different types of individuals and groups. In foregrounding four mechanisms whereby interpretive implementation practices affect the process and outcomes of immigration policymaking, the framework presented here provides a tool for comparing and contrasting empirical findings in the historical Canadian case with those from other national contexts and/or time periods.

Focusing on Overlooked Archival Data

The empirical findings and arguments presented in this book are based on an application of the cultural sociology of immigration policy approach to a qualitative content analysis of both familiar and over-looked archival data. While many existing historical accounts of the postwar emergence of universal immigration policies in Canada and other Global North countries draw on a range of archival records from immigration bureaucracies, this book uniquely includes archi-val records of implementation practices. Data for this book comprise archival records from the Department of Citizenship and Immigra-tion for the period 1952 to 1967, pertaining both to general policy dis-cussions and policy implementation. While details are discussed in the Methodological Appendix, it is worth mentioning here that these data included a range of documents, from draft versions of immi-gration policy (speeches, reports, legislation, etc.) to correspondence regarding: (1) how to interpret general statements of political purpose made by elected politicians; (2) how to formulate written regulations; (3) descriptions of, and thoughts on, individual immigration applica-tions referred to the minister and his/her advisers for admission via order-in-council; (4) deportation appeals; and (5) demands made on the Department of Citizenship and Immigration by other Canadian government departments, representatives of other governments, and organized interests (particularly groups representing particular racial/ ethnic communities).

The analysis presented here focuses on three important sites of dis-cretion in immigration policy implementation. The first is the vague language in which selection principles were formulated in Canadian immigration law and regulations (e.g., "merit," "interests," "suitabil-ity"), and which required interpretation on the part of implementing bureaucrats applying those laws and regulations to particular cases. The second comprises summaries and discussions of admissions that took place outside the scope of provisions in immigration law, via an order-in-council. The third is the consideration of deportation appeals, another area in which immigration law gave full discretion to the minister and his/her advisers within the Department to decide whether someone could remain in the country, irrespective of immigration law violations. The second and third sites – admissions and deportations – are two sides of the same coin. Both are about deciding who may or may not become part of the national collective. Including both is important, due to the centrality of race to immigration policy change in the postwar era. Immigrants from non-European, non-Western Hemisphere countries were overrepresented in order-in-council admissions, while immigrants from European, Western Hemisphere countries were overrepresented in deportation appeals. Including both therefore gives a more complete picture of how interpretations of race, vis-à-vis admissibility, evolved in the context of case processing. Overall, this book shows that the inclusion of data pertaining to all three sites of discretionary practices provides invaluable insights into how the day-to-day interpretive practices of high-level bureaucrats fundamentally affected the postwar policy formulation process and its outcomes.

Overview of the Book

Chapter 2 introduces the theoretical and empirical case for seeing the interpretive practices of high-level immigration bureaucrats as an important component of immigration policy formulation in postwar Canada. It begins by introducing the reader to the Department of Citizenship and Immigration and outlining the legal and organizational factors that made implementation practices a powerful policy tool in the hands of high-level immigration bureaucrats. It then proceeds to consider the standard historiography of immigration policy change in Canada in the 1950s and 1960s. This historiography emphasizes macro-level and meso-level pressures for policy change (e.g., shifting global norms, economic development, organized domestic interests) and depicts immigration bureaucrats as mainly resistant to change. Finally, the chapter pivots to foregrounding the perspective of high-level bureaucrats as they faced the dual challenge of transforming Canada's immigration policy while managing daily operations, which included processing individual immigration cases. It concludes with an overview of the scope and scale of these case-processing activities (i.e., order-in-council admissions and deportation appeals). These activities, it is argued, represent empirical evidence that does not fit with existing accounts of postwar immigration policy formulation in Canada. They shift the timeline according to which skilled workers and extended family members from non-European and non-Western Hemisphere countries were permitted to immigrate to Canada in larger numbers. They also show that high-level immigration bureaucrats cannot be depicted as simply continuing with the kind of systematic, behind-the-scenes racial exclusion via implementation that they engaged in prior to, and during, the Second World War. This empirical challenge suggests the need to adjust existing theories to better account for the role of micro-level implementation practices in immigration policy formulation, a task that is taken up in the following chapter.

Chapter 3 situates the book's narrow focus on the historical Canadian case within the context of two broader scholarly concerns. The first is with the evolving nature of race as a social distinction used by states in nation-building and population management. In the period under consideration, Canada and other states were experiencing a fundamental shift in widely held ideas about race, away from biological racialism toward the notion of race as a social construct. The second is about the function of race and other social group distinctions in universal, merit-based immigration policies that emerged in Canada and elsewhere in the postwar era. The chapter argues that, in both sets of debates, analytical emphasis has been placed on macro- and meso-level impulses for ideational change, while micro-level mechanisms of change operating within states have received less attention. It furthermore argues that inattention to the micro level in these debates represents a missed opportunity to examine two things. One is the finer-grained distinctions built into states' ideas about the place of race in nation-building. The other is the extent to which symbolic distinctions produce socially stratified material outcomes in the course of implementation. When viewed through an appropriate theoretical lens, immigration policy formulation, including implementation, can serve as a useful object of study for addressing these broader theoretical concerns about states' constructions of race within nation-building and the effects of those constructions.

The chapter subsequently builds on existing theories of immigration policy formulation and studies of immigration policy implementation to construct such a theoretical lens: a cultural sociology of immigration policy. This lens allows implementation practices to be conceptualized as part of immigration policy formulation, in a way that foregrounds the role of interpretive meaning-making undertaken by state actors. It draws analytical attention to four mechanisms that work together to influence the policy formulation process and its outcomes. The first is the presence of cultural repertoires, which contain ideas, values and understandings shared across a given cultural space, and which inform immigration bureaucrats' perceptions of immigrants. The second is the boundary work conducted by immigration bureaucrats in reference to those cultural repertoires. Boundary work denotes the interpretive process through which immigration bureaucrats distinguish between admissible and inadmissible individuals and groups in concrete economic, racial, moral, and other terms. The third mechanism is idea "recasting," which refers to the process whereby pre-existing elements of an idea (e.g., race) can be reprioritized in the course of boundary work. The fourth and final mechanism is the institutionalization of the cumulative results of boundary work conducted during policy formulation. This includes, for example, its codification in immigration laws, regulations, and implementation guidelines. The chapter concludes with an overview of how a reading of archival materials pertaining to immigration bureaucrats' policy formulation activities (especially case processing), through the lens of a cultural sociology of immigration policy, changes our understanding of the role these state actors played in the creation of Canada's universal immigration policy as well as our understanding of that policy itself.

Chapter 4 examines in detail how micro-level bureaucratic practices paved the way for, and shaped the content of, new selection criteria for immigrant skilled workers. Since "merit" is a central concept in the evolution of skilled worker policy, the chapter starts by examining the assumption that this term has come to denote deservingness in relation to human capital and economic utility. It also situates the chapter in reference to existing scholarship on immigration policy in the historical Canadian case, which depicts "merit" as a tool used to exclude non-White immigrants. Against this backdrop, the chapter offers an analysis of order-in-council admissions and deportation appeals through the lens of a cultural sociology of immigration policy, in order to show how immigration bureaucrats' interpretations of "merit," "race," and "admissibility" evolved as they created Canada's universal immigration policy.

The analysis reveals that "merit" and other discretionary concepts were used by high-level immigration bureaucrats to experiment with increasing racial diversity in skilled worker admissions. Drawing on elements of the Canadian national cultural repertoire, immigration bureaucrats perceived "merit" in terms of instrumental human-capital indicators, like education and occupation, as well as moral and status-oriented evaluations of individuals' economic, social, and cultural capital. In other words, it was not just the possession of certain qualifications that made immigrants "meritorious." Culturally valued middle-class qualities like entrepreneurial spirit, industriousness, thrift, reliability, and social responsibility were valued alongside education, occupational status, and wealth. At the same time, the Canadian national cultural repertoire allowed immigration bureaucrats to conceptualize "race" as a bifurcated idea denoting both biological traits and a group's socio-economic position in the global economic and political order. In conducting boundary work around the admissibility of racially diverse skilled workers, this idea became "recast," to emphasize its socio-economic element, making middle-class socio-economic, cultural, and moral traits the perceived common ground for admitting immigrants from diverse origins. During this process, individual-level and group-level admissibility diverged. In the case of immigrants from non-European, non-Western Hemisphere countries, individuals' perceived class and status compensated for their group-level racial inadmissibility, leading to inclusion. Likewise, the group-level admissibility of immigrants from European and Western Hemisphere countries became attenuated by individual-level assessments of class and status, leading to exclusion. Finally, the chapter shows how the cumulative results of this boundary work became institutionalized in the "points system" for skilled workers in the 1967 immigration regulations.

Chapter 5 focuses on the generative role of immigration bureaucrats' interpretive practices in establishing new and universal categories for family immigrants. Since family immigration policies and policy implementation in that area are most commonly depicted as sites of intersectional (primarily racial and gendered) exclusion, the chapter begins by situating the historical Canadian case within scholarship on this topic. It highlights the potential contribution to be made by expanding these intersectional analyses to include perceptions of social class, defined as both market position and socio-economic status, which the previous chapter had revealed as central to the formulation of Canada's universal immigration policy for skilled workers.

The chapter then illustrates how high-level immigration bureaucrats' experimentation with admissions practices universalized family immigration policy. It focuses on three cases: Asian fiancé(e)s, adopted children, and the sponsored dependent/nominated relative distinction in general family admissions. In all three cases, immigration bureaucrats drew on normative ideas about family in the course of boundary work around family admissions, in ways that resulted in increased racial inclusion. They also drew on the bifurcated notion of race present in the Canadian national cultural repertoire, "recasting" it to emphasize class and status in their discussions of family immigrants. This resulted in the racialization of "the immigrant family" as a racially diverse status group that was fundamentally inadmissible in terms of economic utility and socio-economic status. As individual-level admissibility became decoupled from group-level family inadmissibility, immigration bureaucrats experimented with selection procedures for admitting family members whose class and status made them compatible with the emergent middle-class Canadian nation. These selection procedures were subsequently institutionalized in the 1967 immigration regulations.

Finally, chapter 6 offers a summary of the book's main arguments and contributions as well as reflections on the potential long-term material and symbolic implications of the middle-class multiculturalism created by Canadian immigration bureaucrats in the postwar era. Regarding material implications, it contemplates how the immigrant selection principles put in place sixty years ago paved the way for increasingly exclusive access to admission for immigrant workers and family members alike. Drawing on recent quantitative analyses of linked administrative and tax records, it also shows how the intersectional logic of immigrant selection has affected immigrants across all major permanent entry categories for skilled workers and family over the past thirty years. The long-term effect of middle-class multiculturalism has been to ensure that ascribed social group memberships (e.g., race, gender, class) affect whether and how immigrants are selected for permanent settlement as skilled workers or family members. The result is a policy that generates substantial social inequalities that tend to be overlooked when the "Canadian model" is touted as "best practice."

Turning to the normative legacy of middle-class multiculturalism, the chapter considers how the findings presented in the book add to our understanding of multicultural citizenship in the Canadian context. Here the chapter argues that the effect of middle-class multiculturalism has been to circumscribe membership in the national community. This has the potential to mute concerns – among immigrants and native-born alike – about socio-economic inequalities and financial redistribution. Drawing on recent research on perceptions of national belonging, the chapter furthermore argues that not even the promise of full symbolic inclusion in the national community has been fulfilled for highly integrated immigrants and their descendants. Thus, in both material and symbolic terms, the legacy of middle-class multiculturalism is one of intersectional inclusion and exclusion that has the potential to generate substantial social costs across Canadian society.

The legacy of middle-class multiculturalism is important not just for Canada but also for other national contexts. The "Canadian model" of mass, merit-based immigration is touted as a case of international "best practice" in policy circles (OECD et al. 2018) because its high level of selectivity along human capital lines is perceived as an efficient means of ensuring the economic utility of immigrants and thereby generating economic and social prosperity for receiving societies and immigrants alike. Since politicians in other OECD countries regularly call for the adoption of a "points system" like Canada's as a panacea for perceived immigration-related woes, this book concludes with thoughts on why they might do well to reconsider.

Chapter Two

Bureaucratic Discretion in the Historical Canadian Context

Late one evening in the summer of 1963, Tom Kent, adviser to Prime Minister Lester B. Pearson, entered Guy Favreau's office to round off a long day of collaboration with a nightcap. He later described the scene in his memoir, *A Public Purpose*, as follows: "There was nowhere to sit down. The chairs all had files piled on them. Guy Favreau had been Minister of Citizenship and Immigration for three months. He had inherited a system under which there was little definition of rules to determine who was admissible to Canada and who was not" (Kent 1988, 243). The heaps of files that made it impossible to sit down in the new Minister of Citizenship and Immigration's office were an outward manifestation of the burden of administering an immigration policy that did not "in any real sense" express the purpose of the program (407). Kent, who would later serve as deputy minister in a restructured Department of Manpower and Immigration (1966–8), described the scale and scope of that burden in his memoir. According to him, immigration policy in the 1960s was an "extreme example" of how a "vague" government policy can lead to the overcentralization of its administration (401). The vagueness of the policy impacted the decisions made by high-level immigration bureaucrats tasked with devising an administrative way to execute it. It also permeated the instructions given to lower-level bureaucrats for the purpose of processing applications. These instructions contained procedural rules that allowed implementing bureaucrats to deal with a certain proportion of cases "mechanically"; however, in the absence of a clearly articulated purpose, "a good many decisions, not determined by the rules, [would be] referred back to higher levels of the bureaucratic structure" (407). Hence, the stacks of files in Favreau's office.

Inside the Department

The federal Department of Citizenship and Immigration, created in 1950, had an expansive network of domestic and foreign processing offices that, in theory, made immigration case processing geographically decentralized.[1] The Immigration Branch of the Department comprised five administrative divisions: settlement, admissions, operations, administration, and inspection. The Operations Division was responsible for the management of field operations across Canada and overseas. Canadian operations were further subdivided into five geographic districts: Pacific, Western, Central, Eastern, and Atlantic. In 1953, there were 327 officially designated ports of entry in Canada, 124 of which were staffed by full-time immigration officers trained by headquarters. The other 203 were staffed by customs officers of the Department of National Revenue, who had the status of ex officio immigration officers, and who reported directly to either the district superintendent for their area or to the officer in charge of the nearest fully staffed port of entry. In addition to the district offices, two administrative units were designated for managing operations overseas (one for the United Kingdom,[2] and one for all other offices abroad). Each individual processing office (or port of entry) in Canada was separated from the deputy minister by four administrative units (three in the case of processing offices abroad). The Admissions Division furnished the content of the Department's immigration operations. It was responsible for matters regarding the admissibility of immigrants and non-immigrants, the preparation and maintenance of admission regulations, appeals, and deportations. Figure 2.1 provides an overview of the structure of the Department as it stood in 1953.

Set up in postwar emergency conditions, one notable feature of the Department was its relatively stable base of employees. Hawkins (1988, 247) describes them as a "special cadre of immigration officers who, to a considerable extent, managed the immigration operation in the postwar period." The basic educational requirement for immigration officers was a Grade 12 education, although wartime experience was also taken into consideration. Very few were university graduates. Many of the first members of the Department were ex-servicemen seeking quick employment, especially ones wishing to remain overseas. Hawkins (1988) attributes their willingness to remain long term, despite the relatively low profile and pay scale of the Department until the mid-1960s (especially compared to the Departments of External Affairs and Trade and Commerce), to their interest in the job itself.

Figure 2.1. The organizational structure of the Department of Citizenship and Immigration in 1953

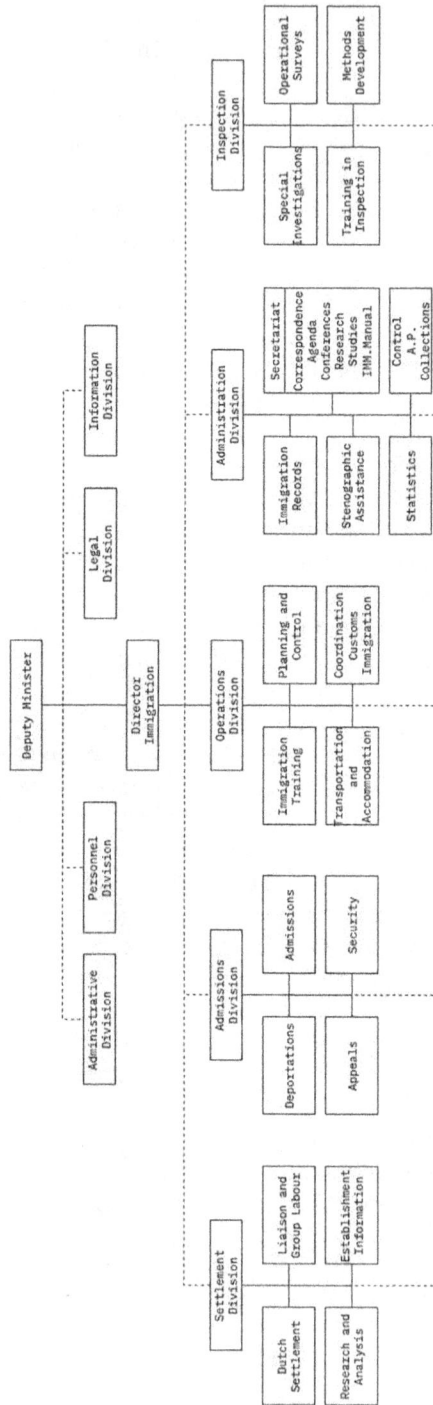

Advisory Communications

Advisory Communications

Operations Communications

Advisory Communications

Advisory Communications

Supt. Pac. Dist.

Supt. West. Dist.

Supt. Cent. Dist.

Supt. East. Dist.

Supt. Atlantic Dist.

Supt. United Kingdom

Officers i/c Post Abroad Other Than UK

Regional Settlement Supervisor

Assistant Dist. Supt.

District Inspector

Occupational Surveys

Settlement Training

Periodic Inspection

New Procedure Implementation

Supervision of Placement Officers

Liaison with Other Agencies

Administrative Services

Admissions Deportations and Investigations

Immigration Training

Ports

Ports

Ports

Ports

Ports

Ports

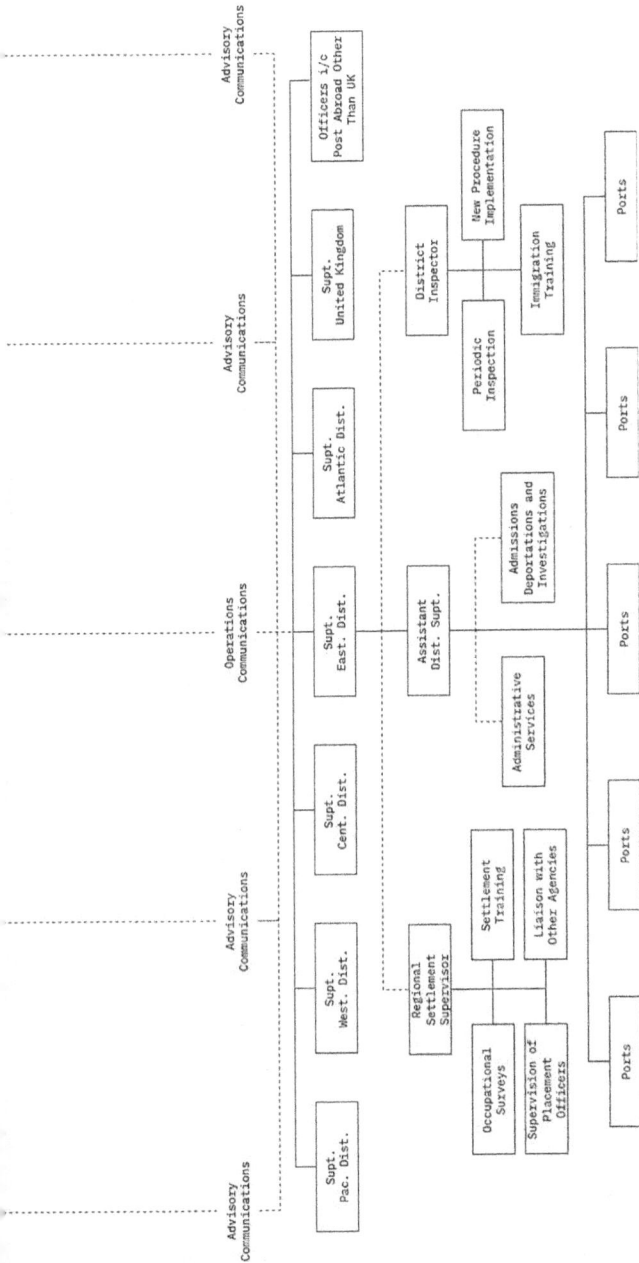

Source: Recreated from the figure included in documents prepared for the Meeting on Immigration Matters between Canadian Government Officials and Government of Ontario Officials, 8 June 1953. In RG 26, Vol. 134, File 3–36–1 Part 1.

Despite the wide geographical distribution of offices, the running of the immigration program was relatively centralized in the hands of high-level bureaucrats and the ministers they served (Hawkins 1988). The post of director of immigration was particularly important, with the incumbent being directly responsible to the deputy minister and, through him, the minister, for all functions of the Immigration Branch. In terms of duties, this included: overseeing the administration of the Immigration Act and Regulations as well as implementation; preparing, interpreting, and distributing rules, regulations, and directives governing immigration procedures; preparing and disseminating information on the program; maintaining official landing records; and coordinating and supervising the activities of field services in Canada and abroad. The director of immigration was not alone in discharging these duties. Fellow members of the Departmental Advisory Committee on Immigration leant support. Along with the director of immigration, the committee included the deputy minister and the chiefs of each of the five major divisions of the Immigration Branch (administration, inspection, admissions, operations, and settlement). Some of the committee's responsibilities included considering, and advising the minister on, immigration policies and procedures, as well as approving or refusing applications for the admission of bulk labour groups submitted by firms or organizations in Canada. Its activities informed the initiation, development, and institutionalization of most immigration policy developments in the immediate postwar era. With new policies taking the form of immigration regulations rather than legislation to revise the Immigration Act, the Department was (and continues to be) the locus of immigration policy formulation (Ellermann 2021). With the exception of the discussion of family sponsorship restrictions proposed by the Department in 1959 and 1967,[3] there was little intervention by Parliament in the Department's policy formulation activities.

Immigrant admissions were more centralized in practice than the official organizational division of labour with its multiple ports of entry implies, for two reasons. First, thousands of cases that could not be adjudicated in a straightforward manner according to instructions were referred back up the hierarchy for a decision. Would-be permanent immigrants submitted application forms and supporting documentation to apply for landing at a port of entry in Canada or offices abroad. These were reviewed by lower-level immigration officers using guidance provided by the First Immigration Manual.[4] The preface of the manual made it clear that the process would not always be straightforward: "Officers will read these instructions in the light of their intent, bearing in mind that instructions, however elaborate, cannot envisage every contingency and are not a substitute for sound judgement."[5] This "sound judgement" was put to the test in several provisions for determining immigrant admissibility. For example, in 1962 immigration officers were instructed to review applications from Canadian residents to sponsor fiancé(e)s that were not explicitly covered in the immigration regulations and to "satisfy [themselves] as to the bona fides of the application,"[6] without a clear articulation of what those would comprise. Regarding the "personal qualities" of skilled worker applicants, a 1963 amendment states that, among other criteria, "in the selection officer's judgement, immigrants must be generally suitable and not undesirable as future Canadians."[7] Immigration officers could use personal interviews to clarify information about applications, but uncertainty was built into the adjudication process. It is thus understandable that the "vague" nature of the immigration policy of the day (as attested to by Tom Kent and discussed further in the next section), combined with increased pressures to avoid explicit racial discrimination in codifying and operationalizing that policy,[8] made it relatively common for files to be passed up the hierarchy for adjudication.

The second reason why admissions were centralized in practice is that immigration policy at the outset of this period, especially the 1952 Immigration Act, reinforced the high level of executive control over immigration policy that had been given to Cabinet in the 1910 Immigration Act. Knowles (1997, 84) describes the 1910 act as conferring on the Cabinet "virtually unlimited discretionary powers allowing it to issue orders-in-council to regulate the volume, ethnic origin, or occupational composition of immigrants destined to Canada." The 1952 Immigration Act and 1953 immigration regulations (Order-in-Council P.C. 1953–859) reinforced the broad power of the Cabinet. In doing so, they also reinforced the discretionary powers of the high-level bureaucrats under the Cabinet's command to admit or exclude, *notwithstanding the Immigration Act and regulations*, any individual or group for any length of time. The principal policy instrument for these admissions and exclusions was the order-in-council. As the deputy minister's notes on immigration policy from 1961 state plainly:

> There is no specific policy laid down respecting the admission of persons by individual order-in-council. The Governor in Council has authority to admit any person who does not come within the prohibited classes set out in the Immigration Act and whose admission is not specifically provided for in Sections 20 or 21 of the Immigration Regulations. Cases usually dealt with in this manner are those having exceptional merit or those which are of a compassionate nature.[9]

In other words, this policy instrument gave high-level immigration bureaucrats an absolute carte blanche in determining immigrant admissions.

The Department did not shy away from using orders-in-council as a policy instrument to steer admissions. In some cases, the First Immigration Manual instructed lower-level officers to forward files to Immigration Branch Headquarters (BHQ) for consideration. For example, an Operations Memorandum[10] from 1957 noted that "many applications are received for immigrants on behalf of whom it is necessary to ask for the authority of the Governor in Council ... e.g. close relatives in the British West Indies." Immigration officers were instructed to submit such requests at a particular point in the application process to ensure that they could be processed in time.[11] In another example, immigration officers were instructed to partially process applications for permanent stay from non-immigrants in Canada (i.e., people with temporary permits) who were holders of National Research Council fellowships or university students. If those cases were considered to have "merit," officers were instructed to "process to the point of landing" then forward them to the chief, Admissions Division, to begin obtaining order-in-council authority to admit them. They were furthermore advised to forward all other cases of non-immigrants applying for permanent residence directly to BHQ.[12]

Throughout the period under consideration, ministerial discretion also provided one of the few avenues for appealing immigration decisions. Until the passing of the 1967 Immigration Appeal Board Act, which gave legal recourse to Canadian citizens to appeal family sponsorship denials, only individuals ordered deported could have their case reconsidered by an Immigration Appeal Board (see the section on deportation appeals below). Anyone else facing a negative outcome could only forward their case to the minister directly, in the hope that the immense discretionary powers invested in him/her would be used to make an exception on humanitarian and compassionate grounds (Kelley and Trebilcock 2010).

The combination of vague language and wide discretionary powers left ministers, deputy ministers, and directors of individual immigration offices in Canada and abroad with a burdensome number of individual cases to process (Hawkins 1988). These were either forwarded up the chain of command by immigration officers who were uncertain how to proceed, sent to them directly by applicants and/or their lawyers, forwarded by Members of Parliament who channelled requests from constituents, or presented by ethnic organizations like the Chinese Benevolent Association (CBA) and the National Japanese Canadian Citizens Association (NJCCA). Indeed, Hawkins (1988) argues that the processing of individual case requests was one of only two areas (lobbying for family sponsorship rights being the other) in which the exercise of political pressure on the Department was relatively strong. Organizations like the CBA and NJCCA regularly submitted briefs, including compilations of individual immigration cases, directly to the minister.[13] In some cases, the organizations identified individuals whose leave to enter or remain in Canada had, in their eyes, been wrongfully denied in light of regulatory changes, like ones involving the repatriation of Japanese-Canadians during the Second World War. In other cases, these organizations were nominating individuals for admission as immigrants. One memorandum describes twenty-three out of forty cases contained in one brief from the NJCCA as involving individuals "who are debarred from admission to Canada as immigrants through the force of present immigration regulations," making them "entirely an immigration matter."[14]

It was not just Minister Favreau in 1963 whose office was filled with individual case files. As Hawkins (1988, 103) documents, Minister J.W. Pickersgill estimated in 1954 that 90 per cent of his time was devoted to dealing with "mountains of cases," and Minister Richard Bell, in office from 1962–3, complained of "the inexorable flow of individual files across the Minister's desk, preventing constructive administrative action." This was despite the fact that the 1952 Immigration Act offered a means of relieving pressure on the minister. It allowed the minister to designate immigration officers as special inquiry officers (SIOs), who enjoyed exceptional powers to inquire into individual cases. These powers included the ability to summon individuals for an interview under oath and to determine whether a person could enter or remain in Canada. But the assistance of SIOs did not alleviate the case processing burden of senior members of the Department.

The untenable nature of the situation was clear to all involved: the vague and discretionary character of Canada's immigration policy had been criticized in a Supreme Court decision in 1956. It would also be made the subject of the 1965 evaluation of departmental operations carried out by Toronto lawyer Joseph Sedgwick. As deputy minister, Kent would oversee the passing of the 1967 immigration regulations, which were, in part, intended to ameliorate the situation.

According to Kent's (1988, 411) assessment, the 1967 immigration regulations accomplished not one but two notable feats: (1) they entrenched, for the first time, many details of the immigration process as regulations under a statute of law, rather than leaving it a matter of pure internal administrative direction; and (2) they "removed all traces of discrimination because of an intended immigrant's country of origin and therefore, in effect, race." However, as a cursory review of immigration law from 1952 to 1967 shows, vague language inviting discretionary interpretation and potential racial discrimination was hard to erase entirely.

The Evolving Vague Language of Canadian Immigration Policy

Racial discrimination and vague language allowing for maximal discretion had long coexisted in Canadian immigration law, and they were evident in the 1952 Immigration Act passed at the beginning of the postwar period. The act defined "admissibility" broadly in terms of national origins. Under section 61 of the act, the Governor in Council was given authority to issue regulations prohibiting or limiting admissions of individuals, including, under subsection (g): nationality, citizenship, ethnic group, occupation, class, geographical area of origin, "peculiar customs, habits, modes of life or methods of holding property"; "unsuitability having regard to the climatic, economic, social, industrial, educational, labour, health or other conditions or requirements"; or "probable inability to become readily assimilated or to assume the duties and responsibilities of Canadian citizenship within a reasonable time after their admission." While they did not explicitly use the term "race," the scope to define admissibility in reference to nationality, citizenship, ethnic group, geographical area of origin, ways of life, and "climatic" suitability provided plenty of scope for selecting by racial origins.

Building on section 61 of the 1952 Immigration Act, section 20 of the 1953 immigration regulations (P.C. 1953–859) laid down "Norms of Admissibility" in terms of national origins. According to section 20(1), the following classes of persons were eligible for admission to Canada: British subjects by birth or by naturalization in the United Kingdom, Australia, New Zealand, or the Union of South Africa; citizens of Ireland and the United States; and French citizens by birth or naturalization in France or in the Saint-Pierre and Miquelon Islands. As Kelley and Trebilcock (2010, 327) point out, the distinction the British and French citizens "born and naturalized" in particular geographical areas was made to ensure that citizens from "undesirable" regions like India, Hong Kong, West Indies, and French North Africa were not eligible for admission. While section 20(1) did not distinguish between skilled workers and family, section 20(2) explicitly limited the immigration of "any Asian" to spouses and unmarried children (under age twenty-one) of Canadian citizens. Section 20(3) limited the admission of citizens of India, Pakistan, and Ceylon in numeric terms but left the use of quota admissions open to workers and their families.

Most controversially, in terms of its scope for discretionary interpretations and potential for racist exclusion, section 20(4) of the 1953 immigration regulations awarded SIOs the authority to deny admission to anyone on any of the following grounds: (a) peculiar customs, habits, modes of life, or methods of holding property; (b) unsuitability with regard to the economic, social, industrial, educational, labour, health, or other conditions in Canada; or (c) probable inability to become readily assimilated or to assume the duties and responsibilities of Canadian citizenship within a reasonable time after his/her admission. This wide-ranging discretionary power became the subject of a case before the Supreme Court, which, in its 1956 *Brent* decision, declared that this power exceeded the provisions of the Immigration Act (Kelley and Trebilcock 2010).

Another vague concept through which the Minister of Citizenship and Immigration could exercise his/her exceptional authority over immigrant admissions was "merit." Order-in-Council P.C. 2856 allowed the Minister of Citizenship and Immigration to exercise his/her sweeping authority to admit individuals as "cases of exceptional merit." As Minister Edward Harris outlined to the House of Commons on 4 July 1952, this category could be used to admit individuals from select countries of origin. It could be applied to non-nationals in (i.e., persons who were not citizens of) the United Kingdom, Australia, New Zealand, South Africa, Ireland, the United States, France, Belgium, Luxembourg, Norway, Denmark, Sweden, Switzerland, Holland, Germany, Austria, Greece, Finland, and Italy (citizens of these countries were generally eligible for admission). It could furthermore be applied to citizens of Israel, Turkey, Syria, Lebanon, Iran, European countries not explicitly named, South America, and the British West Indies.[15]

Forced by the 1956 *Brent* decision to make selection criteria more transparent, the Department revised the immigration regulations (through Order-in-Council P.C. 1956–785) to further specify the classes of admissible immigrants, which it divided into four groups (Kelley and Trebilcock 2010, 328–9). The range of countries whose citizens (by birth or naturalization) were generally eligible for admission under the previous regulations (as workers or family members) was retained and comprised the first of the four new groups. The second group comprised citizens (by birth or naturalization) of the following countries, who were eligible to immigrate if they were seeking employment under the auspices of the Department or looking to establish themselves in a business, trade or profession: Austria, Belgium, Denmark, West Germany, Finland, Greece, Iceland, Italy, Luxembourg, the Netherlands, Norway, Portugal, Spain, Sweden, and Switzerland. The third group included citizens of European countries, the Americas, Egypt, Israel, Lebanon and Turkey, who were deemed eligible to enter Canada if they had relatives there who could sponsor them. The fourth category was a residual one, specifying that citizens of all other countries (e.g., Asian ones) could be admitted only if they were the close relative (husband, wife, unmarried child under the age of twenty-one, or parent over the age of sixty-five) of a Canadian citizen sponsor.

The 1962 immigration regulations (P.C. 1962–86), which were credited with introducing the first iteration of a universal worker admissions policy, still contained the kind of vague language that carried with it potential for discretionary racial exclusion. Section 31(a) made admissible any person "who, by reason of his education, training, skills or other special qualifications, is likely to be able to establish himself successfully in Canada," including his/her spouse and unmarried children under the age of twenty-one. Note that the threshold levels of education, training, and skills needed for successful establishment were not specified. Nor were "special qualifications" defined.

The 1967 immigration regulations (P.C. 1967–1616) introduced the "points system" according to which workers ("independent immigrants") and a range of extended relatives ("nominated relatives") could be selected based on individual human capital and family ties. They also equalized family reunification provisions across all origin groups. This first attempt to codify in detail the immigrant worker selection process did not eliminate the discretion accorded to lower-level bureaucrats in adjudicating cases. Points were awarded to independent worker and extended family applicants for years of education; employment opportunities in their intended occupations; present occupation; age; arranged employment; knowledge of English and French; the general level of employment in the area of Canada the immigrant was destined for; and relevant personal qualities. This last measure in particular still gave a lot of interpretive authority to the lower-level bureaucrats applying the policy. According to the assessment criteria for independent applicants (i.e., skilled workers) set out in the Regulations, the "personal assessment" involved a consideration of "adaptability, motivation, initiative, resourcefulness and other similar qualities," and the allocation of points would reflect the visa officer's "judgment of the personal suitability of the applicant and his family." Yet for other qualities there emerged an unprecedented level of codification in comparison to the previous system. For example, for education and training, one point was to be awarded for each year of formal education, training (professional, vocational, trades), or apprenticeship. This was a marked improvement from the previous practices established for assessing skilled workers, which Kent (1988, 410) described as "the rule of thumb of eleven years' schooling plus highly arbitrary other judgments."

By 1967, immigration policy as it was articulated in the immigration regulations (the Immigration Act would be revised later in 1976) had undergone a substantial transformation. Explicitly racial discrimination had been eliminated and the scope for bureaucratic discretion reduced. Legal and organizational impulses help explain the curtailment of the discretionary powers that had created such a high case-processing load for the minister and raised the ire of the judiciary. The factors driving the effort to eliminate explicit racial discrimination at the same time are the subject of extensive scholarly discussions.

Explaining Postwar Policy Change

Existing scholarship on the emergence of Canada's universal immigration policy generally sees the elimination of explicitly racially discriminatory clauses as a process driven by impulses that were exogenous to the Department and the policymaking process itself. While scholars sometimes disagree on the relative weighting, a range of macro- and meso-level impulses is consistently assigned causal significance in explanations of policy change.

Macro-Level Impulses for Change

Scholars seeking to explain the emergence of universal immigration policies from the 1950s to 1970s unanimously emphasize the causal role played by the emergence of a new normative political context emphasizing human rights as well as changing international relations within that context. From a world society perspective, Triadafilopoulos (2012) attributes the demise of racially discriminatory clauses in Canadian immigration policy to the emergence of a global, normative political context emphasizing liberal values and human rights in the postwar era. World society theory in general posits that nation states and, by extension, their actions and policies, are shaped by exogenous cultural forces. These forces ensure a certain degree of isomorphism in the organization and structure of states (e.g., models of government, citizenship, economic development, and justice) as well as their underlying values (e.g., human rights) (Meyer et al. 1997). For immigration policy, these dynamics mean that "race was outlawed as a legitimate ordering principle of the social world" (Joppke 2005b, 49). The diffusion of shared values of human rights, which emerged in the wake of the Holocaust and were codified in the United Nation's 1948 *Universal Declaration of*

Human Rights, made it inevitable that states like Canada would abolish immigrant selection practices emphasizing racial and national origins and converge in their policymaking around non-discriminatory alternatives.

Canada's domestic macro-economic context is also widely acknowledged as an important impulse behind the development of its universal immigration policy. In the 1950s and 1960s, Canada's rapidly growing and changing economy created a perceived need for an influx of appropriately skilled workers (Green 1976). Between 1950 and 1960 Canada's gross national product doubled, from $18 to $36 billion; it produced half of the world's newsprint; natural resource exports boomed; and $60 billion worth of houses and other buildings were constructed, over double the value of buildings constructed from 1925 to 1950 (Kilbourn 1968, 315). With skilled immigrants from the United Kingdom increasingly unwilling to immigrate following that country's postwar economic recovery, the Department of Citizenship and Immigration was certainly under domestic economic pressure to consider the admission of immigrants from non-traditional and non-favoured source countries, in order to maintain economic growth. Domestic macro-economic developments therefore help explain the substantive emphasis in these policies on human capital indicators (age, education, occupation, language) as selection criteria for skilled workers and extended family members. In other words, they explain why Canada moved "from the principle of race-based to skills-based selection" (Ellermann 2021, 3).

Meso-Level Impulses for Change

Closely related to the macro-level shift in the global normative context described above, a number of scholars see meso-level institutional responses by different branches of the state as key to explaining the emergence of Canada's universal immigration policy. For example, FitzGerald and Cook-Martín (2014) argue that the removal of racially discriminatory clauses from Canada's immigration policy was driven by the government's overarching foreign policy ambitions within the international relations context that emerged after the Second World War. By all historical accounts, Canada assumed a unique position among Western liberal-democratic states in the 1950s. Despite having less than half of 1 per cent of the world's population, Canada became the fourth most powerful nation state on earth for a time, following the United States, the USSR, and the United Kingdom. As Kilbourn (1968, 327) puts it, "because she was not one of the great powers, and because she possessed the unique if unearned advantage of being a wealthy western nation without an imperial past, Canada had an important role to play as a presence in international disputes" and in the reshaping of the Commonwealth in the 1950s. Canada's ambition to maintain its newfound power on the global stage made it imperative for the country to break with its explicitly racist past, especially its racist immigration policy, which was a potential threat to its position as a power-broker within the Commonwealth. FitzGerald and Cook-Martín (2014, 142) argue that, "without significant military or economic power, Canada attempted to secure the world's respect by its good deeds," and these good deeds could not be done with racist policies on the books. Bloemraad (2015, 64) similarly speaks of Canada's strategic concern with its "moral and political standing in the international community." Canada was acutely aware of the political penalties faced by its more powerful allies due to their histories of colonialism and slavery and had every interest in avoiding those penalties. Ellermann (2021) concurs, attributing Canada's relatively rapid transition to a universal immigration policy to the government's lack of insulation from significant diplomatic pressures rooted in the country's Commonwealth ties and foreign policy ambitions.

Since states are not monoliths but sets of institutions with "many hands" and potentially competing interests (Morgan and Orloff 2017), it is important to note that the Department of Citizenship and Immigration and the Department of Foreign Affairs were not alone in shaping the Canadian government's response to changing global contexts. One aspect of changing patterns of international relations in the postwar era – the Cold War – placed the Department of Citizenship and Immigration's efforts to establish a universal immigration policy at odds with security interests of the Royal Canadian Mounted Police (RCMP). As Whitaker (1987, 22) states, the Cold War led to the "systematic application of specifically political criteria as a basis for mass exclusion from Canada of categories of persons," particularly Chinese. Political fears interacted with the negative racialization of Chinese as immoral and lawless (see, e.g., K. Anderson 1995) to construct this group as a political threat, especially in the eyes of the RCMP. Already faced with the difficult task of verifying family relations in the course of family sponsorship, the Department was pressured by the RCMP in the early 1950s to restrict family admissions, due to a perceived "Communist conspiracy to substitute trained agents for bona fide sons sponsored by Chinese Canadians." While the RCMP insisted in 1952 that up to 85 per cent of future Chinese immigration "would be persons substituted or trained in subversive activities," without the Chinese-Canadian parents noticing, no such case was ever uncovered (Whitaker 1987, 97).

The Chinese were not the only group targeted by the RCMP for exclusion. In a confidential memorandum from 1952,[16] RCMP Commissioner Nicholson suggested to Deputy Minister Fortier that the definition of "prohibited classes" in the Immigration Act be amended to encompass "persons who by reason of religion, race, creed, etc. have indicated specifically or generally that they will not bear arms in the defense of Canada," based on "the troubles that the country [had] experienced from the Doukhobour sect." In the margins, the deputy minister's simple handwritten response of "No" indicates that the Department did not bend to the RCMP's restrictive impulses on this matter. According to Whitaker (1987), the Department was also ultimately able to resist the RCMP's attempts at increased scrutiny and control over admissions practices pertaining to the Chinese. These examples show that the Cold War aspect of the macro-level context in which immigration policy was changing had a complicating effect on meso-level responses to that context in terms of racialization and security-related impulses to include/exclude immigrants.

Meso-level institutional responses on the part of the Canadian state were also influenced by other collective actors. As pluralist models of immigration policy would predict (see chapter 3), the emergence of a universal immigration policy in Canada was influenced by organized interests, although scholars of this era generally concur that this influence was muted relative to other national contexts. Unlike in the United States and Australia, lobbying on the part of businesses, unions, or ethnic community groups was not particularly strong in postwar Canada, although there are notable exceptions (Hawkins 1988). Unions were relatively active in attempting to limit an influx of non-White immigrants. Triadafilopoulos (2012, 61–3) shows that this was the thrust of submissions made by the Canadian Congress of Labour (CCL) and the Trade and Labour Congress (TLC) to the Standing Committee of the Senate on Immigration and Labour between 1946 and 1953. While political pressure from racial and ethnic groups to create a more inclusive immigration policy is not considered to have been very strong (Hawkins 1988), Italian, Chinese, and Japanese groups actively lobbied for changes to family sponsorship provisions (Madokoro 2012; Roy 2007). Roy (2007) points out that these lobbying efforts included not just arguments for changing provisions in the immigration regulations, but also the forwarding of individual cases to the minister and deputy minister for consideration.

In sum, the standard historiography of postwar immigration policy change places explanatory emphasis on macro- and meso-level factors that were exogenous to the policymaking activities of the Department of Citizenship and Immigration. The macro-level cultural shift towards a global human rights culture and meso-level foreign policy objectives formulated against that macro-cultural backdrop are identified as the main drivers of immigration policy change. Macro-level economic factors help explain the origins of the new policy's substantive emphasis on skills-based rather than race-based selection.

Micro-Level Resistance to Change

The standard historiography outlined above does not see micro-level factors, such as the actions of immigration bureaucrats, as an important impulse behind Canada's postwar immigration policy change. On the contrary: high-level immigration bureaucrats are depicted as reluctant to universalize policy, that is, to decouple immigrant selection criteria from social distinctions like ascribed racial or national group membership. Triadafilopoulos (2012) employs the terms "policy stretching," "unravelling," and "shifting" to describe the efforts of Canadian immigration bureaucrats to maintain the racist status quo for as long as was politically possible. The term "policy stretching" captures the obdurate stance attributed to immigration bureaucrats: "stretching is not so much about 'muddling through' policy challenges as it is about deflecting them in the name of staying true to [previously] established goals" (Triadafilopoulos 2012, 11). It is only when the stretched policy began to unravel (i.e., become politically untenable in light of exogenous political pressures) that a shift occurred. This tripartite process of stretching, unravelling, and shifting is argued to be the reason behind the two-step introduction of universalized immigration regulations in 1962 (for skilled workers) and 1967 (for family).

The 1962 immigration regulations in particular are depicted as a turning point at which Canadian immigration bureaucrats prevented policy from actually turning. Triadafilopoulos (2012, 94) calls the 1962 regulations that eliminated racial restrictions on skilled worker admissions "Janus faced" for only "formally rejecting the principled use of race, nationality, and culture in determining the suitability of immigrants." With regard to immigration from the West Indies, FitzGerald and Cook-Martín (2014, 177) call the 1962 regulations a "charade played for an international audience" that was designed to mask what would remain exclusionary practices toward black would-be immigrants "at least until the end of the decade."

Existing scholarship shows that, in addition to resisting and delaying formal policy changes, high-level bureaucrats took steps to maintain racially exclusionary selection practices by moving them "behind the scenes" to policy implementation (see, e.g., K. Anderson 1995; Hawkins 1988; Knowles 1997; Wolgin and Bloemraad 2010; Triadafilopoulos 2012). For example, the Department continued to limit the size of, as well as the staff and resources allocated to, case processing offices in non-desirable regions of origin, as Satzewich (1989) demonstrates with regard to the British West Indies. Additionally, immigration officers could continue to use the vagueness of the new regulations (e.g., regarding the definition of skills, qualifications, and satisfactory means of family support) and the 1952 Immigration Act to exclude non-White immigrants as they saw fit, without fear of sanctions from higher-ranking department officials. The picture that emerges is one of high-level bureaucrats as relatively autonomous individuals acting strategically to maintain racialized selection in part by leaving enough room for discretion in implementation that – they appear to have presumed – would lead to racial exclusion in practice, irrespective of policy on the books. Indeed, the accusation that personal racist commitments consistently lead to discriminatory practices under Canadian immigration law is one that persists to this day (see, e.g., Aiken 2007; Sharma 2006).

The origin of this presumed racism on the part of implementing bureaucrats is generally left unspecified but could be accounted for by either of the two most common ways of conceptualizing individual actions in the bureaucratic context. Both interpretations imply, as legal scholarship on discretionary decision-making often does (see, e.g., Pratt and Sossin 2009), that state actors are autonomous individuals who are free to make rational choices about how to align their actions, regardless of the context they are working in. According to the first interpretation, racist outcomes of discretionary implementation practices could be the result of a principal-agent problem (Ellermann 2009; Lahav and Guiraudon 2006; Satzewich 2015). In this scenario, the agent (the implementing bureaucrat) refuses to follow the instructions of the principal (the government), due to personal preferences that conflict with higher-ups who are issuing instructions. In the Canadian historical case, this would mean that high-level bureaucrats were counting on anyone in charge of applying policy (including themselves) to act on racist preferences that they either possessed innately or acquired during their tenure in a department that had traditionally served the mandate of building a White Canadian nation. Alternatively, many empirical studies of bureaucracies in the field of immigration and elsewhere have concluded that bureaucrats, rather than seeking to diverge from policy instructions, have been keen to follow their departments' mandates (Eggebø 2013; Ellermann 2009; Satzewich 2015; Wilson 1980).

In postwar Canada, this would have meant that high-level bureaucrats presumed racist exclusion would persist until full legislative change occurred, due to adherence to the exclusionary mandate set out in the 1952 Immigration Act and 1953 regulations and/or behind-the-scenes instructions from senior officials in the Department to stay the course.

There are certainly well-documented historical precedents in Canada, pre-dating the postwar era, for presuming a certain path-dependent adherence to the project of White nation-building on the part of state actors. The most prominent example is the use of bureaucratic discretion to restrict the entry of European Jews before and during the Nazi persecution. The legal basis for restrictive practices against Jews was laid with Order-in-Council PC 1931–695 of 31 March 1931. This order-in-council, recognized as "the tightest immigration admissions policy in Canadian history" (Kelley and Trebilcock 2010, 216), did not name Jews specifically as a policy target. Rather, it limited the range of admissible immigrants to American citizens and British subjects from Britain, Ireland, the Irish Free State, Newfoundland, New Zealand, Australia, and South Africa, provided they had sufficient funds to maintain themselves until obtaining employment. Also included in the admissible classes were "agriculturalists with sufficient means to farm in Canada," and the wives and minor children of Canadian residents (Kelley and Trebilcock 2010, 216).

The racial exclusion of Jews under this order-in-council was shaped most clearly by the practices of Canadian immigration bureaucrats, particularly Frederick Blair, the director of the Immigration Branch (then part of the Department of Mines and Resources) from 1936 until his retirement in 1943. In 1938 Blair assumed personal responsibility for processing applications made by European Jews to enter Canada as agriculturalists, in addition to reviewing cases processed by lower-level immigration bureaucrats. Of the thousands of files he processed and reviewed, very few were approved. Also from 1938 onward, Blair issued a series of directives to immigration officers overseas, raising the capital requirement for Jews from $5,000 to $20,000; Jewish industrialists with as much as $170,000 to invest in Canada were turned away (Kelley and Trebilcock 2010, 261). He summarized his activities thus in personal correspondence with a colleague: "Pressure on the part of Jewish people to get into Canada has never been greater than it is now, and I am glad to be able to add, after 35 years' experience here, that it was never so well controlled" (quoted in Abella and Troper 1991, 3). These are only a few of the practices that ensured that the admission of European Jews before and during the Holocaust would remain tragically low, despite the absence of explicit measures to bar their entry.

Notwithstanding the history of racist practices by Canadian immigration bureaucrats, it is important to note that the path-dependent continuation of such practices in the period from 1952 to 1967 is something that has been presumed in the absence of analyses of their case processing activities. In other words, historical work on the postwar era begs the question of how racially exclusionary these practices were, and data on implementation that could shed light on how individuals within the state conceptualized race in practice have not been taken into account.

Explaining the Absence of Implementation from Historical Analyses

Why have historical accounts begged the question of how racially inclusive or exclusionary the implementation practices of immigration bureaucrats were during this era? I propose that these practices have remained unexamined for two reasons. First, there is a bias in immigration policy analyses in general – and historical accounts of the postwar era in particular – towards privileging immigration laws and regulations as a source of information on immigrant inclusion and exclusion (Fox 2015; Motomura 2015). This bias is firmly rooted in legal theorizing more generally, which treats law as the primary instrument of regulation and discretion exercised in the course of applying the law as a "residual category" (Pratt 2005, 53). Scholars who have explored the transition from racially exclusionary to universal immigration policies generally rely on publicly available legal documents as indicators of change. In the Canadian case, the transition begins with the 1952 Immigration Act and 1953 immigration regulations, which maintained Canada's historically racist approach to immigrant selection. It ends in stages, with the 1962 and 1967 immigration regulations, followed eventually by the 1976 Immigration Act. As Triadafilopoulos (2012, 2) states in his analysis, "the introduction of a universal admissions policy in 1967 and its entrenchment in the Immigration Act, 1976, shattered the foundations of 'White Canada' and created the conditions for Canada's development into one of the most culturally diverse countries in the world."

For their study of the evolution of racially discriminatory immigration policies in twenty-two major countries of the Western Hemisphere between 1970 and 2012, FitzGerald and Cook-Martín (2014, 34) examined whether "laws were in effect to select ethnic groups, such as Spaniards, Jews, Chinese, blacks, whites, and so forth." These included both laws that defined these groups in "strictly racial terms, in the sense of groups defined by phenotype and/or notions of immutable biological characteristics," and ones that "based their categories on legal nationality or country of birth or distinguished groups by their language, religion, or culture." The year in which all such clauses were removed from laws and regulations was chosen to mark a given country's transition away from racial exclusion. The authors go on to state explicitly that their analysis was restricted to "laws that were publicly available at the time that they were enacted, such as constitutions, statutes, published regulations of immigration and nationality, published bilateral and multilateral treaties, and court cases." Even if not discussed explicitly, other accounts of the postwar introduction of universal immigration policies in Canada and elsewhere follow the same practice (see, e.g., Ellermann 2021; Hollifield 1992; Joppke 2005b).

Second, there are practical limitations to data collection, particularly in comparative-historical studies. Whether comparing two (Triadafilopoulos 2012) or twenty-two (FitzGerald and Cook-Martín 2014) national contexts, it is challenging enough to analyze large volumes of archival material documenting general policy discussions that help trace the motivations of lawmakers and social influences on their decisions without turning to the matter of policy implementation. In response to critiques about the absence of implementation practices from their analysis, Cook-Martín and FitzGerald (2015) point to the practical limitations of fieldwork across multiple national contexts. They furthermore invite future efforts by other scholars to address potential gaps between written policy and implementation practices in assessing the postwar introduction of universal immigration policies and the evolving nature of race as a selection principle therein. The present study takes up this call. However, it also illustrates the challenges of accounting systematically for immigration policy implementation in a single national context and over a relatively limited period of time (see the Methodological Appendix).

Re-examining Policy Change from the Micro-Level Perspective

This book places the Department of Citizenship and Immigration and the state actors inside it at the centre of the narrative of postwar immigration policy change in Canada. It is clear that these actors were empowered to formulate legislative change in response to external pressures while simultaneously adjudicating individual immigration cases. Theoretically and empirically, there is every reason to see these practices as a site where Canada's universal immigration policy took shape. This is because, whether devising legislation or processing cases, immigration bureaucrats were responsible for deciding which attributes made someone worthy of admission when membership in a racial or national group could no longer be the decisive factor.

From the perspective of state actors inside the Department, managing the daily operation and transformation of immigration policy in the context of navigating external pressures was hardly straightforward. According to Kent (1988, 408), Canada's immigration policy – that is, the "political statement of purpose" according to which the immigration program was to be administered – was as follows during this time: "It was a rate of immigration in line with the 'absorptive capacity' of the country. It was to facilitate the reunion of families of people already here. It was to accept immigrants who could readily adapt to Canadian life. It was to be open to refugees, in numbers that did not greatly conflict with other criteria." Here, the notions "absorptive capacity" and ability to "readily adapt" stand out as requiring a significant level of interpretation. According to Kent, responsibility for interpreting the core of Canadian immigration policy was left largely to the "unfettered judgment" of immigration officers. The notions were, however, also broadly determined at the political level – and in subsequent administrative instructions – by concerns related to two issues: the economy and national identity.

The importance of these two issues for determining immigration policy is not unique to the Canadian context or to this period of history. Zolberg (2006, 1999) refers to them as the "economic axis" and "identity axis" of immigration policymaking. Immigration scholars generally agree that these two axes are essential to understanding the content and contours of immigration policymaking across Western liberal-democratic states (see, e.g., Boswell 2007; FitzGerald and Cook-Martín 2014; Hampshire 2013; Sciortino 2000).

In terms of the "economic axis" of policymaking, the rapid expansion and transformation of the Canadian economy since 1950 meant ensuring that immigrant workers could find an appropriate place in the workforce. Immigrants would thus need to have education levels and other attributes relevant to their labour market integration. If codification of attributes denoting economic utility remained somewhat vague, the general direction of travel for policy change was at least relatively clear. The emergent "manpower orientation" (Hawkins 1988, 72) of 1960s immigration policy in Canada was further reflected in the 1966 transformation of the Department of Citizenship and Immigration into the Department of Manpower and Immigration.

In terms of the "identity axis" of policymaking, notions of "absorptive capacity" and ability to "readily adapt" at the core of Canadian immigration policy in the early 1960s were much woollier and more difficult to codify than economic utility. As Kent (1988, 408) explains, there were "even deeper concerns about people with strange languages, customs and appearances upsetting Anglo-Saxon communities" than about immigration and the economy. The idea that immigration policy needed to protect and further the nationalist and racist goal of Anglo-conformity, in the interest of social and political stability, had had a long history in social and political thought in Canada by the time Kent took office. Some of the first popular books on immigration warned of the dangers of diversity if large-scale settlement of non-European races occurred (Palmer 1998, 129). The Conservative R.B. Bennett, speaking as a Member of Parliament before becoming prime minister in the 1930s, stated with regard to the excellent settlement trajectories of continental Europeans: "We must still maintain that measure of British civilization which will enable us to assimilate these people to British institutions, rather than assimilate our civilization to theirs" (quoted in Palmer 1998, 131). Possibly the most famous articulation of concerns about racial and cultural diversity being brought about by immigration was made by Prime Minister William Lyon Mackenzie King in the House of Commons in 1947. The quotation reads as follows: "The people of Canada do not wish to make a fundamental alteration in the character of their population through mass immigration. The government is therefore opposed to large-scale immigration from the Orient, which would certainly give rise to social and economic problems" (quoted in Hawkins 1988, 93). Immigration bureaucrats in the Department at the outset of the period in question thus inherited a long-standing tradition of seeing the immigration of groups defined as racially different as a threat to the national collective. By the mid-1960s, Kent (1988, 412) viewed the task of managing "absorptive capacity" as involving the imposition of "limits to the speed at which the composition of a community can change, bringing new people and unfamiliar life-styles, without creating tensions." Immigrant admissibility, long determined by the compatibility of somatic features ("appearances"), culture ("customs," "life-styles"), language, and nationalities with an Anglo-Saxon norm, would have to become more inclusive of difference, due to the macro- and micro-level impulses outlined in the previous sections. However, there was no ready strategy for managing that inclusivity effectively, meaning that one needed to be formulated on the ground.

Although it would not necessarily have been understood in such terms, Kent was describing what cultural sociologists call "boundary work" (Lamont 2000): deciding immigrant admissibility was a matter of categorizing and classifying immigrant groups in concrete racial, ethnic, moral, and other terms as compatible or incompatible with the ascribed traits of a White Anglo-Saxon nation. This boundary work was conducted not just in the context of policy formulation but also during policy implementation, as immigration bureaucrats classified and categorized individual immigrant applicants whose files filled the minister's office. How this boundary work informed the creation of the 1962 and 1967 immigration regulations is an overlooked part of the historiography of Canada's universal immigration policy that this book seeks to reconstruct.

The Empirical Challenge to the Historiography of Postwar Policy Change in Canada

Centring the role of immigration bureaucrats in the emergence of Canada's universal immigration policy involves accounting for their wide-ranging implementation practices – especially case processing activities – as an aspect of policy formulation. The remainder of this chapter provides an overview of the empirical basis for this undertaking as well as a sense of how it challenges the established historiography of immigration policy change in postwar Canada.

In order to understand how immigration bureaucrats' perceptions of immigrant admissibility, especially with regard to race, evolved on the ground, it is necessary to account for two main types of implementation practices: admissions by order-in-council and deportation appeals. This is necessary because each type of practice applied to different immigrant groups. As non-European and non-Western Hemisphere origin groups were subject to numerous legal barriers to entry, orders-in-council had to be used to admit individuals from these groups. This was less often the case for immigrants from European and Western Hemisphere origin groups. Members of these groups, however, were frequently the subjects of deportation appeal cases. The combined focus on order-in-council admissions and deportation appeals illuminates the boundary work conducted by immigration bureaucrats in relation to immigrants from a fuller range of racial, ethnic and national origins.

Order-in-Council Admissions: Determining the Admissibility of Immigrants from "Non-preferred" Countries of Origin

Most archival records in which individual order-in-council admissions are discussed are spread across a wide range of thematic files in Library and Archives Canada, making the process of finding them somewhat "archeological" (see the Methodological Appendix for details). Only one memorandum, from 1961, contains an overview and assessment of the Department's order-in-council admissions, covering the period from 1950 to 1960. While the in-depth analysis of available order-in-council admissions is reserved for chapter 4 and chapter 5, some details from this memorandum are offered here to give a sense of the extent to which these practices deviated from admissibility provisions in the Immigration Act and Regulations.

As Tom Kent's anecdote about chairs covered in files suggests, and figure 2.2 (reproduced from the 1961 memorandum) shows, a substantial number of individuals (32,584) were admitted by order-in-council, notwithstanding admissibility provisions in the Immigration Act and regulations, between 1950 and 1960. Unfortunately, no similar overview could be found for the years 1961 to 1967, that is, the remainder of the period covered in this book.[17] While these admissions by order-in-council comprised a relatively small percentage of overall admissions (see the comparison in figure 2.2), this book demonstrates that they nevertheless carried powerful implications for immigration policy reform in postwar Canada.

The Department's assessment of admissions made by order-in-council from 1950 to 1960 indicates that these orders-in-council were often used to admit individuals who were formally and legally inadmissible due to their ascribed racial group membership.[18] For example, the Department attributes the substantial decrease from 1,381 such admissions in 1952 to 579 in 1953 to the removal of Lebanese, Syrian, Armenian, and other nationals of Near Eastern countries from the regulations governing Asian immigration. In its words, "the Department had been admitting a substantial number of these people by individual Order-in-Council prior to that time," and special accommodations had become unnecessary. In other words, a regulatory change was preceded by the large-scale circumvention of the admissibility criterion (in 802 cases) that was subsequently changed. Similarly, the decline of order-in-council admissions by approximately 1,000 in 1960 is attributed to a policy amendment pertaining to passport and visa requirements earlier that year, which allowed the minister to admit Chinese and Japanese fiancées without order-in-council action. Furthermore, individual admissibility, once established as a pattern, remained in effect even if the regulations were amended in such a way as to exclude the racialized groups those individuals belonged to. According to the report, the increase from 858 to 7,015 admissions by order-in-council between 1955 and 1957 occurred because Order-in-Council P.C. 1956–785 of 24 May 1956, had defined the admissible classes more clearly, limiting the discretionary powers of the Department, which then had to use

Figure 2.2. Total number of persons admitted by order-in-council authority, 1950–1960, compared to total admissions

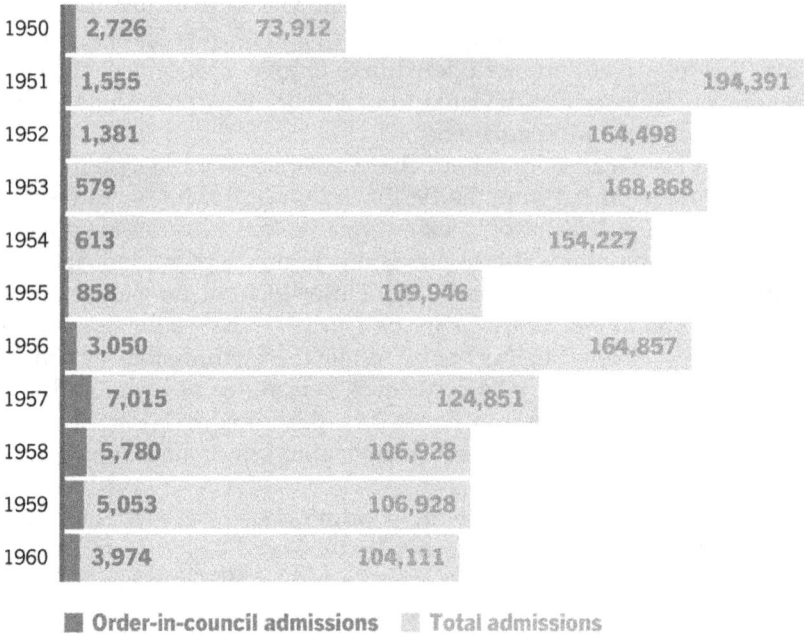

Year	Order-in-council admissions	Total admissions
1950	2,726	73,912
1951	1,555	194,391
1952	1,381	164,498
1953	579	168,868
1954	613	154,227
1955	858	109,946
1956	3,050	164,857
1957	7,015	124,851
1958	5,780	106,928
1959	5,053	106,928
1960	3,974	104,111

■ Order-in-council admissions ▨ Total admissions

Source: Numbers of order-in-council admissions from 1950 to 1960 are taken from the following document: Notes on Canadian Immigration Policy, Deputy Minister's Copy, Revised January 1961, in RG 26, Vol. 133, File 3–35–2 Part 8. Numbers of permanent residents admitted are taken from Citizenship and Immigration Canada (2013): Backgrounder – 2014 Immigration Levels Planning: Public and Stakeholder Consultations, https://www.canada.ca/en/immigration-refugees-citizenship/news/archives/backgrounders-2013/2014-immigration-levels-planning-public-stakeholder-consultations.html, accessed on 3 August 2021.

orders-in-council to continue admitting individuals from groups that were suddenly excluded. Thus, according to Department records, they "continued to admit basically the same classes of immigrant but it was necessary to obtain order-in-council authority in a far greater number of cases either to waive the Regulations governing the admissible classes or the passport or visa requirements." Although it does not give a clear indication of the Department's motivations for contradicting its own policies, this internal document shows the limits of basing historical analyses of race as a determinant of admissibility on readings of immigration laws and regulations. It also attests to the very early emergence (in 1950) of the distinction (in practice) between individual-level

Figure 2.3. Year of first admissibility of select immigrant groups according to the immigration regulations versus in practice

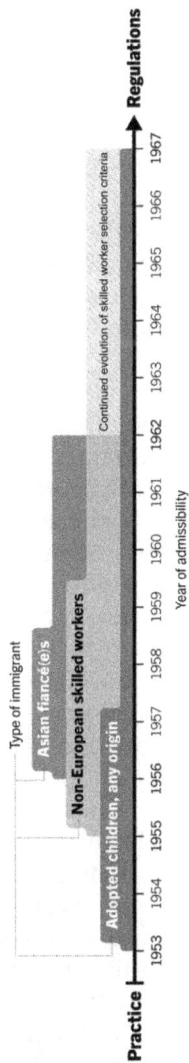

Source: Author's summary of the timing of order-in-council admissions in relation to formal policy changes.

and group-level admissibility that is considered a hallmark of universal immigration policies.

As outlined in the Methodological Appendix, the analysis of order-in-council admissions presented in this book is based on a range of files containing varying degrees of depth and detail. For example, rich discussions of individual cases were sometimes found among memos pertaining to broader issues of policy formulation in files dedicated to a particular national origin group. These types of documents provide deeper insights into the boundary work carried out by immigration bureaucrats in deciding admissibility; however, beyond occasional reference to previous cases, they do not deliver insights into the scale of order-in-council admissions. Other types of documents, like the overviews of batches of order-in-council admissions (1,731 in total) carried out between 1954 and 1964, give a sense of scale but few details about the cases that give insights into the interpretive work that went into deciding each case.

A brief look at the broad patterns of admissibility evident in the 1,731 order-in-council admissions issued in batches between 1954 and 1964 illustrates two important aspects of how these implementation practices related to the policy formulation process in the postwar era. First, they show that the distinction between individual-level and group-level admissibility emerged in implementation practices, *prior to* the creation of universal admissions policies for skilled workers and family members. It was thus not the 1967 immigration regulations that marked the transition from group-level to individual-level assessments. Second, they were used to admit individuals from groups considered formally inadmissible on racial grounds under the prevailing Immigration Act and regulations. Notably, Chinese individuals – members of one of the historically most heavily excluded groups in Canadian immigration policy – were admitted systematically well in advance of the 1962 immigration regulations (that universalized skilled worker admissions) and 1967 immigration regulations (that universalized family admissions). For example, in the years 1954 and 1955 alone, 632 out of 660 individuals who were admitted notwithstanding section 20 of the immigration regulations (the section explicitly regulating the admission of racially and nationally defined groups) were listed as being of "Chinese" or "Asian" "race." Furthermore, despite the fact that section 20(2) limited the immigration of "any Asian" to the wife, husband, and unmarried children under the age of twenty-one of any Canadian citizen, 605 of these 632 Asians were family members who were legally inadmissible under that section, including over-age children (463), parents (45), spouses or children of non-citizen sponsors

(58), and step-children (16). This pattern of exemption for individual racialized family members continued through to 1964, the last year for which these batch records are available. Though on a smaller scale, at least 319 individual skilled workers from racially inadmissible groups were admitted prior to the 1962 amendment to the immigration regulations that allowed for the entry of skilled workers of any origin. When these and additional archival records are taken into account, it becomes evident that at least three types of individuals became admissible in practice before legal limitations on their group-level admissibility were lifted: Chinese and Japanese fiancé(e)s, adopted children (of all ascribed racial origins), and skilled workers (see figure 2.3).

Deportation Appeals: Determining the Admissibility of Immigrants from "Preferred" Countries of Origin

Under section 31 of the 1952 Immigration Act, individuals ordered deported by an SIO had the right to appeal the decision to the Minister of Citizenship and Immigration. The minister, in turn, had the authority to adjudicate the appeal himself/herself, or to refer the case to an Immigration Appeal Board (IAB), which was comprised of three members of the Department. Both the IAB and the minister had full discretion to confirm, quash, or substitute their own decision for the original recommendation made by an SIO. The minister, in turn, had the power to alter a decision of an IAB as he/she saw fit; as Kelley and Trebilcock (2010, 334) state, "a prospective immigrant's best hope lay with the minister." Whereas the 1952 Immigration Act specified that only the minister could refer cases to the IAB, the 1962 immigration regulations gave all individuals subject to deportation the right to appeal their case to the IAB.

For the period from 1956 to 1967, there are a total of 961 appeal decisions in files pertaining to the Immigration Appeal Board.[19] All are cases of individuals ordered deported for being in violation of the Immigration Act or regulations, which were reviewed by an IAB. By far the most common immigration law violations for which a person had been ordered deported were becoming an inmate of a penitentiary, reformatory, or prison; becoming committed to an asylum or hospital for mental illness; Criminal Code violations, like theft, possession of a firearm, etc.; drug possession and/or use; and having been a member of a "prohibited class" upon entry to Canada, for example, by having been physically or mentally ill at the time of entry.[20] Reflecting dominant immigration patterns at the time, the main countries of origin and citizenship represented in these files were Germany (139 individuals);

the United Kingdom (123 individuals); Hungary (118 individuals); and the United States (116 individuals).

The deportation appeal files are remarkable for three reasons. First, without exception, the assessment submitted by the IAB to the minister did not call into question whether an individual had violated immigration law and thus made themselves subject to removal from Canada. In all cases, consideration of whether the person deserved a chance to remain in the country was given notwithstanding the fact that (as far as the IAB was concerned) they were legally deportable. Second, a large proportion of individuals who had been ordered deported for violating immigration law were granted leave to remain: in only 580 of 961 cases (60 per cent) was the decision to deport upheld without qualification. Like the order-in-council admissions of individuals deemed inadmissible based on their racial or national origins, these deportation appeal cases reveal a substantial disconnect between immigration laws and implementation practices. They point to the need to take implementation into account when assessing the degree to which individual and group-level distinctions actually lead to inclusion or exclusion. Third, with decisions rooted in lengthy discussions of an individual's "record" in Canada (e.g., education, occupation, work record, family, general behaviour), the admissibility of an individual did not (in most cases) map cleanly onto national origins, age, the nature of the immigration offence, or the person's occupation. These decisions thus complement order-in-council admissions practices as a source of information on the role of bureaucrats' micro-level interpretive practices in shaping the process and substance of Canada's postwar immigration policy shift.

Based on this empirical evidence, which cannot be explained by existing theories of postwar immigration policy change, this book aims to revise and extend those theories. It does so by seeking answers to the following research questions. What was the scope of the implementation (case processing) activities engaged in by high-level immigration bureaucrats in the Department? What role did these practices play in the process of devising Canada's new universal immigration policy? Finally, what did these practices mean for the substance of the new policy, particularly the evolution of the role of race in defining immigrant admissibility?

Conclusion

A substantial number of order-in-council admissions and deportation appeals were used by high-level immigration bureaucrats to flexibly interpret nationally defined (and, by proxy, racially defined) admissions preferences in the postwar era. Rather than reluctant high-level bureaucrats dragging their heels in the face of macro-level and meso-level pressures for change and capitulating only when all other options became political impossibilities, the prospect emerges that these state actors played a proactive role in change management. The following chapters propose a theoretical approach to conceptualizing such implementation practices as an aspect of policy formulation (chapter 3) and apply that approach to analyses of implementation practices as they relate to the emergence of Canada's merit-based admissions policy for skilled workers (chapter 4) and family immigrants (chapter 5).

In drawing attention to the role of micro-level interpretive practices in immigration policymaking and implementation, this book does not claim that these practices can be divorced from the important macro- and meso-level social contexts that existing scholarship identifies as essential impulses behind the creation of Canada's merit-based immigration policy. A different role is simply attributed to them here. Whereas existing scholarship sees macro-level and meso-level impulses as the ultimate drivers of change, they are treated throughout the present analysis as factors taken into consideration by immigration bureaucrats as they formulated notions about who White/non-White immigrants were and what characteristics made them admissible or not. These notions were important not just in terms of their effects on immigration, but also because they came to shape the broader relationship between race, nation, and state in Canada.

Chapter Three

State Actors Shaping the Nation:
A Cultural Sociology
of Immigration Policy

While this book focuses empirically on immigration policy change at a single historical juncture in one national context, its theoretical concerns are much broader. This is because immigration policies are tools used by states to manage the composition of their populations, and the policy change of interest involved a renegotiation of how to manage the racial composition of a White settler nation in the Global North. How race, as a social distinction, is used by states in nation-building and population management is a perennial concern. Given the implications for racialized social stratification, it is particularly important to understand how state policies that formally claim to be "race free" – like the universal immigration policy established in postwar Canada – emerge and what material and symbolic effects they have on populations. The role of immigration bureaucrats in shaping Canada's postwar immigration policy is an object of study that can address these concerns. This is due to the fact that their actions were part of a broader historical shift in states' thinking about, and managing, the relationship between race and nation in the Global North.

Immigration Policy, Race, and Nation-Building

Immigration policies fundamentally define the kinds of characteristics that prospective members must display to be considered a part of the nation. By extension, they define the nation itself (Zolberg 2006). They are thus important tools with which the state can shape the social and political contexts they govern, both materially and symbolically. This is the case because states are generally considered to be what Bourdieu (1994) terms "superordinate classifiers," that is, institutions at the pinnacle of social construction. They formalize, codify, and objectify culturally informed notions of who is who. States are not the only actors – institutional or individual – to engage in social construction, but they are considered among the most powerful. This power derives from states' status as institutions that hold a monopoly over the legitimate use of force within a given territory, as sociologist Max Weber put it (Weber 2007b). This force can be physical or symbolic, and the regulation of populations – including via symbolic classifications – is an important means by which states pursue political interests (Brubaker and Cooper 2000; Hacking 1986; Loveman 2014; Steinmetz 1999). Having the power to lend symbolic and legal force to particular social classifications does not mean, however, that states can classify their populations any which way, according to arbitrary distinctions. On the contrary, states emphasize (or challenge) distinctions rooted in everyday social life.

Race and related categories like ethnicity and nationality are key categorizations used by states to describe and manage their populations. Given the centrality of these terms, it is worth elaborating briefly on their relationship to one another in the context of this study. I follow Brubaker (2009), Loveman (1999, 2014), and others in seeing race, ethnicity, and nation as functionally equivalent categorizations. In other words, they all group human beings together in oversimplified ways in reference to phenotype (race), culture (ethnicity), and/or geo-political region of origin (nationality) in ways that imply shared origins and traits. Each one of these social categories, in the hands of the state, creates an administratively visible population whose social inclusion or exclusion is shaped by political discourse, policy, and the treatment of group members in everyday life. Thus, when it comes to examining the changing idea of race and its relationship to immigrant inclusion and exclusion in the postwar era, it is the drawing of categorical distinctions and how they are linked to processes of social stratification that is important, and not whether these distinctions are consistently made using the language of race, ethnicity, or nationality.

In the nineteenth and early twentieth centuries, immigration policy in Canada and other settler-colonial states was largely designed to bring in members of European "races" who could help establish and solidify dominance over Indigenous peoples. This pursuit of dominance, including physical and cultural genocide, was based on the idea that Indigenous people were innately deficient beings in cultural, political, and moral terms (Thompson 2016, 75). As non-White immigrants were brought in to fulfill manual labour needs in the railroad and other industries, racialized nation-building efforts expanded to manage the growth of those populations. The 1910 Immigration Act was the first general Immigration Act to codify race as a selection criterion in immigration law. It gave Cabinet the power to prohibit the entry of immigrants "belonging to any race deemed unsuitable to the climate and requirements of Canada or immigrants of any specified class, occupation or character" (quoted in Kelley and Trebilcock 2010, 137). Japanese and East Indians were considered the primary targets of this unspecified racial exclusion. (Chinese were covered separately under the 1885 Chinese Immigration Act and its increasingly restrictive amendments in 1887, 1892, 1900, and 1903.) This was evident in bureaucratic practices immediately prior to the passing of the 1910 Immigration Act. In 1908 the Canadian government had negotiated a backstage gentlemen's agreement with Japan – the Hayashi-Lemieux Agreement – to limit Japanese immigration to Canada by restricting the number of passports issued to Japanese who wished to emigrate there to 400 a year (Kelley and Trebilcock 2010, 146). Also in 1908, the Immigration Act of 1906 was amended by order-in-council (i.e., without debate in Parliament) to give full authority to Cabinet to prohibit the entry of any "specified class of immigrants who have come to Canada otherwise than by continuous journey from the country of which they are natives or citizens and upon through tickets purchased in that country" (quoted in Kelley and Trebilcock 2010, 149). Which "class" of immigrants was meant became evident when a directive was issued to Canadian Pacific Railway (CPR) outlets in India, prohibiting the sale of direct passage tickets to Canada (Kelley and Trebilcock 2010, 148). The fact that East Indians were, like Canadians, British subjects at the time did nothing to mitigate their group-level inadmissibility; it merely forced the Canadian government to develop more creative control measures than an outright ban, which would have caused diplomatic problems. The explicitly racially exclusionary bent of Canadian immigration policy – in both law and practice – continued until the repeal of the Chinese Immigration Act in 1947, which was the first step towards the dismantling of this policy.

In the 1950s and 1960s, different branches of the Canadian state were engaged in efforts to redefine the relationship between race and nation, in light of world-historical events and rapid economic change. Doing so in areas of government that were intricately entwined with population growth and management meant reconsidering the place of race within that definition of nation. When it comes to characterizing and explaining changes in ideas of who racialized groups were at the time, and whether they could be part of a particular nation, arguments have converged around two levels of analysis: the macro and meso levels. This has resulted in theoretical and empirical gaps in our understanding of the evolving relationship between state, race, and nation.

Race in the Postwar Era: From Macro-
and Meso- to Micro-Level Ideational Change

For the postwar era, Thompson (2016) argues that macro-level and meso-level dynamics were the principal forces behind changes in how race was conceptualized and used in population management. At the macro level, wider structures of thought and discourses of race permeated states and international organizations, informing ideas of what types of action are legitimate.[1] On a meso level, institutions like national statistics agencies and international organizations like the United Nations (UN) were actively interpreting and acting on these macro-level ideas and discourses in efforts to further their own agendas.

In terms of macro-level shifts, there is a strong scholarly consensus that a broad shift occurred in thinking about race from the late 1940s to the 1960s. It was prompted by world-historical events, including the Holocaust and decolonialization movements, as well as changes in scientific thinking about race. In the late nineteenth and early twentieth centuries, the global consensus had been that race was a category denoting biological differences between groups of humans that were linked, immutably, with particular character traits, values, norms, and behaviours; these groups, in turn, were ordered along a hierarchical spectrum of moral worth. Thompson (2016, 50) and others call this notion of race "biological racialism." As Saini (2019) argues, biological racialism had been in place since the height of colonialism. The belief that the human race contained biologically distinct groups of more or less intelligent and moral beings offered a more pleasant justification to Europeans for acquiring non-White colonies (saving and civilizing savages) than the alternative (hunger for political and economic power). It also led to the nineteenth-century fashion of "human zoos," in which groups of Indigenous or African-origin people were put on display alongside animals. Biological racialism was lent additional force and plausibility through rationalist, "scientific" measurement techniques, including in the field of anatomy, during the nineteenth century. This scientific racialism (and racism) generated a large volume of institutionalized knowledge about races.

In Canada, the common-sense nature of biological racialism and its implied hierarchical relationship between racial groups was exemplified by J.S. Woodsworth's 1909 widely read book *Strangers within Our Gates*. A minister, social activist, and later co-founder of the Co-operative Commonwealth Federation (CCF), the predecessor of today's National Democratic Party (NDP), Woodsworth was keen to enumerate immigrant groups of varying geographic origins living in Canada. He did this with a view to gauging the social challenges brought about by mass immigration. His description of immigrants from varying national-origin groups reflects the biological racialism of the time in its description of the racial groups originating from different regions. These racial groups are depicted as possessing immutable traits, and as standing in hierarchical degrees of proximity to Canada's White settler majority, which had its roots in the United Kingdom and France. At the top of Woodsworth's (1909) hierarchy, Scandinavians are described as "clean-blooded, thrifty, ambitious, and hard-working" (132); and Germans are considered "white people like ourselves" (100). Further down the hierarchy, Eastern and Southern European groups are held in less regard. Hungarians are described as a "race of farmers" who are "more intelligent and less industrious" than other Slavs and can "easily adapt" to life in Canada (143). Southern Italians possess intelligence levels "not higher than one could imagine of the descendant of peasantry illiterate for centuries" (168). Even further removed from the White settler ideal are the "Levantine races," which included Greeks, Turks, Syrians, and Armenians, who are described as "most undesirable" due to their low intelligence and their "dangerous" susceptibility to disease (168).

The biological racialism of the pre–Second World War era was subsequently replaced by a different global idea of race: one emphasizing the shared human condition, human rights and racial equality. As Thompson (2016) details, this transition began in the early twentieth century, with challenges to the "scientific" foundation of biological racialism from within the scholarly community. Scholars across a number of contexts advocated for a social constructivist rather than biological understanding of racial groups. In the wake of the Holocaust, the barbarism that had been justified through scientific racism leant political force to, and accelerated, the intellectual transition towards a new macro-level cultural framework for understanding race. The emerging global discourse of human rights was institutionalized internationally in the form of the 1948 *Universal Declaration of Human Rights*. The following year, UNESCO formed an expert committee of sociologists and anthropologists to study the concept of race. The resulting publication in 1950 of *The Race Question*, in which Gunnar Myrdal and others argued for discontinuing use of the word "race" in scientific discourse, in favour of "ethnicity," leant institutional force to this new, non-biological conceptualization. At the same time, decolonialization movements were underway in Africa, which would lead, in 1960, to the adoption of the *Declaration of the Granting of Independence to Colonial Countries and Peoples* by the UN General Assembly. These intellectual and political shifts, in turn, changed the normative framework against which the legitimacy of individual states' actions and policies were judged. Western liberal-democratic states vying for moral supremacy against the Soviet Union came under increasing pressure to reconcile their desired global image as protectors of individual rights with their highly racially discriminatory domestic policies and practices. Racially exclusionary immigration policies in particular posed a problem (FitzGerald and Cook-Martín 2014; Joppke 2005a; Thompson 2016; Triadafilopoulos 2012). For Canada, membership in the Commonwealth made the situation particularly uncomfortable. How could the country justify continued restrictions on immigration from India and the British West Indies while at the same time championing human rights and decolonialization movements on the world stage? Likewise, how was it possible to deny full citizenship to Chinese and Japanese populations in Canada in the form of reduced family reunification privileges?

Meso-level racial projects within state institutions played an important role in mediating how changing macro-level notions of race affected population management in different national contexts. At this level, census bureaus and the census categories produced by them have received the most scholarly attention. As Starr (1992, 265) argues, statistics, as a form of official categorization, are an important part of the "process by which the state 'edits' an official version of the social world." A growing body of scholarship examines how states contribute to processes of racialization in society by officially classifying their populations according to racial and ethnic categories (see, e.g., Kertzer and Arel 2002). The state's role in creating social classifications along racial lines is determined strongly by political elites. These actors decide how to classify populations, how to sort individuals into those classifications, what names to give them, and how to order or rank available categories (Starr 1992, 294). Once established, states use officially sanctioned racial and ethnic classifications to support discourses about race and race relations that then inform policymaking. For example, Nobles (2000) shows how racial statistics in the United States and Brazil have made race a salient social distinction in different ways over time, and how they have been used to support political discourses pertaining to the nature of race relations (e.g., the "Whitening" of Brazil). These discourses then serve as support for particular policies (e.g., the recruitment of European farm labourers to facilitate "racial uplift").

Insofar as policies and discourses fuelled by racial and ethnic statistics affect social and political inclusion and exclusion, they are intricately linked to citizenship. Citizenship refers here to an individual's relationship to the state, including legal status, rights, participation, and a sense of belonging (Bloemraad, Korteweg, and Yurdakul 2008).

Racial and ethnic statistics affect citizenship because they do not simply reflect demographic facts. Rather, they affect the distribution of material resources (e.g., state funding, labour market access) and symbolic notions of who is entitled to make claims on the state.

In the postwar era, census bureaus in countries like Canada changed how they enumerated racial groups. They did so in light of the aforementioned macro-level shift in thinking about race. At the start of the twentieth century, in the spirit of biological racialism, the Canadian census classified the population by colour. Individuals were defined as white, red, black, or yellow, to correspond with the "race of man" to which they belonged: Caucasian, American Indian, African or Negro, or Mongolian (Japanese/Chinese), respectively (Shanahan 2014, 297). Tracking racial difference, especially growth among immigrant populations, was deemed important in light of the explicitly racial understanding of nation motivating what was then the Dominion Bureau of Statistics (Boyd, Goldmann, and White 2000). As the 1921 Census report stated, the racial origins question was justified on the basis that "the constitution of Canada is based on the presence of two dominant races [Anglo- and French-Canadians]" (quoted in Shanahan 2014, 302). Changes to this explicitly racial naming and monitoring in response to macro-level normative pressures have been accounted for in terms of organizational and individual-level interests within the Bureau. Under the leadership of statistician Herbert Marshall, who had been involved in the UN Statistical Commission in the late 1940s, the decision was made early on, for the 1951 Census, to remove references to "race" and replace them with "origins." As Thompson (2016, 120) documents, enumerators were instructed that origin referred to "the cultural group, sometimes erroneously called 'racial' group." This early, relatively uncontested shift from the language of race to the language of ethnicity places the actions and political stance of the Dominion Bureau of Statistics in stark contrast to depictions of the Department of Citizenship and Immigration at that time. Thompson (2016, 123–4) argues that the Bureau was the institutional leader when it came to changing the idea of race articulated by the Canadian state: "Alone, the census has been at the forefront of the shift to the social construction of race, changing its language well in advance of other policy spheres and dominant social norms … [This] demonstrates the willingness of the Canadian state to change its use of racial discourse and language at the same time it proved hesitant to make substantive legal or policy change in other political realms, such as immigration law or Aboriginal affairs, that featured virulent and rampant racial discrimination." Thus meso-level institutional change in the idea of race is attributed to the Dominion

Bureau of Statistics and the census, with the Department of Citizenship and Immigration and immigration policy serving as a foil.

Compared to census bureaus and censuses, immigration bureaucracies and policies have not featured as prominently in analyses of meso-level changes in states' racial projects. Thompson (2016) and others who focus on the census as an object of study acknowledge the power of immigration policy for defining populations along racial lines. For example, Loveman's (2014, 22) work on the evolution of racial and ethnic classifications in censuses in Latin American countries acknowledges that immigration policies, too, are vehicles through which states define what she calls the "ethnoracial" foundations of membership in the polity, that is, which groups can be considered part of the national self or foreign other. However, immigration bureaucracies and the policies they produce have not been the main objects of study for scholars interested in state categorization and classification practices aimed at managing racial diversity.

This relative inattention to immigration bureaucracies and policies represents a missed opportunity for adding a micro-level perspective to the macro- and meso-level ones that are prioritized in discussions of the changing role of race in population management in the postwar era. There are two reasons for this. First, at least in the Canadian case, high-ranking members of the Department of Citizenship and Immigration served simultaneously as policymakers and implementers.[2] In their function as implementers, these state actors were required, on a regular basis, to articulate their understandings of immigrants' racial classifications and their significance *in practice*, not just abstractly. In contrast, the Canadian census was administered by enumerators who recorded responses from interviews with households. This was the case until 1971, when self-enumeration (i.e., respondents completing their own questionnaires) was introduced. Creating categories and classifications is one thing, but how do people get slotted into one or the other? The deliberations about how to apply classifications to individuals and groups that occur in immigration policy formulation and implementation can reveal fine-grained information about the nature of the social distinctions underpinning those classifications. Second, and relatedly, the application of classifications in immigration policy implementation can yield more powerful insights into the actual material effects of symbolic distinctions. In immigration policy, racial classifications and other social distinctions are associated with decisions about the admissibility of groups and individuals, that is, whether they may enter or remain in the territory and polity. They also affect the distribution of material resources when immigrants in particular racial groups (or their national proxies) are given differential access to settlement services. The Assisted Passage Loan Scheme, which was reserved for European-origin immigrants to Canada until 1970, is one example of such a material effect. In other words, looking at immigration policy – particularly its implementation in concrete cases – provides an opportunity to see whether/when racial and other distinctions are associated with actual inclusion or exclusion. It thus, arguably, becomes the more strategic site for not only examining the evolving relationship between racial classifications and population management but also how such classifications produce or maintain patterns of social stratification.

As chapter 2 argued in reference to the case of postwar immigration policy formulation in Canada, bringing the micro level into explanations of the evolving relationship between race, nation, and state in the mid-twentieth century is not just a response to a theoretical puzzle. It is also an empirically motivated necessity. The implementation practices of immigration bureaucrats diverged from, and moved ahead of formal changes in, immigration law when it came to admitting members of hitherto inadmissible groups. Therefore, we cannot fully understand what happened to race as a principle of inclusion and exclusion in the transition to a universal immigration policy during that period without accounting for the interpretive practices of these state actors.

Reconsidering the Meaning of Race in Merit-Based Immigration Policies

While rooted in a case study of Canada, the argument presented in this book speaks to a broader concern in the social sciences about the role of race in immigrant selection in Western liberal-democratic states. The 1960s and 1970s saw the introduction of universal, or "merit-based," immigrant selection policies in countries like Canada, the United States, and Australia. These policies are called "universal" because they are theoretically open to any individual in the world (with the appropriate human capital and/or social ties) irrespective of their ascribed social group membership, that is, race, gender, or social class. But the nature of discrimination – particularly racial discrimination – that occurs under these policies is still a matter of scholarly debate.

According to Joppke (2005a), immigration policies like Canada's allow for only two legitimate distinctions for deciding the terms of entry and settlement. The first is a group-level distinction based on citizenship status (i.e., between citizens and non-citizens); the second is an individual-level distinction based on individual characteristics like human capital and social ties to family or employers (see also

FitzGerald et al. 2018). Of the four commonly identified dimensions of citizenship – legal status, rights, political participation, and belonging (Bloemraad, Korteweg, and Yurdakul 2008, 54) – the notion of citizenship status here emphasizes legal status. In other words, it emphasizes state classifications of individuals as citizens or non-citizens and, within the non-citizen category, distinctions between permanent residents, temporary residents, those immigrating for economic or family purposes ("immigrants"), and those immigrating for the purpose of seeking refuge ("refugees" or "asylum seekers"). It can also encompass an absence of status, or the state of being "undocumented" or "irregular," as even the absence of formal status is a particular relationship between an individual and a state (Menjivar 2006; Zolberg 1999). The legitimacy of discriminating based on citizenship lies in the internationally agreed right of states to territorial sovereignty, which includes the power to decide whether non-citizens may enter/exit that territory and under what conditions. Citizenship status is considered "non-discriminatory" because it is a "formal legal category" that does not map onto "particular group characteristics," especially racial and ethnic ones (Joppke 2005a, 49). In other words, this group-level distinction in immigration policy is one in which, theoretically, ascribed group memberships (e.g., race, class, gender) are irrelevant.

The second legitimate distinction – individual traits like human capital and social ties – is also regarded as "non-discriminatory" because such characteristics are likewise divorced from ascribed group memberships (Joppke 2005a, 49). The legitimacy of discriminating based on human capital, particularly "skills" (using proxies like education, occupation, and language) rests arguably on two premises. The first is that "skill" is commonly understood from an economic, human capital perspective as something that results from individual investments of time, effort, and money that anyone can make regardless of social class, gender, and race. The second premise, again reflecting a (neoclassical) economic perspective, is that admitting non-citizens selectively according to particular skill levels is an effective means of meeting domestic labour market needs, while allowing non-citizens the opportunity to improve their economic position. Taken together, these two premises emphasize individual agency, equality of opportunity, and "win-win" outcomes for receiving states and immigrants (Boucher 2020, 1; see also Boucher 2016).

The facial neutrality of the main distinctions embedded in the universal immigration policies – citizenship status (at the group level) and human capital and social ties (at the individual level) – has led many scholars to argue that these policies represented the demise of racist immigration policies (FitzGerald and Cook-Martín 2014; Joppke 2005b; Reitz 2012; Triadafilopoulos 2012). The strongest evidence offered in support of this argument are the demographic changes in immigrant admissions that occurred once universal selection policies had been implemented. In Canada, for instance, statistics show that whereas almost 80 per cent of all immigrants in 1971 had been born in the British Isles or Europe, fewer than 30 per cent had those regions as a place of birth in 2016 (Statistics Canada 2017a). In 2016, Asian countries comprised seven out of ten top countries of origin for immigrants arriving within the previous five years: the Philippines, India, China, Iran, Pakistan, Syria, and South Korea (Statistics Canada 2017b, 5). FitzGerald and Cook-Martín (2014, 181) make this argument most directly, stating: "The most obvious flaw in the argument for racist continuity in Canadian immigration policy is the dramatic transformation in the origins of *permanent* immigrants" (emphasis added). In other words, claims about the universal nature of immigration policies in Western liberal-democratic states focus on the multicultural character of legally privileged entry categories for skilled workers and family members that grant permanent resident status to a significant proportion of the immigrant population.

Scholars working from a critical race perspective disagree (see, e.g., K. Anderson 1995; Aiken 2007; Jakubowski 1997; Simmons 1999). They see racial distinctions as fundamental to power dynamics and social stratification in societies and their institutions.[3] In the Canadian case, these scholars argue that immigration policy continues to operate in racially exclusionary ways, either directly (i.e., through intentional racist exclusion) or indirectly (i.e., through the racialized effects of universal policies). When it comes to direct racial exclusion, racist biases are argued to persist among individual immigration bureaucrats responsible for processing applications from majority non-White origin countries. The unequal geographic distribution of visa processing centres and resources like personnel is also seen as an institutional choice motivated by racial discrimination. K. Anderson (1995, 180) provides a clear statement of this view: "although 'race' was exorcised from statutes, it was by no means erased from the administrative practices of the Canadian government."

One phenomenon presented as evidence of indirect racial exclusion is the expansion and racialization of temporary migration programs. In reference to the introduction of the 1973 Non-Immigrant Employment Authorization Program (NIEAP), Sharma (2006, 23) argues that racist "nationalist practices" by the immigration bureaucracy led to the expansion of temporary admissions categories in which non-White immigrants from less developed countries of origin are over-represented. According to her, the "problem of permanence of non-whites within Canadian society" (22), following postwar changes to immigration policy, was solved by "differentially" including them in the economy while excluding them from long-term membership in the national collective. Similar arguments have been made in reference to the Live-In Caregiver (LIC) program (e.g., Bakan and Stasiulis 2012; Tungohan et al. 2015); the Seasonal Agricultural Worker Program or SAWP (e.g., Gabriel and MacDonald 2012; Preibisch and Hennebry 2012); and the Temporary Foreign Worker Program (TFWP), which has grown markedly over the past decade (Boucher and Gest 2018; Goldring and Landolt 2013; Lenard and Straehle 2012).

Another example of indirect racial exclusion is the unequal distribution of educational and occupational opportunities between the Global North and (majority non-White) Global South. Scholars working within a critical race perspective argue that this unequal distribution makes it more difficult for non-White immigrants to acquire the human capital required under more legally privileged entry categories for skilled workers (Galabuzi 2006; Simmons 1999). Cashmore (1978) and Abu-Laban (1998a) both argue that language requirements have particularly strong exclusionary effects along racial lines.

While "immigration policy universalists" acknowledge that the expansion and racialization of temporary migration programs may represent a form of ongoing racial exclusion, they are less inclined to accept arguments about systemic racial discrimination operating through selection criteria applied to permanent skilled worker or family immigrants (see, e.g., FitzGerald and Cook-Martín 2014, 182–3). Here they cite the aforementioned evidence of racial diversity among immigrants selected into those categories. The debate about the role of race in selecting permanent skilled worker and family immigrants is thus arguably at an impasse.

This apparent impasse is rooted in how the idea of race is conceptualized in studies of the postwar era, especially on the part of immigration policy universalists. There are two related issues with how race is conceptualized. First, it is often treated as analytically separate from other social distinctions that are associated with social inequalities, like gender and class, especially outside scholarly communities that adopt a critical race or intersectional perspective. This means that "universality" and "non-discrimination" are evaluated in terms of the presence or absence of explicitly exclusionary clauses related to race (and its ethnic/ national proxies).[4] This is perhaps unsurprising given how immigration policy is often linked, conceptually, to nationalism, colonialism,

and the racial management of nation-states' demographic composi-
tions. Immigration policies are widely understood to be instruments
used by states to classify populations to nation-building ends. This
conceptual link between immigration policy and nation lends itself to
a focus, in empirical research, on social group memberships that are
strongly embedded in theorizations of that concept. For example, Tilly
(1999, 413) defines the nation as a "categorical relation in which agents
on one side of a boundary claim (1) common historical origins, culture,
and destiny for all persons on their side of the boundary and (2) dis-
tinctness from others beyond the boundary." As the reference to common historical origins suggests, notions of who belongs to a nation are
strongly linked to racial distinctions. This link derives from the state-
formation phase experienced by modern nation-states, during which
the rhetorical congruence between race, ethnicity, and nation became
the basis from which the state (as a representative of the nation) drew
its legitimacy (Gellner 1983; Smith 1998; Brubaker 2009; Wimmer 2008).
If race as a distinctive means of social classification is associated with
racially exclusionary nation-building practices, the key to universalizing immigration policies in the mid-twentieth century can, by logical
extension, be seen as the removal of national and racial distinctions.

Second, race is often treated as a coherent idea about the existence of
biologically distinguishable groups that stand in hierarchical relation to
each other. In other words, the idea of race as biological racialism that
scholars have identified as prevalent at a macro-cultural level in the
mid-twentieth century is used as a category of analysis and ascribed
category of practice in describing the idea of race as it operates in
immigration policymaking. The conceptual transition in macro-level
ideas of race around the mid-twentieth century described earlier in
the chapter is then presumed to have been mirrored at the meso level,
in branches of the state and the policies they developed. As a result,
the entire debate about the changing nature of race as an organizing
principle in immigration policy begs the question of what race actually
meant, in practice, to those responsible for making and implementing
that policy.

The distinction between categories of analysis and categories of
practice is useful in drawing attention to how scholarly work can
inadvertently reify the concepts it aims to scrutinize, particularly race
(see, e.g., Brubaker 2009; Jenkins 1994; Loveman 1999). From a social
constructivist perspective, identity categories in the social world, that
is, processes that lead to a sense of "groupness," are the result of self-
classifications and other-classifications. In other words, they are the
result of iterative, micro-level practices, which are informed by existing

macro- and meso-level principles of classification, but which do not necessarily reflect them perfectly. Social constructivist approaches to race see racial groups as the outcomes of social practices that demarcate the boundary between groups. These boundaries can be drawn in terms of "folk" understandings of these groups that emphasize biological traits such as phenotype; they may also be drawn in cultural, socioeconomic, moral, religious, or other terms. Adopting a clearly defined, biological idea of race as a category of analysis leads scholars to ask limiting questions of data pertaining to the categories of practice that are actually generative of that category. It also implicitly treats the idea of race as stable and coherent, which makes it difficult to conceptualize ideational change beyond having race "disappear" or be displaced elsewhere in the system, for example, from permanent to temporary entry schemes.

Race has been operationalized in analyses of postwar immigration policy change as a coherent, biological idea about who people are that is analytically distinct from other social ascriptions due, in part, to a weakness of standard theoretical approaches to conceptualizing immigration policy and policymaking. These approaches provide little room for exploring the emergent quality of ideas and meanings that shape policy. Therefore, a new approach is needed to account for how the micro-level actions of state actors affect the *process* of immigration policy formulation as well as the *substantive meanings* given to selection principles under that policy, for example, the meaning of "race" in relation to "admissibility."

Evolving Approaches to Theorizing the Role of States and State Actors in Immigration Policy Formulation

Theories developed to explain immigration policy formulation have long focused on how sources of power and meanings that are exogenous to the policymaking process itself lead to particular policy outputs, that is, laws, regulations, and formal policy statements. It is possible to distinguish three broad theoretical approaches, and each has distinct implications for conceptualizing the role of states and individual state actors in policy formulation. The first are pluralist approaches, which see interest groups in society as key forces that sway states towards policies that reflect those interests. The second are institutional approaches, which locate the main source of political power in particular institutions or constellations of relationships between institutions. The third are state-centred approaches, which see states as institutions that can wield power in the service of their own interests.

Pluralist approaches see policy as the result of political pressures emanating from organized groups in society. The state is mainly a broker between competing interests in society, foremost economic and cultural ones, and it parlays the most powerful interests into immigration policy. The works of Freeman (1995) and Hollifield (1992) are exemplary in this vein. On the economic side, the impulses coming from society at any given time will be influenced by whether pro-immigration business interests or organized labour, wary of the effect of imported workers on domestic ones, are more powerful. On the cultural side, the outcome of struggles between pro-immigration ethnic lobbies and anti-immigration nativist sentiments at any given time will affect policy choices. A frequent, predicted outcome of this model is that the degree of organization matters: more organized groups that stand to reap clear benefits from immigration (e.g., business and ethnic groups) will prevail over less organized groups who stand to gain less (e.g., the general public or workers), leading to the expansion of legal channels for immigration seen in North America and Europe in recent decades. In this work, the state's brokering activities – especially the degree to which they are likely to parlay restrictive impulses into admissions policies – are also influenced by broad ideational currents. As they pertain to immigration policymaking from the mid-twentieth century onward, these models presume that states broker between interests against the backdrop of liberal principles and norms, like the primacy of universal individual rights. Here Hollifield (1992) speaks of "embedded liberalism" whereas Freeman (1995) evokes the existence of an "anti-populist norm." Whether institutionalized at the domestic or international level, the purported effect of such norms has been to push states toward inclusion by ensuring that restrictive impulses from society cannot be acted on by states to a strong extent. Critiques of these models abound; these focus on their underlying assumptions, like the distinction between societal groups and the state as well as the consistency of group interests over time (see, e.g., Boswell 2007; Tichenor 2002). As regards the scope for theorizing the state and its interests, critics note that pluralist models do a poor job of explaining both why states would choose to respond to organized interests generally, and how precisely variations in substantive policy content occur.

Institutionalist approaches to theorizing immigration policy formulation are capable of addressing these lacunae, as they attribute the political power to define policy content to institutions and constellations of institutions. A very broad range of scholarly approaches falls under the institutionalist umbrella, focusing on different state and non-state institutions. For example, Joppke's (1998, 2005b) work highlights the power of the judiciary in forcing states to extend the scope of labour immigration from non-White source countries based on the courts' interests in advancing norms of non-discrimination. One of the more complex theoretical models in the intuitionalist vein is Tichenor's (2002) historical intuitionalist account of immigration policy outputs in the United States and their oscillation between more expansionist or inclusive and more restrictive or exclusionary tendencies. In this model, immigration policy results from a complicated interplay between the interests and goals of governing institutions (i.e., branches of the state), interest groups outside the state, ideational currents manifest in institutionally generated knowledge or expertise (e.g., government agencies and commissions), and international political developments that affect how state actors, interest groups, and societies in general understand their relationship with (and obligations to) the rest of the world. This model is a dynamic one in which both the interests and goals of institutions (state or non-state) and the degree of political power they can muster in championing particular policy outputs are subject to change over time in response to the four above-mentioned factors. Even if, as Boswell (2007) argues, institutionalist approaches are most useful for explaining immigration policy outputs post hoc, from a historical perspective, they do have an advantage over pluralist models in that they provide a means for conceptualizing states (treated as unitary actors or a collection of competing actors) as active participants in the policy formulation process.

In contrast to both pluralist and institutionalist accounts, so-called state-centred approaches have gone furthest in attempting to specify the interests and actions of states. One strand of these accounts is characterized by Sciortino (2000, 218) as "neo-corporatist," to denote its emphasis on how states, within the confines of international constraints, mediate among conflicting cultural and economic interests at the domestic level, in ways that suit their own interests and goals. Zolberg (1999) provides one of the earliest examples of this approach, arguing that those in positions of power within states are vote maximizers, aiming to produce immigration policies that balance a range of interests in ways that appear politically expedient. These interests include aforementioned economic and cultural ones, as well as the state's own foreign policy ambitions (which can play strongly into the admission of otherwise "undesirable" groups like refugees), and desire to maintain the exclusivity of the national community. In a similar vein, Boswell (2007) argues that states will adopt immigration policies that allow them to maintain legitimacy in the eyes of voters, which rests on the state's perceived performance in four dimensions: security, accumulation, fairness, and institutional legitimacy. The substantive type of immigration policy to emerge in a given state at a given time will, according to this perspective, depend on the extent to which that state seeks to realize each of those imperatives, which it might choose not to do. Thus, substantive policy outcomes can be expected to vary based on the broader historical and institutional contexts that help define what the maintenance of state legitimacy entails. Focusing on different branches of state (executive and legislative), Ellermann (2006, 2021) explains immigration policy formulation and implementation in terms of the ability of states to insulate themselves from external interest groups. This can be done by shifting the locus of decision-making to a branch of government to which interested non-state actors (e.g., business or community groups) do not have ready access, for example, by moving responsibility for a policy with visible local impacts to a regional government office, as in the case of some German states' approaches to deportation. It can also be accomplished by placing immigration policymaking powers in the hands of the executive rather than the legislature. While perhaps gaining in predictive power, these neo-corporatist state-centred approaches are still open to the critique of ascribing relatively constant interests to both societal actors and the state (Sciortino 2000, 218). In other words, there is little room to account for variability in the stances held by organized interests like employers and trade unions, the state itself, and the vision all parties share for creating mutually beneficial policies.

This critique has been addressed to some extent by state-centred theories that have been characterized as "realist" to denote their focus on the emergence of endogenous interests within the state (or one of its branches). These endogenous interests, in turn, are seen as key to explaining immigration policy formulation and implementation. Scholarly work in this vein tends to be based on detailed archival research and/or ethnographic fieldwork, and has allowed the broadest scope for conceptualizing the micro level of immigration policy formulation. It emphasizes how different levels of the organizational hierarchy and different types of actions within immigration bureaucracies are relevant to policy formulation. Looking at the historical case of the "Bracero" guest worker program in the United States, Calavita (2010) argues that higher-level "state managers," that is, actors in federal agencies like the Immigration and Naturalization Service (INS), are able to take their agencies in particular directions based on career and organizational interests. This focus on particular actors reveals that "the state" is less a monolith than a collection of institutions at different levels of government, whose competing interests will shape the direction of immigration policy. Paquet (2015) makes a similar argument, highlighting the role of provincial governments in shaping Canadian immigration policy from the 1990s onwards, particularly "policy entrepreneurs," that is, bureaucrats who act autonomously to bring about policy change. Relatedly, Boucher's (2013) comparative analysis of changes to "points systems" for skilled workers in Canada and Australia shows that another way high-level bureaucrats affect policy formulation is through efforts to keep policy debates and decisions within venues under their control. They do this by making executive decisions via regulations, and by preventing non-state actors from shifting debate to a more public venue like Parliament. For Bonjour (2011), moral obligations and immaterial values such as the ethical norm of equal treatment – not just strategic political interests – inform the policy formulation activities of higher-level immigration bureaucrats.

Moving down the organizational hierarchy, Paquet (2019) shows how the aggregate work of "middle-ranking" immigration bureaucrats in one Canadian province (Quebec) shapes policy formulation at the essential level of problem definition and consensus building. Looking at Germany, the United Kingdom, and the European Commission, Boswell (2009) highlights the work done within immigration bureaucracies to generate and use research and expert knowledge in formulating "evidence-based policymaking" practices. She argues that such knowledge is used to legitimize claims to resources, jurisdictions, and authority, and to substantiate organizational interests. Slaven and Boswell (2019) examine the work of immigration bureaucrats in balancing their own ideas and beliefs about appropriate policy interventions with mandates from elected officials and public expectations. They show how this interpretive and cognitive work can result in symbolic, rather than instrumental, policies, that is, ones that signal commitments to values or goals rather than affect target populations in the stated way. In sum, this line of scholarship shows that high- and mid-level immigration bureaucrats are responsible for a lot of "what happens after an election and before policy implementation" (Paquet 2019, 168). One conclusion to be drawn from this is that it is impossible to understand the policy formulation process and its outcomes fully without examining the iterations, interactions, and interpretations of state actors within immigration bureaucracies.

One important development in state-centric theorizing of immigration policy has been the reconceptualization of the nature of immigration bureaucrats' actions. These actions have often been depicted as rational and based on clear understandings of both the goals of policymaking and means of achieving them. More recently, scholars have become attentive to the possibility that the actions of immigration bureaucrats can be creative, improvised, and pragmatic in the sociological sense. This means that they are based on evolving interpretations of issues and events that manifest in concrete situations (Joas 1996).[5] Slaven and Boswell's (2019) study of immigration policymaking, described above, embraces such a pragmatist stance in its emphasis on ideas, framing, and immigration bureaucrats' creative actions. Pragmatist cultural sociologists like Ann Swidler (1986) posit that social actors draw creatively on cultural resources (e.g., prevailing ideas, norms, and values) to interpret and classify elements of a situation and devise a course of action. Note that pragmatist approaches do not propose that actors exercise their creativity in a vacuum, but that they do so in reference to general and immediate social contexts. As Emirbayer (1997, 294) states: "Agency is always a dialogic process by which actors immersed in the *dureé* of lived experience engage with others in collectively organized action contexts, temporal as well as spatial." These structural environments include macro-level (e.g., societal, cultural) structures and meso-level (e.g., organizational) ones. In this sense, a pragmatist approach to understanding the actions of immigration bureaucrats complements immigration policymaking theories that highlight how external social forces (e.g., interest groups or macro-cultural contexts) shape policymaking. It adds to those theories a mechanism for explaining how external social forces are translated into immigration policy.

The pragmatist conceptualization of immigration bureaucrats' actions in policymaking has the built-in potential to be especially useful for understanding paradigmatic policy shifts. According to pragmatist social theorists, the creativity of action is particularly marked in situations where routines have broken down, forcing actors to reflect on their situation and experiment with a course of action (see, e.g., Dewey 1988; Emirbayer 1997; Joas 1996; Schneiderhan 2011).

The historical Canadian case at the heart of this book illustrates this pragmatist claim. By all existing accounts, the postwar context in which immigration bureaucrats were tasked with creating universal immigration policies was one in which a routine (that of White nation-building through immigration) was breaking down in light of changing international and domestic contexts. New policy solutions needed to be found while daily operations were kept up and running. As archival records show, this situation prompted frequent ruminating on the nature and purpose of different immigration streams. In 1959, the Deputy Minister of Citizenship and Immigration encouraged the Director of Immigration to admit that the immigration program was based less on "empiricism" than on "intuition," and that it really amounted to an "educated guess."[6] In 1961, the deputy minister admitted that the "chief dilemma" regarding the Department's policy towards immigrants from the British West Indies was that it was "ambivalent as to what [they were] trying to do"; this ambivalence led him to wonder: "Are we trying to pick domestics whose attitude to household service is good and who will be content to remain in household service and be good domestics on a career basis? Or are we using the domestic movement as a means of selecting a higher class of girl who will not stay in domestic service any longer than necessary?"[7] This uncertainty finds one of its clearest expressions in 1961 over the issue of how to manage family immigration from India. In a series of memoranda, the deputy minister stated openly that he was at a loss for how to proceed, in part because "the problem [had] not really crystalized in [his] mind."[8] In an effort to move forward, he sought input from members of the Immigration Branch on the matter: "The answer may be to turn loose one of your own people on this, in order to research the subject and determine what the problem really is … I frankly do not know what the answer is at the present time."[9]

Despite their lack of clarity about the situation, however, high-level bureaucrats were intent on giving people outside the organization the impression that those at the helm were acting deliberately and decidedly, as the following quotation illustrates: "It seems that we should at the moment neither close our eyes to the impending problems nor get into a panic, but that it is essential to give everyone the impression that we are acting quite lucidly and that we are in full command of the situation."[10] The actions of immigration bureaucrats in the policy formulation process may appear rational and goal-oriented in public statements and documents, but empirical attention to deliberations in uncertain situations may reveal moments of heightened creativity that leads to the emergence of new ideas, practices and policies.

The historical Canadian case shows how the pragmatist focus on creative action during periods of rupture can illuminate the *process* of developing and institutionalizing new practices. Given their lack of a clear vision, members of the Department described the admissions practices they developed during the postwar era as "experimental." They came to see order-in-council admissions of individuals from legally inadmissible groups as a tentative solution to practical problems associated with moving from a racist to a universal immigration policy. This was the case, for example, with the admission of Chinese and Japanese fiancé(e)s, who were admitted on an "experimental basis" from 1956 and 1957 onward, respectively.[11] Experimenting was an important means of testing policy solutions, as evidenced by the Department's description of the gradual inclusion of adopted children in the range of legally admissible immigrant family members (see chapter 5). In 1960, after years of admitting adopted children exceptionally by order-in-council, the Department stated that the gradual institutionalization of that practice would be "begun on an experimental basis so that careful control [could] be exercised in the initial instance."[12]

The pragmatist approach to seeing action as situational, relational, and interpretive may also help illuminate the role of immigration bureaucrats in shaping the *substance* of policies as they emerge in practice. This is due to its aforementioned attention to the creative use of cultural resources by actors to interpret, categorize, and classify elements of a situation, and in devising a course of action. Rather than asking what state actors aim to do and why, this approach prompts us to ask what meanings they attach to their actions and to the people who are the intended targets of their policies. If meanings, and related interests and goals, are emergent in situations, it is possible to theorize ideational innovation as endogenous to the policymaking process, and as having the potential to shape the policy formulation process and its substantive outcomes.

Efforts to centre state actors' creative use of cultural elements like ideas and meanings in the immigration policy context are well established. However, they are to be found in scholarship on immigration policy implementation, which is treated as conceptually and empirically distinct from the immigration policy formulation literature reviewed above. In moving towards a theory of immigration policy formulation that includes implementation (for the theoretical and empirical reasons outlined previously), it is thus possible and useful to draw on insights from the literature on immigration policy formulation.

Adding Insights from Studies of Immigration Policy Implementation

Studies of immigration policy implementation in the areas of deportation, border control, and family/marriage migration have shown how state actors creatively interpret concepts in immigration law in the course of applying that law to individual cases. Legal scholars have long noted the importance of state actors' interpretations of immigration law in shaping its substance. As Motomura (2014, 4) states, the "gap between law on the books and law in action is filled by countless government decisions that reflect the exercise of discretion."

Building on Lipsky's ([1980] 2010) influential study of "street-level" bureaucrats, scholarship on immigration policy implementation shows how these discretionary decisions shape the effects of immigration laws and regulations. The vague language and discretion built into government policies mean that implementing bureaucrats must develop cognitive routines for interpreting the meaning of key concepts in order to function efficiently under organizational constraints such as high caseloads and processing targets. In turn, these cognitive routines come to define the very content of policy itself. As Lipsky states, "The decisions of street-level bureaucrats, the routines they establish, and the devices they invent to cope with uncertainties and work pressures, effectively become the public policies they carry out" (xiii). Feminist welfare state scholars have illustrated this scaling up of routines in reference to how low-level bureaucrats define what kind of people are considered the legitimate recipients of welfare benefits (Adams and Padamsee 2001; Korteweg 2003). Likewise, in the area of immigration, case processors define who can be considered a legitimate immigrant, by giving meaning to key concepts like "family," "marriage," and "highly skilled" (see, e.g., Bhabha 2006; Bouchard and Carroll 2002; Kim 2011; Eggebø 2013; Friedman 2010; Gilboy 1991; Pellander 2015; Pratt 2005; Satzewich 2015; Scheel and Gutekunst 2019).

The work of interpreting and defining concepts in immigration law and regulations is not conducted in a vacuum. Scholars show that macro-cultural contexts, meso-level organizational factors, and individual traits play a role in shaping implementation practices, although the relative weighting and effect of each of these aspects is a matter of debate. Much of this literature relies implicitly on a pragmatist view of bureaucratic actions as relational, situational, and contingent.

On a macro-cultural level, studies of the implementation of family reunification policies in Norway (Eggebø 2013), Finland (Pellander 2015), Canada (Satzewich 2014a), and Germany (Scheel and Gutekunst 2019) show how normative ideas of family and marriage present in the receiving-country's culture affect whether bureaucrats perceive a marriage between an immigrant and a non-immigrant to be "genuine" (and thus grounds for admission). Not just receiving-country norms but also perceived sending-country norms around marriage and migration can shape such assessments (Pellander 2015; Satzewich 2014b).

Some scholars focus on organizational configurations and cultures in bureaucratic agencies responsible for immigration regulations as social determinants of the interpretive practices of case processors. In her study of street-level bureaucrats responsible for detecting, detaining, and deporting irregular immigrants in Switzerland, Borrelli (2021) highlights how formal and informal on-the-job training socializes individuals to make discretionary decisions in patterned ways. Looking at the adjudication of family reunification applications in Canadian visa processing centres abroad, Satzewich (2014b, 1459) argues that the organizational imperative that "you don't want to embarrass the Minister" by falling short of processing quotas creates an incentive to approve applications and avoid time-consuming interviews and secondary screenings. In their study of French consulates, Alpes and Spire (2014) argue that organizational elements like time pressures, divisions of labour in visa processing, professional socialization into a "culture of distrust," and the French state's diplomatic and economic interests in the state where a consulate is located are strong determinants of implementation practices. Ellermann's (2009) work on deportation implementation in Germany and the United States shows that organizational configurations can shape outcomes insofar as they insulate front-line implementers from – or make them susceptible to – direct public and political attention and interventions.

The degree to which individual-level factors like personal attitudes and role conceptions shape implementation outcomes is another area of investigation. In their work on German immigration authorities, Scheel and Gutekunst (2019, 857) paint the picture of relatively autonomous bureaucrats engaging in practices that "go well beyond their competences" in adjudicating marriage migration cases: they demand additional evidence of "real" relationships in the face of suspicions that "naive" European women are being preyed upon by "ruthless" foreign men from non-European countries. Similarly, Pellander (2015, 1481) argues that Finnish bureaucrats explicitly see themselves as moral gatekeepers. According to her, their personal efforts to police marriage migration involving "vulnerable" Finnish or foreign women duped into "marriages of convenience" or "forced" migration are constrained only by anticipated judicial constraints. In contrast, Eule (2018) characterizes frontline immigration bureaucrats involved in policing irregular migration in Germany as pragmatic and not overly invested in achieving a particular outcome. He states that, "more often than not, they favour convenience over politics, realism over law, going home over wearing themselves down on an impossible mission" (2781). Both the degree of autonomy afforded individual low-level implementers, and the quality of preferences and interests they would act on if they had it, remain a matter of debate.

One overarching question in studies of immigration policy implementation, which is also relevant to this book, is whether the interpretive outcomes of discretionary implementation practices tend to be exclusionary or inclusive, and towards whom. Studies of immigration policy implementation practices most often characterize them as exclusionary, especially along the lines of race, gender, or class (Scheel and

Gutekunst 2019). However, without negating the potential for exclusion, it is important for researchers to remain open to the possibility that the outcomes of discretionary practices can also be inclusive. For example Satzewich (2014b, 1464) shows that, in contrast to many of their European counterparts, Canadian visa officers' assessment of whether a marriage is "genuine" can be flexible when a couple's situation does not conform exactly to expectations rooted in the social norms in Canada and/or an immigrant's country of origin. He argues that officers tend to interpret cases "in the spirit of" immigration law, which can be more inclusive than the letter of the law. Similarly, Ellermann (2006) illustrates how lower-level state officials in Germany draw on moral assessments of deservingness to override the absence of legal status and provide exceptions from deportation enforcement. As Pratt and Sossin (2009, 302) argue, "Discretion may mean beneficence or tyranny, justice or injustice, reasonableness, or unreasonableness." The degree to which the outcomes of discretionary implementation practices lean toward inclusion or exclusion – and on what grounds – is an important empirical question that cannot be overlooked in characterizing the substantive nature of immigration policies.

This review of immigration policy implementation studies shows how they complement state-centred theories of immigration policy formulation that focus on the role of ideas and state actors' interpretations of them. Discretion, interpretive practices, and meaning-making are clearly seen as central to the activities of immigration bureaucrats at different levels of the organizational hierarchy and different policy stages (formulation and implementation). In both literatures, these activities are seen as taking place in concrete situations that are structured by macro- and meso-level contextual factors like cultural and political currents and organizational cultures. The extent to which the individual characteristics of bureaucrats affect outcomes, and whether those outcomes are inclusive or exclusionary, are open empirical questions. Importantly for the project at hand, the documented effect of interpretive implementation practices on shaping the substance of policy *after* it has been formulated and institutionalized means that these practices – if carried out by high-level bureaucrats – can shape policy substance *during* the policy formulation process. The effect of discretionary interpretations of entry criteria like "admissibility," "family," and "skill" would be even greater in the hands of high-level bureaucrats. If these actors are using implementation to experiment with policy, the substance of their interpretive practices will become institutionalized and ultimately affect a larger number of people through further implementation over time.

We therefore need a state-centred theory of immigration policy for-mulation that is capable of conceptualizing implementation (case pro-cessing) as an element of policy formulation, and not just as something that occurs afterwards. Such a theory would generate a fuller under-standing of the micro-level aspect of immigration policy formula-tion, including, potentially, the "bottom-up" generation of admissions criteria and other policy elements. I am not the first to propose that immigration policy can be formulated on the ground, in the course of implementation. Kang (2017) shows how local branches of the INS in the US–Mexico border region developed enforcement practices on the ground that were later scaled up and included in federal legisla-tion. She makes this argument in reference to "rule-making processes," for example, the preparation of internal agency regulations, based on experiences in exercising administrative discretion in a particular social and political context. However, her study does not take into account the individual case adjudications that implementation scholarship has shown to be highly relevant to shaping the substantive content of laws and regulations. In the following section, I propose a theoretical approach that can account for case processing as an aspect of policy formulation.

A Cultural Sociology of Immigration Policy

The approach proposed here for a fuller theorization of bureaucratic practices in policy formulation – including implementation – is a cul-tural sociology of immigration policy. At its core, this approach builds on existing work that highlights the role of culture (e.g., ideas, cogni-tive schemas, paradigms, and frames) in policymaking (see, e.g., Bleich 2003; Skrentny 2002; Steensland 2006; DiMaggio 1997; Goldstein and Keohane 1993; Hall 1993). The fundamental insight from this work is that culturally informed notions of *who* people are influence how state actors conceptualize both the policies they create and how those poli-cies are applied – or not – to different types of individuals. Following Steensland (2006), the cultural sociology of immigration policy pro-posed here points to three mechanisms through which cultural mean-ings affect policy formulation.

The first mechanism, which operates as a background assumption in the model, is the presence of cultural repertoires,[13] on which immigra-tion bureaucrats draw while formulating policy. The term cultural rep-ertoires (Swidler 1986; Lamont 1992) refers to a shared stock of ideas, understandings, and values that are available to individuals within a given cultural space. Actors draw on these repertoires selectively and creatively in making or justifying decisions and actions. As the scholarship on immigration policy implementation reviewed above shows, immigration bureaucrats can draw on multiple cultural repertoires. These can be from their own national cultural context (e.g., normative ideas of family in Canada) or other national contexts (e.g., normative ideas of family elsewhere). This mechanism makes it possible to conceptualize the relationship between macro-level cultural factors (e.g., ideas about the nature of race or normative definitions of family), meso-level organizational factors (e.g., established routines of practice or "ways of doing things"), and the micro-level interpretive actions of immigration bureaucrats. In carrying out routinized actions pertaining to policy formulation (including case processing), these state actors are neither conduits through which prevailing cultural, social, and political impulses automatically shape policy outcomes, nor are they completely autonomous in relation to those impulses.

The second mechanism is the "boundary work" conducted by immigration bureaucrats in reference to cultural repertoires. In cultural sociology, the term "boundary work" denotes the process by which everyday people draw distinctions between themselves and others, thereby creating a system of symbolic stratification. Far from describing in abstract terms how a "self" is defined in opposition to an "other," boundary work explores how groups "concretely define 'us' and 'them,'" by identifying the "most salient principles of classification and identification" deployed from available elements of cultural repertoires (Lamont 2000, 4). These repertoires contain moral, racial, ethnic, socio-economic, gender, class, and status-based distinctions that underpin shared ideas and understanding of who people are. While this line of investigation within cultural sociology has focused on the boundary work of non-state actors, Skrentny (2002, 2006) argues that policymaking is a form of boundary work whereby state representatives draw on salient principles of classification and categorization in deciding whether to extend the application of existing policies to new target groups. The idea that formal immigration policy reflects the outcome of boundary work has been put forward by many scholars in relation to multiple national contexts (see, e.g., Bridget Anderson 2013; Bail 2008; Chauvin, Garcés-Mascareñas, and Kraler 2013; Zolberg 1999). In making this point, they have generally focused on formal policies (as articulated in legal, parliamentary, and media documents) rather than implementation. However, immigration policy implementation studies (e.g., on entry denial, detention, and deportation) show how boundary work – especially around notions of moral deservingness – operates in the interpretive practices of low-level, frontline immigration officials in ways that can uphold or attenuate the effects of legal clauses (see, e.g., Ellermann 2009; Pratt 2005). Within a cultural sociology of immigration policy, different levels of boundary work conducted by state actors (e.g., in general policy deliberations and case processing) can be seen as an important aspect of the policy formulation process and its outcomes.

The third mechanism is the institutionalization of the results of boundary work. This refers to the process whereby the concrete terms in which individuals and groups are categorized and characterized during policy formulation activities become formalized and codified. In the case of immigration policy, this institutionalization can manifest in immigration laws and regulations, as well as manuals and instructions issued to "street-level" bureaucrats charged with adjudicating cases. It is through this mechanism that boundary work on the part of state actors becomes applicable to cases beyond the ones that were the object of the original boundary work, amplifying its material and symbolic effects.[14]

The cultural sociology of immigration policy approach developed here adopts the general framework and mechanisms proposed by Steensland (2006), but it also modifies that framework in two ways. First, it points to policy implementation – in addition to policy debates and political discourse – as a key site within the state where the second and third mechanisms operate. Second, it includes the possibility of a fourth mechanism whereby cultural meanings affect policy: the evolving substance of ideas themselves at the hands of state actors. This is an important addition insofar as it integrates the pragmatist approach to seeing meanings and ideas as contingent, situational, and relational, which has been gaining ground in state-centred theories of policy formulation.

This additional mechanism has its provenance in the branch of policy studies referred to as "discursive institutionalism." Discursive institutionalism is broadly concerned with the ideational aspect of policy-making, including the question of what constitutes an "idea" in public policy, and how changes to ideas and the policy paradigms built on them can be conceptualized (see, e.g., Baumgartner 2014; Berman 2013; Béland 2009; Blyth 2013; Schmidt 2010). A lot of work in this field – like work on the role of culture in immigration policy – treats ideas and related concepts like schemas and frames as relatively coherent, stable, and well defined (e.g., the notion of "biological racialism"), and policy change as the substitution of one idea with another (e.g., "biological racialism" being substituted by "universal human rights"). Identifying and arguing against this tendency, Carstensen (2011, 2015) makes the case for treating ideas as sets of relational ideational elements tied together by political actors, with no coherent beginning or end. In other words, ideas are social constructs that not just shape – but are shaped by – the policymaking process (Schmidt 2010). Building on Schmidt (2002), Carstensen (2015) posits that ideational change can take place at the micro level of policymaking through mechanisms that affect the relationship between different constituent elements of an idea. The three main mechanisms he identifies are the "recasting" of the relation between elements of an idea; the "renewal" of one element of an idea; and the "revolutionizing" or wholesale change of elements in the idea. Which of those particular mechanisms drive policy change at the level of ideas is an open empirical question that a cultural sociology of immigration policy can better answer than existing theories of immigration policy formulation.[15]

Viewing Canada's Postwar Policy Shift through the Cultural Sociology of Immigration Policy Lens

Examining the emergence of Canada's universal immigration policy from the perspective of a cultural sociology of immigration policy provides a means of conceptualizing interpretive implementation practices as a generative element of the policy formulation process and its outcomes. While the role of the four mechanisms in this process is demonstrated in more detail in the chapters that follow, the argument can be summarized as follows.

Beginning with the first mechanism, high-level immigration bureaucrats in the Department of Citizenship and Immigration were embedded in cultural repertoires that contained a shared stock of ideas about the characteristics of immigrant groups. Within the Canadian national cultural repertoire, the idea of race, in relation to immigrant admissibility, appears to have been a bifurcated one. In other words, it had two elements: the narrow biological meaning associated with "biological racialism" and a meaning rooted in notions of social class and status. This bifurcation can be attributed to what Wallerstein (1991) argues has historically been the function of racial groups as status groups associated with higher/lower levels of development in the global economic and political context. The perceived "moral worth" of particular national, ethnic or racial groups rests on physical, cultural, and behavioural markers that are inextricably linked with the group's (real or imagined) place in the international political and economic hierarchy.

Two famous and widely read books suggest that the dual notion of race as both a biological and socio-economic distinction was common enough in the Canadian context to be an established part of the repertoire used to categorize and classify immigrants in the 1950s and 1960s. The first is Woodsworth's (1909) social history of immigration to Canada entitled *Strangers within Our Gates*. This work, which enumerates class and status traits among the hereditary features of different ethnic and racial groups in Canada at the turn of the twentieth century, was discussed earlier in the chapter. The second book is Porter's ([1965] 2015) *The Vertical Mosaic: An Analysis of Social Class and Power in Canada*, originally published in 1965 using data from the 1931 Census. The book's argument that Canada's national structure of class and power was stratified along ethnic and racial lines, with White British elites at the top of the hierarchy, was illustrated in part with data on the ethnic distribution within occupations considered as denoting high, medium, and low levels of status. Porter found that individuals of Jewish, Scottish, English, and Irish origin were over-represented in both high-level professional and financial occupations and mid-level clerical occupations; in contrast, individuals of Asian, Eastern European, Italian, "Other Central European," and "native Indian" origins were most strongly over-represented in primary occupations (logging, fishing, and mining) and unskilled labour (80). This suggests that, beyond any statistical or historical knowledge of the subject, the association between racial group membership and social class was visible in Canada's occupational hierarchy, and likely informed broadly held ideas and perceptions of "who people were" in the cultural repertoire available to immigration bureaucrats at the time when they were experimenting with a new admissions policy.

The second mechanism was the boundary work conducted by immigration bureaucrats in discussions of immigrant groups and individual immigrants during the postwar period. Adjudicating the admissibility of individual immigrants in order-in-council admissions and deportation appeals involved talking about the qualities of individuals in terms of race gender, class, morality, and other social distinctions. Operating in a context of rupture, in which routine practices of nation-building through racist immigration policies were breaking down, this boundary work created a *process* of low-risk experimentation. Experimenting with admissibility in individual cases allowed new principles for selecting immigrants from hitherto "non-preferred" (non-European and non-Western Hemisphere) source countries to emerge gradually over time. This process subsequently paved the way for sweeping changes to formal policy in 1967.

The *substance* of the selection principles that emerged through immigration bureaucrats' experimental and interpretive practices was generated through this second mechanism (boundary work), in concert with a third: idea "recasting," or the process whereby the relation between elements of a concept changes while the elements themselves remain the same (Carstensen 2015, 292). The substance was marked by a growing distinction in practice between individual-level and group-level admissibility. Additionally, the bifurcated idea of race (as a biological and socio-economic distinction), which was present in the Canadian national cultural repertoires, allowed bureaucrats to "recast" that idea in relation to admissibility. Whereas race in the sense of biological racialism prevailed in many national contexts until the postwar era (see the discussion earlier in this chapter), immigration bureaucrats came to emphasize race as socio-economic status in their deliberations. In their eyes, this "recast" idea of race emerged as the common ground on which immigrants from "non-preferred" (i.e., non-European, non-Western Hemisphere) countries could be seen as compatible with the hitherto White Canadian nation. Through these two mechanisms (boundary work and idea "recasting"), bureaucrats' experimental implementation practices resulted in the admission of individuals who displayed middle-class attributes and behaviours (e.g., those with higher education, financial capital, entrepreneurial spirit) well ahead of the 1962 and 1967 policy changes. Here they were attentive to different forms of capital displayed by individual immigrants: economic,[16] social,[17] and cultural[18] capital. In terms of cultural capital, bureaucrats' considerations went beyond the kind of institutionalized cultural capital (e.g., formal educational qualifications and certified language abilities) to look at what Bourdieu (1986, 48) calls embodied cultural capital or one's *habitus*. This form of cultural capital comprises internalized cultural signals (e.g., attitudes, preferences, knowledge, behaviours) and reflects "external wealth converted into an integral part of the person." In other words, immigration bureaucrats were attentive to the presence or absence of appropriately middle-class behaviours and values, like entrepreneurial spirit, in files they were processing. The practices developed by these state actors for admitting skilled workers and families from racially diverse backgrounds were not "race blind": they defined admissibility intersectionally, in terms of race and class.

Turning to the fourth and final mechanism, both the distinction between individual-level and group-level admissibility, and the substantively intersectional selection principles that emerged alongside it, were subsequently institutionalized in the 1967 immigration regulations. This is visible in the language of selection criteria for the admission of skilled workers and extended family members under the "points system." Where these are couched in vague language, for

example, the "personal assessment" criterion under the points system, the boundary work performed around individual immigrant
admissibility can be taken as a good indication of what this criterion
denoted. The institutionalization of the cumulative, substantive selection principles that emerged in immigration bureaucrats' micro-level
interpretive practices has given these practices long-lasting material
and symbolic effects. Given the broad shifts in immigrant origins away
from European, Western Hemisphere source countries and towards
non-European, non-Western Hemisphere ones, one of the biggest material effects of this institutionalization was the creation of a demographic
multiculturalism along middle-class lines (i.e., in terms of immigrants'
human, social, and cultural capital). Symbolically, this has made Canadian multiculturalism – as a defining feature of the imagined national
community – a fundamentally middle-class multiculturalism, with
attendant effects on defining who can or cannot be perceived as belonging to the multicultural Canadian nation.

Conclusion

There are strong theoretical reasons to strengthen the micro-level
perspective in debates about the evolving place of race in the nation-
building projects of Global North states in the postwar era. States are
institutions that have the power to define their populations along
racial and ethnic lines. Existing literature shows that such classification processes are influenced by macro-level cultural shifts, which can
legitimate or delegitimate particular policies and practices. Meso-level
organizational interests in certain branches of the state like census
bureaus and immigration departments may affect how macro-level
impulses are parlayed into policy. However, there is substantial scope
in discretionary policy areas such as immigration to add an important
layer of meaning to the kinds of racial and other boundaries articulated
in state policies and laws. This is a layer of meaning that emerges situ-
ationally and relationally as individual actors within the state develop
new practices and policies. In other words, this is a layer of meaning
that emerges at a level of analysis – the micro level – that is either theoretically overlooked or conceptualized in such a way that makes it
difficult to examine ideas and meanings as emergent properties of policymaking situations.

This chapter has made the case for increasing attention to the micro-
level aspect of the broad postwar shift from "biological racialism" to
universalism in state policies directed at population management. It
has argued that immigration policy is a strategic object of study for

furthering this agenda, when examined through an appropriate theoretical lens. The theoretical lens proposed – a cultural sociology of immigration policy – draws attention to the generative potential of immigration bureaucrats' interpretive practices in the course of policy formulation, which is considered to include implementation (case processing).

The theoretical approach introduced here and applied to the historical Canadian case adds a new explanatory layer to the story of postwar ideational change regarding the place of race in Western conceptualizations of nation. It becomes possible to see not only how political and cultural impulses at the macro- and meso-level shape policy formulation at the micro level but also how meanings generated at the micro level and subsequently institutionalized in laws and regulations can shape macro-level contexts. In the historical Canadian case, we can see how micro-level negotiations around the meaning of race in relation to admissibility created a demographic multiculturalism that ushered in the era of multicultural politics and policy. Applied to case processing as an aspect of policy formulation, this analytical approach can also reveal links between the symbolic and material aspects of the state classification processes. This is because the boundary work conducted by immigration bureaucrats in the course of adjudicating immigration cases literally determines a person's material position (e.g., legal right to enter and work) in the state and nation.

The following two chapters illustrate in more detail the results of applying the cultural sociology of immigration policy approach to reassessing the role of immigration bureaucrats in immigration policy formulation, including implementation, in the historical Canadian case. They demonstrate how the interpretive practices of these state actors affected both the policymaking process and its substantive outcomes via the four mechanisms identified in that theoretical approach: cultural repertoires, boundary work informed by them, idea "recasting," and institutionalization. This is done for skilled workers (chapter 4) and family immigrants (chapter 5).

Chapter Four

Individual Merit and the Making
of Multicultural Skilled Workers

For many people, the notion of a universal and "non-discriminatory" immigration policy is equated with selecting immigrants based on individual traits and social ties, irrespective of social group memberships. In policies directed at skilled workers, selection based on individual traits is furthermore associated with "merit," a concept with a complicated history in the field of sociology. In general, it denotes individual characteristics that mediate between one's social background and social attainment. Often associated with "meritocracy," a term invented by Michael Young in his 1958 book *The Rise of the Meritocracy*, merit refers to specific inner capacities of individuals, foremost intelligence and effort. According to Young ([1958] 2017), a meritocracy is a society in which these capacities are identified and used systematically to allocate occupational positions and related awards in a just and efficient manner that eschews the reproduction of social stratification along group (i.e., social class) lines. The concepts of merit and meritocracy have been taken up by sociologists like Daniel Bell and Talcott Parsons, who argue that they are defining features of rational, modern society. As Bell (1972, 30) puts it, in post-industrial societies, "differential status and differential income are based on technical skills and higher education, and few high places are open to those without such qualifications." Following this logic, it seems natural that the solution to the mid-twentieth-century problem of immigration policies that selected people primarily based on national and racial group membership was to transform them into instruments for selecting on individual merit. To date, national governments and international organizations refer quite naturally to the existence of "merit-based migration systems" (OECD et al. 2018, 17) when describing the kind of policy pioneered by Canada.

Unfortunately, Young's ([1958] 2017) original formulation was meant ironically. According to his (misunderstood) argument, meritocracies only appear to allocate hierarchical social positions on the basis of individual ability and effort, generally certified by educational credentials. Ultimately, they serve to legitimize older forms of class stratification, because the achievement of appropriate educational credentials and, later, occupations of high status, remains contingent on wealth, status, and networks. Meritocracy does not ameliorate so much as mask processes of social stratification rooted in social positions.

In historical work on race and immigration policy in Canada, the term "merit" has generally been conceptualized in this pejorative sense, as a means of limiting the entry of non-White workers. Calliste (1993, 88) points out that, prior to the 1962 immigration regulations that universalized skilled worker admissions, Black nurses from the Caribbean were admitted only as "cases of exceptional merit," based on their nursing qualifications and an offer of employment from a hospital that declared itself "aware of their racial origin." In contrast, White nurses from the United Kingdom were generally admissible as skilled workers. As a result, only 475 Black nurses from the Caribbean, or an average of fifty-nine a year, were admitted between 1954 and 1961, despite there being a shortage of nurses in the country. Also, compared to White nurses from the UK, the qualifications of Black nurses from the Caribbean were subjected to greater scrutiny. Looking at the immigration of "coloured persons" in general, and of farm labourers in particular, Satzewich (1989) similarly argues that the concept of exceptional merit was generally used as a tool for racist exclusion, as it was one of the few provisions under which individuals from predominantly non-White countries of origin could apply to immigrate to Canada.

While Canadian immigration policy was undeniably geared towards racist exclusion until 1967, treating the cases of non-White admissions under the exceptional merit clause prior to 1967 as an example of this exclusionary bent misses a more interesting point about them. Why did immigration bureaucrats consistently admit smaller numbers of non-White workers when they were not legally obliged to admit any at all? Canada was facing a significant shortage of appropriately trained personnel in the 1950s (Calliste 1993; Mullally and Wright 2007), so domestic economic concerns about a shortage of skilled workers certainly provided an incentive to recruit foreign-trained doctors and nurses from outside preferred racial groups. However, since shortages in high-skilled occupations like medicine remained constant, one would expect higher numbers of admissions than actually occurred. In the case of Commonwealth countries, diplomatic relations provided a political motivation to provide small concessions (Satzewich 1989), but this does not explain the consistent admission of non-White workers from non-Commonwealth countries, like China, over the course of the 1950s.

As this chapter argues, exceptional merit and other discretionary concepts in Canadian immigration policy were used *experimentally* to *include* individual non-White immigrants in – and to *exclude* individual White immigrants from – the Canadian nation, and to ultimately reshape immigrant inflows along intersectional lines. It also argues that the cumulative result of discretionary practices in response to vague legal concepts like merit was twofold: the emergence of individual-level assessments of human capital as a defining feature of universal immigration policies (later codified in Canada's "points system") and the creation of a multiculturalism (demographic and notional) that is middle-class. It furthermore shows that merit did not merely denote possession of instrumental markers like occupation and education that generate economic utility; it was also defined in moral and cultural terms that reveal class-based notions of what kind of people could be considered members of the Canadian nation.[1]

Cases of Exceptional Merit

One of the vague concepts written into Canadian immigration law from 1950 onward that was open to discretionary interpretation on the part of high-level immigration bureaucrats was that of "cases of exceptional merit."[2] Merit, exceptional or otherwise, is a nebulous concept. In economic theory, it is most commonly used to describe actions that are considered valuable to society in terms of their consequences. The precise meaning of "merit" is thus contingent on social valuation processes that are necessarily informed by prevailing social contexts and the negotiation of meaning within them. As Sen (2000, 9–10) states, from this point of view, "there is no escape from the contingent nature of its content, related to the characterization of a good – or an acceptable – society and the criteria in terms of which assessments are to be made." Insofar as this social valuation is directed at *actions*, and not at the essential qualities of *persons*, there is the potential for it to be applied in a universal, non-discriminatory way to people of different ascribed group memberships. Theoretically, the idea of merit, understood in instrumental terms, as pertaining to socially valuable actions, has the potential to contribute to non-discriminatory outcomes by focusing attention on what individuals do rather than on who they are.

Archival records pertaining to immigration policy implementation suggest that, from the early 1950s onward, the (anticipated) actions of individuals were indeed meant to be at the heart of assessments of cases of exceptional merit. This is evident in the First Immigration Manual, a twenty-one-volume set of instructions first created in 1952 for low-level bureaucrats on how to apply the Immigration Act and Regulations. It consolidated existing policy statements, circulars, and instructions into thirty chapters. Those chapters laid out formal instructions on how to interpret immigration policy, which criteria to apply to the selection and admission of immigrants, and other, more technical administrative aspects of procedures and documentation. Amended at regular intervals until it was superseded by the Second Immigration Manual in 1971, a version of the First Immigration Manual from 1954 defines "cases of exceptional merit" as follows:

> a case which is being dealt with (i) on humanitarian grounds when rigid application of the regulations would result in personal or financial hardship to the prospective immigrant or the applicant, or (ii) by executive direction, or *(iii) for public benefit, which includes cases where, in view of the special qualifications or achievements of prospective immigrants, their admission is in the public interest; i.e., they will contribute appreciably to the social, economic or cultural life of Canada.*[3] (emphasis added)

This wording suggests that case processors were directed to evaluate individual qualifications and achievements in terms of their putative economic, social, or cultural value to Canadian society, with nothing to suggest that there were limitations, based on social group distinctions, on what kinds of individuals qualified for consideration.

However, as Sen (2000, 12) notes, real world practices often diverge from theory when it comes to the non-discriminatory potential of the idea of merit. In practice, the attribution of merit to *actions* is often intertwined with the attribution of merit to *people*, that is, its association with personal traits like intelligence or talent, which are conceptualized as innate. The innate qualities of individuals are then commonly linked to ascribed group memberships, foremost racial and ethnic ones. This is evident in Canada's postwar provisions for "cases of exceptional merit." As Minister Edward Harris explained to the House of Commons in July of 1952, citizens of European origin countries did not need such a clause, as merit was a presumed quality of those groups. However, this was not the case for non-citizen residents of European countries, citizens of countries further down the hierarchy of preferred origins (e.g., Lebanon or Turkey), and citizens of the British West Indies. Individuals from these groups could be considered for admission based on merit. At the bottom of the racial hierarchy, groups like Indians, Pakistanis, Ceylonese, and "other Asians" (a common descriptor used to denote Chinese and Japanese) were considered as innately lacking in merit, and individuals from these groups were formally precluded from being considered for admission on that basis.[4] Since the British West Indies was the only majority non-White country of origin whose citizens qualified for consideration as cases of exceptional merit under the immigration regulations in the early 1950s, this clause was clearly not officially intended to be a tool for large-scale racial inclusion.

However, a reading of formal policy in the early 1950s does not provide a full understanding of the actual valuations behind group-level and individual-level conceptualizations of "merit," "special qualifications," "special achievements," "public interest," and (economic, social, cultural) "contribution." These are terms that gained meaning – and legal force – in the interpretive practices of the high-level immigration bureaucrats responsible for both policymaking and case processing. It is only by examining the cumulative meanings that emerged in these practices that it becomes possible to understand how the attribution of merit based on *actions* became possible for non-White individuals historically considered non-meritorious *persons* in terms of their ascribed group-level traits. Likewise, this is the only way to see how an ascribed lack of merit based on actions led to the exclusion of persons who were otherwise considered meritorious persons in terms of their ascribed group-level traits. At the same time, examining the micro-level attribution of meaning in processing individual cases reveals the nature of individual merit to be not purely about instrumental notions of what actions are desirable. In other words, it is not purely about the value of those actions for pursuing a policy aim, for example, the economic utility of someone's training. Merit is also a non-instrumental, immaterial quality with a moral, cultural, and status-related valance. Ultimately, these practices illustrate how the distinction between individual-level and group-level assessments emerged as an essential feature of the prototypical "merit-based" migration management system. They also reveal the original function of this distinction to be racial diversity management rather than the elimination of race as a distinction that influenced admissibility.

Defining Meritorious Groups in Practice

The famous immigration policy statement made by Prime Minister Mackenzie King in the House of Commons in 1947 reveals that racial group membership was a central concern in defining immigrant admissibility in the immediate postwar era. The quotation reads as follows: "The people of Canada do not wish to make a fundamental alteration in the character of their population through mass immigration. The government is therefore opposed to large-scale immigration from the Orient, which would certainly give rise to social and economic problems" (quoted in Hawkins 1988, 93). Read alongside the first postwar Immigration Act (1952) and regulations (1953), in which "admissible" classes of immigrants are defined according to national and racial origins, this quotation is generally parsed by scholars as evidence that group-level admissibility was defined in terms of biological racialism (Bloemraad 2015; Kelley and Trebilcock 2010; Triadafilopoulos 2012). As discussed in chapter 3, biological racialism refers to the belief that the human race comprises biologically distinct groups with innate characteristics (e.g., intelligence) that can be placed in a hierarchy of worth. King's statement reflected such hierarchical thinking, which placed White, Anglo-Saxons at the top and Asians at the bottom.

It is evident in immigration bureaucrats' boundary work around group-level admissibility that biological racialism influenced how these state actors conceptualized the goals of the policy they were tasked with administering. In 1955, the acting deputy minister of immigration communicated in a memorandum to the minister a more explicit version of Prime Minister Mackenzie King's 1947 sentiments, writing:

It is true that Asian immigration is, and always has been, more restricted than non-Asian. The primary reason for this long-standing policy is obvious – this country would have been over-run by Asian hordes long ago if the door were open. Until and unless the people of Canada signify a desire to change the ethnic character of our population by a stronger infusion of Asian blood, Asian immigration must be restricted.[5]

Despite use of the term "ethnicity," the reference to blood and insinuation that blood mixing would change the character of the Canadian population makes it clear that "Asian" is being given a biological meaning. There is further evidence of this in a 1954 excerpt from the First Immigration Manual, which contains detailed case processing instructions for immigration officers. There the term "Asians" is defined as follows: "'Asian' means, for immigration purposes, a person of Asiatic *race*, i.e. a race whose homeland is in the continent of Asia; persons of Arabian race and persons whose racial homeland is Iraq, Iran, Israel, Lebanon, Syria or Turkey and persons of Armenian race are NOT dealt with as Asians"[6] (emphasis added). In this example, references to races with distinct "homelands" clearly indicate a belief in the existence of groups with common ancestries that exist independently of political constructs like nation states.

Given external pressures to universalize immigrant selection, how (if at all) did the micro-level interpretive practices of immigration bureaucrats in the postwar era change this notion of group-level admissibility rooted in biological racialism? If change is understood simply as the disappearance of explicit references to race, a cursory review of archival records shows that this was achieved (see also Satzewich 1989). For example, explicit references to race permeated the earliest records of order-in-council admissions compiled by the Department for the years 1954 to 1964. In 1954 and 1955, all 660 such admissions contained the term "race," for example, in references to immigrants being "of Japanese race," "of Chinese race," or "of Anglo Saxon race." In 1956, only half of the 610 order-in-council admissions contained the word "race." From 1957 onwards, "race" was replaced completely by "citizenship." The term was, however, nominally retained in the First Immigration Manual, until final substantive revisions reflecting the 1967 immigration regulations were completed in 1971.[7] Compared to other state institutions, foremost the Dominion Bureau of Statistics, the Department of Citizenship and Immigration changed its nomenclature rather late. The word "race" had been dropped in favour of reference to "origins" much earlier from the Canadian census, starting with the census in 1951 (Thompson 2016, 120). This relative reluctance to abandon the vocabulary of race could be interpreted as evidence supporting the common portrayal of immigration bureaucrats as resisting changes to the explicitly racist policies to which they had long adhered.[8]

However, when archival records are analysed through the cultural sociology of immigration policy lens, the story becomes more complicated. Boundary work around immigrant admissibility reveals that the notion of race available to immigration bureaucrats in the postwar policy formulation context was bifurcated. It contained not just a biological element, but also a socio-economic one. In 1955, Minister of Citizenship and Immigration J.W. Pickersgill delivered a speech in Victoria, BC, that elaborated on the cornerstones of Canadian immigration policy. In it, he described some of the characteristics that he associated with immigrant groups who were considered compatible with the White settler nation-building efforts:

> When I meet, for instance, a Danish immigrant, only three years in Canada, who had built up the aerial photography of Canadian farms into a business providing jobs for seventy people – when I hear of a Greek who five years ago was a chauffeur for an ambassador to Canada and who now has a poultry farm in which he produces 50,000 broilers a year – when I am told of Dutch family after Dutch family which in two or three years in

Canada have progressed from farm labourers to farm proprietors, it gives
me pretty convincing proof that there is a very real place in this country
for newcomers and a very real need for their services and the things that
they can bring to us.[9]

This statement illustrates that the racialization of groups by immigration bureaucrats – in this case the positive racialization[10] of European-
origin groups – was tied to signifiers of social class at the outset of the
period under consideration. The concept of "class" is understood here
as a relational attribute ascribed to an individual or group based on
socio-economic distinctions (e.g., perceived success, wealth, power);
moral distinctions (e.g., perceived work ethic); and cultural distinctions
(e.g., perceived level of education). These descriptions reflect the concept of class as laid out by sociologist Max Weber (2007a), which has two
components. The first is one's material position in the socio-economic
order (e.g., the possession of property, occupation, employment status,
educational attainment). The second is the status and honour attributed to one's membership in social groups (e.g., occupational, racial/
ethnic, gender groups). This refers to the "social ranking of individuals,
groups, or objects as superior or inferior according to a shared standard of social value" (Ridgeway and Nakagawa 2015, 3–4). It is thus
the combination of perceived economic capital and symbolic esteem
that determines the relative standing of a group in the social hierarchy.

Immigration bureaucrats positively racialized European-origin groups
by ascribing to them innate socio-economic characteristics and practices
that were "deemed as potentially to the wider good" (Kushner 2005, 211).
These new "good Canadians" are described as "good farmers," "good
carpenters," "good engineers," and business owners.[11] Beyond indicating
the successful material position of these immigrants – implied by steady
employment in recognized occupations – the adjective "good" indicates
a symbolic moral judgment about their work ethic. In two of the three
examples named, Dutch and Greek immigrants transitioned from simple
employment in low-status jobs (i.e., chauffeur, farm labourer) to owning
and operating businesses. While the previous employment status of the
Danish immigrant is unclear, he, too, is valued for establishing a business
and growing the Canadian economy by providing jobs for others. Thus
being a new European-origin (White) Canadian, who was a "decent,
conscientious citizen," meant behaving in a manner that reflects what
Lamont (1992) identifies as middle-class values such as entrepreneurial
spirit, ambition, drive for self-actualization, and taste for upward mobility. In other words, the admissibility of European immigrant groups was
tied to their positive racialization as possessing innately middle-class

traits: education, stable employment, assets, ambition, and an orientation toward improving one's position in society.

Conversely, immigration bureaucrats negatively racialized non-European immigrant groups as possessing innate low-class qualities that made them inadmissible to the national collective. In particular, they highlighted non-Europeans' lack of education and skills as well as their poor employment records or prospects. In a piece of internal correspondence from 1955, the Director of the Immigration Branch of the Department of Citizenship and Immigration justified the exclusion of "coloured or partly coloured persons" in terms of socio-economic and moral distinctions: "Coloured people in the present state of the white man's thinking are not a tangible community asset ... they do not assimilate readily and pretty much vegetate to a low standard of living."[12] Here the term "vegetate" suggests that non-Whites lack the ambition and work ethic that makes someone a "tangible community asset," like the Danish, Greek, and Dutch immigrants who "progressed" from their original starting positions in Canada. This negative moral classification, in turn, is linked with a "low standard of living," a term that connotes more than inhabiting a low material position in the economy. Understood as "the necessities, comforts, and luxuries enjoyed or aspired to by an individual or group,"[13] the passive acceptance of a low standard of living attributed to non-White immigrants suggests that they lack cultural tools (e.g., education, tastes) to aspire to a better lot in life.

In the same year, Minister Pickersgill negatively racialized non-White immigrant groups in the same terms used to describe Canada's First Nations, who were relegated to the lowest rung of the national socio-economic and racial hierarchy: "Far too many of our Canadian Indians have not achieved a standard of living of which we have any right to be proud ... And I do not want to be responsible for bringing immigrants to Canada to live in circumstances which will be no better than those of far too many of our Canadian Indians."[14] The term "achievement" in reference to a "standard of living" that is, in the eyes of the minister, nothing to be "proud of" again suggests that the low-class position of groups racialized as visibly non-White derives from innate moral deficits associated with low social class, such as lack of ambition, that make these groups inadmissible to the Canadian national collective.

Ten years on, in 1965, this negative racialization of non-White groups as fundamentally inadmissible due to innate characteristics related to social class had not changed. It is reflected, for example, in the following statement made by the deputy minister in that year: "As you know, my personal inclination is to be colour blind in respect of immigrants, but I am concerned about the prospect of bringing in large numbers of people whose personal qualifications would give little promise of successful establishment and eventual assimilation."[15] In this case, being non-White is associated with class-related distinctions associated with education, both in the material sense (i.e., as a resource for obtaining material returns on the labour market) and in the symbolic sense of having achieved a desired level of cultural competence.

Here we see what Sen (2000) identified as the inextricable link between merit as a feature of individual actions and merit as a feature of persons defined at the group level as having particular racial origins. As discussed in chapter 3, the idea of race available to immigration bureaucrats in the Canadian national cultural repertoires was bifurcated. It denoted both innate biological characteristics and prevailing perceptions of a given racial group's status and prestige based on its position in the world's political and economic systems (see, e.g., Wallerstein 1991). Due to the link between evaluations of individual "merit" and perceptions of group-level racialized socio-economic status, interpretations of admissibility criteria like "merit" and "economic utility" were not "race blind" in practice, but informed by intersectional social distinctions.

Distinguishing between Individuals and Groups: Order-in-Council Admissions

By definition, admissions decisions under universal immigration policies are based on individual-level assessments of human capital and social ties, irrespective of ascribed social group memberships like race, class, and gender. While this distinction between individual-level and group-level admissibility is widely recognized as a distinguishing feature of universal immigration policies, less is known about the process whereby this distinction emerged. The present study shows that individual-level assessments of admissibility emerged in the experimental practices of immigration bureaucrats. A closer examination of these practices yields invaluable insights into how individual-level admissibility was conceptualized for members of non-White and White immigrant groups alike. It also reveals how these conceptualizations made it thinkable to include non-White workers in the Canadian nation. Through the micro-level mechanism of "recasting," assessments made by immigration bureaucrats that drew on the bifurcated idea of race as both biological and class-based came to privilege the latter over the former. In addition to including individuals from normally undesirable racial groups, this mechanism also had implications for the exclusion of individuals from normally desirable racial groups, ultimately giving the Canadian nation-building project a class-based inflection.

One source of information on individual-level assessments are archived lists of individual order-in-council admissions to Canada, which were issued notwithstanding immigrants' group-level inadmissibility under the Immigration Act and regulations. These lists vary across years in the degree of detail they offer, and it is not possible to tell whether they are comprehensive. Nevertheless, they contain references to a large enough number of cases and therefore reveal some broad patterns. Throughout a given calendar year, the Department would compile cases and issue orders-in-council for batches of individual cases at irregular intervals. Mostly, these lists offer basic details about individuals, including their names, "race" (or citizenship, as vocabulary evolved), age, and occupation, and often point-form notes about factors that were decisive in deciding to admit someone. These details make it possible to get a basic, quantitative sense of the number of individuals admitted outside of immigration law, as well as a basic qualitative sense of the kind of characteristics immigration bureaucrats associated with admissibility.[16]

These records document the admission, between the years 1954 and 1961, of a total of 1,731 individuals, notwithstanding section 20 of the immigration regulations. This was the clause under which admissibility was regulated in terms of national origins.[17] All of these individuals were granted permanent residence status. Although not officially eligible for consideration under the "exceptional merit" clause, the most strongly represented national origin group for each year was the Chinese, who comprised 69 per cent of admissions over that seven-year period, and 86 per cent of admissions in the first two years.

Not all individuals in these files were admitted as skilled workers, although criteria relevant to skilled worker selection (e.g., education, work experience) were applied in almost all cases. From 1954 to 1961 (the year before the 1962 immigration regulations first universalized skilled worker admissions), 278 individuals were admitted as skilled workers notwithstanding their inadmissibility under section 20; a further sixty were admitted as individuals accompanying a skilled worker. Except for 1956, when they were surpassed by East Indians, Chinese and British citizens born in Hong Kong were the most highly represented origin groups, accounting for between 39 per cent and 88 per cent of skilled worker admissions. In 1955, the first year in which skilled worker admissions were noted in overviews of order-in-council admissions, the majority of individuals under this designation had university degrees (e.g., in political science, engineering, medicine, economics) or relevant professional training (e.g., in nursing or teaching). Many also had work experience in Canada and/or elsewhere as well as either ongoing employment in Canada or an offer of employment. While individuals with university education are over-represented in these order-in-council admissions, there are still instances of skilled workers being admitted, without mention of education level, to work in a skilled trade or service, for example, in the restaurant industry. Many individuals had come to Canada as students and wished to remain as workers in their chosen fields. As the years progress, notes on cases expand to include more information on assets (e.g., amount of savings available for transfer to Canada) and income.

Even when not admitted as skilled workers, but as family members otherwise ineligible due to their national origins, indicators of instrumental, economic merit consistently served as factors influencing the decision to issue an order-in-council for admission. Across all years, frequently cited characteristics include having a job or job offer (216 mentions); being in a professional occupation (256 mentions); being a university graduate or student (276 mentions); and owning a business (366 mentions). Some of these criteria (education, occupation, job offer) became part of the original "points system" and contemporary iterations of the Federal Skilled Workers Program. Others, like being a post-secondary student in Canada or owning a business, would later become admissions criteria for economic programs like the Business Class (for investors and entrepreneurs) and the Canadian Experience Class (with its track to permanent residence for graduates of Canadian post-secondary institutions).[18]

While the indicators mentioned above are generally associated with instrumental notions of merit, others suggest that order-in-council admissions were also based on broader moral and cultural assessments of class and status as they manifest in (embodied) cultural and social capital. The most prominent of these indicators is "steady employment" (427 mentions), which arguably signals more than the ability to do a job, like perceived seriousness, loyalty, and commitment.[19] The second most prominent, non-instrumental indicator is the possession of assets, savings and/or property (fifty-five mentions, always including exact dollar values). Again, distinct from attesting to an ability to participate in the labour market, this indicator generally signals status (social standing) and broader moral traits associated with positively racialized groups, like thriftiness. Although mentioned much less frequently, service in the Canadian military (nineteen mentions) emerged as a distinction associated with individual admissibility. As Benedict Anderson (1991) argues, military service is considered the quintessential signal of moral allegiance with the national community. Finally, there are seven cases in which the immigrants' or their families' prominence in the community is mentioned as grounds for admission. Involvement in local organizations like church communities, especially when favourable supporting documents were submitted by prominent members of those communities, signal social capital. That is, they indicate the ability to mobilize resources by virtue of strong social connections, a kind of wealth that is not the same as the ability to do a job that meets economic demand. There are also occasional references to an individual being "of a good type," having "good prospects," or of having made a "favourable impression" on immigration officers, all phrases that suggest a more general assessment of personal qualities and way of being in the world that Bourdieu (1986) calls someone's *habitus*. Recall, from chapter 3, that *habitus* refers to wealth and social status that is embodied, that is, it can be perceived (often unconsciously) by others on the basis of someone's attitudes, knowledge, behaviours, language ability, and other visible characteristics. There are also reasons to see indicators that are, on the surface, even more closely related to economic utility as signifiers of social status and/or of desirable middle-class personality traits. For example, business ownership attests not just to participation in the economic life of the country, but to ambition; holding a university degree (particularly in the 1950s, when university attendance was less common) is likewise a status marker if noted in addition to, or in lieu of, employment details.

Where cases scattered throughout other archival records reveal more in-depth justifications of order-in-council admissions for workers, it becomes even clearer that notions of admissibility rooted in social class went beyond instrumental indicators of potential economic utility. They also included moral judgments about individuals' general compatibility with an aspiring middle-class nation. As discussed earlier in the chapter, the Immigration Act and Regulations in place in the early 1950s allowed immigration bureaucrats to admit individuals from mainly European countries of origin as "cases of exceptional merit." In practice, admission on the basis of merit was extended not only to individuals from those countries (which included, as the only majority non-White country, the British West Indies), but also from majority non-White countries not formally named in this discretionary category. Examining the language used to describe "meritorious" cases illustrates how instrumental and non-instrumental markers of social class were implicated in these decisions. For example, in 1955, the Director of Immigration presented descriptions of multiple possible "meritorious" Indian candidates for permanent settlement, of which the following is representative:

[Name], aged 32, married. This man was allowed temporary entry in July of 1949, to attend the University of British Columbia. At the time of his entry he held a BSc from the University of East Punjab and proposed to take his BA course. We have been advised that his BA course will be completed in August of this year. This man has four uncles resident in Canada who have provided him with $22,000 in assets. Of this, $10,000 is a half-interest in a saw-mill at New Westminster, B.C. Pacific District Superintendent states that this man is well educated, has become Canadianized, and would be a definite asset to the East Indian population of Canada and to this country.[20]

Likewise, status is emphasized in the consideration of twelve out of thirty-nine cases (some involving families rather than individuals) put forward to the minister for potential admission either within or outside the quota system for Indian-origin immigrants. The focus on status manifests in mentions of financial and other assets feature alongside education and employment as positive features.[21] References to education, ambition, and professional status were also used to define "meritorious" Chinese applications for admission. This was the case, for example, for the Chinese engineering student employed by the Ontario government and married to a Chinese medical doctor, and for the Chinese assistant professor of agricultural economics and farm management at the University of Manitoba.[22] In 1961, in an internal memorandum regarding a request from the Japanese ambassador to accept individual Japanese workers as "special cases," the deputy minister stated that the Department was "always ready to look at cases of special merit"; in the Japanese case, these could be "an expert repair man of Japanese cameras [or] a painter, writer, or other specially talented person (university professor, National Research Council research scientists, etc.)."[23] These examples suggest that merit served as an umbrella concept to denote a range of middle-class signifiers that made individuals desirable future members of the Canadian nation. These signifiers included being well-educated (a phrase that has different connotations than purely educational attainment), being professionally successful, building wealth, having a strong work ethic, and seeming to be "Canadianized," a descriptor that hints at a general way of being and acting in society that is not reducible to other indicators.

While individual-level admissibility diverged from group-level admissibility, individuals were not necessarily evaluated in isolation, but in the context of their immediate and extended families, as the "meritorious" case from India above shows. Throughout the lists of order-in-council admissions for workers from inadmissible racial groups, there are multiple examples of couples or entire families being evaluated in reference to merit. Some couples had met while studying in Canada, as was the case in 1961 with one Chinese man from Hong Kong, who had studied engineering at the University of British Columbia and subsequently found employment in his field; his wife (also from Hong Kong) was still working towards her arts degree. The same year, the Department admitted a Chinese family consisting of a man with a PhD working in the United States, his wife, who was attending graduate school in Canada and had a job offer, and their two children, noting that this was a "very well-qualified family." Other Chinese-origin individuals were given permission to settle based on their own educational qualifications and the presence of parents and siblings in Canada.

Distinguishing between Individuals and Groups: Deportation Appeals

The scope and relevance of broader, moral assessments of class in relation to notions of immigrant admissibility becomes even clearer when deportation appeal decisions are examined. As described in chapter 2 in more detail, the 1952 Immigration Act allowed immigrants to appeal a deportation order made by a special inquiry officer (SIO). Appeals were to be directed to the Minister of Citizenship and Immigration, who could direct the appeal to an Immigration Appeal Board (IAB) consisting of at least three officials from the Department selected by the executive (Kelley and Trebilcock 2010). The main countries of origin and citizenship of individuals represented in available deportation appeal records are Germany (139 individuals); the United Kingdom (123 individuals); Hungary (118 individuals); and the United States (116 individuals). Rooted in discussions of an individual's "record" in Canada (i.e., education, occupation, work record, family ties, general behaviour), deportation appeal acceptances and rejections were not consistently associated with national origins, age, the nature of the immigration offence for which they were ordered deported, or the person's occupation. Most strongly and consistently, decisions were based on moral assessments of worth pertaining to the individual's work ethic and the holistic personal impression that individual made on any immigration officers involved in the case.

A closer look at the reasons associated with actual exclusion from Canada (i.e., the decision to uphold a deportation order) can help shed light on the complicated boundary work that shaped these decisions. Beginning with national origins, rates of rejection did not vary strongly among three of the four top origin groups. Germans, Hungarians, and citizens of the United Kingdom were rejected at rates of between 50 per cent and

58 per cent. For citizens of the United States, the rejection rate was much higher (75 per cent), and higher still when these citizens were classified as being of "Negro race" (94 per cent). The higher rejection rates for White and non-White US citizens may partly be explained by the fact that a high proportion of these individuals were visitors or non-immigrants (41 per cent for White US citizens and 44 per cent for non-White US citizens); Canadian officials would arguably have been less invested in the success of temporary immigrants or visitors from across a nearby land border than they were in landed immigrants from farther away, many of whom had financial assistance under the Assisted Passage Loan Scheme to defray the cost of travelling to Canada.[24] However, the exclusion rate for non-White US citizens was still markedly higher, perhaps indicating a particularly strong group-level bias towards this racialized group. For comparison, the rejection rate for Chinese-origin individuals was lower, at 62 per cent. Overall, non-White individuals are under-reported in the appeal records, suggesting that racial discrimination may have played a role at the point of deciding to forward a case for review by the IAB. Nevertheless, in terms of group-level admissibility, the fact that membership in the most positively racialized immigrant groups (e.g., British, German) did not translate into proportionally much higher willingness to overturn a deportation decision (compared to the overall rate of 60 per cent) can be seen as part of the disconnect during this era between perceived group-level and individual-level admissibility.

Turning to the grounds for deportability, aggregate decisions to reverse a deportation that was based on the violation of a clause in the immigration regulations hint at the moral dimension of the boundary work underpinning decision-making. The four most frequently cited legal grounds for deportation were violation of one (or more) of the following clauses in the immigration regulations: (1) section 19(1)(e)(iii), which applied to persons who had become an inmate of a penitentiary, jail, reformatory, prison, asylum, or hospital for mental disease (654 violations; appeal denied in 68 per cent of cases); (2) section 19(1)(e)(ii), which applied to individuals who had been convicted of an offense under the Criminal Code (198 violations; appeal denied in 53 per cent of cases); (3) section 19(1)(d), which applied to those who had violated the Narcotics Act (133 violations; appeal denied in 73 per cent of cases); and (4) section 19(1)(2)(iv) for individuals who had been members of the "prohibited classes" at the time of their arrival, for example, persons who were not legally admissible at the time of arrival but whose grounds for admissibility were either overlooked or left undeclared by the applicant (98 violations; appeal denied in 74 per cent of cases). It is interesting to note the higher rates of rejection for drug-related offences (usually possession and/or use of narcotics such as marijuana) and being a member of the "prohibited classes" at the time of admission (usually on the grounds of poor physical or mental health). These two violations arguably have a different moral valence than the others: drug use implied, in the culture of the time, both a personal moral failure and belonging in a social milieu of poor repute (Becker 1953). Being a member of the prohibited classes at the time of arrival suggests dishonesty on the part of the immigrant for not fully disclosing the details of their case. These two violations signal unfavourable personality traits related to morality and deservingness in ways that the others do not.

With the legal grounds for deportation remaining uncontested in almost all cases by the IAB, the decision to uphold or overturn a deportation order hinged instead on deliberations about what was referred to as the individual's "record in Canada." In general, this term comprised evaluations of the individual's (and sometimes their family's) employment history, occupation, community life, personal relationships, and general perceptions of character noted by SIOs involved with the case. Like the order-in-council admissions of individuals from inadmissible national groups, there was a strong emphasis on traits that could be considered indicative of a person's economic utility, like their educational qualifications and occupation. However, an examination of deportation appeal denials by general type of occupation reveals that there was no straightforward relationship between occupational levels and IAB outcomes and thus no straightforward privileging of instrumental notions of merit. For example, individuals identified as being in professional occupations (e.g., medicine, law, or engineering) had their appeals denied at the same rate (49 per cent) as individuals described as skilled labourers (e.g., tradespeople). The refusal rate for individuals described as general labourers, that is, engaged in work for which no specialized training was required, was only slightly higher, at 54 per cent. The biggest divergence was between individuals engaged in sex work (81 per cent appeal denial rate) and those who were small business owners (33 per cent appeal denial rate). Here again, there are factors associated with these lines of work that go beyond economic utility. Sex work has historically been seen as a morally corrupt occupation; indeed, appeals were rejected in 80 per cent of cases where prostitution was mentioned as part of someone's "record in Canada," regardless of whether it was related to the legal grounds for the deportation order.

On the opposite end of the moral scale, being a small business owner signals status and ambition in a way that employment, regardless of field, does not. Perceived belonging to a middle- or upper-class status group, in terms of assets, property, and so on was most strongly correlated with successful deportation appeals. Appeals were denied in only 27 per cent of cases where an individual's wealth and status markers (e.g., possession and dollar value of significant assets like houses and vehicle) were mentioned, and in 16 per cent of cases where the wealth, status, and social standing of adult family members in Canada (e.g., parents, siblings, aunts, and uncles) were noted.

Finally, interpretation of someone's record in Canada was based to a large degree on assessments of personality traits. These discussions of who someone *was* further reveal the cultural and moral dimension of economic selectivity. As with order-in-council admissions of individuals from inadmissible racial and national origin groups, deportation appeal decisions were strongly influenced by whether someone had demonstrably been in "steady" or "unsteady" employment. This was ascertained in reference to the duration of time spent working for a single employer. This distinction, which signals work ethic and commitment, was much more strongly correlated with the denial of deportation appeals than the occupational levels mentioned previously: 78 per cent of individuals who had been in "unsteady" employment had their appeals denied, compared to 38 per cent of individuals who had been in "steady" employment. Where noted, the personal impressions of any departmental personnel, like the SIO responsible for the case, were very strongly associated with appeal outcomes. For example, positive assessments of general character were correlated with low appeal denial rates, as was the case with the following terms (associated rate of appeal denial in brackets): "willing to work" (14 per cent); "made a good impression" (13 per cent); "hardworking" (10 per cent); and "willingness to establish" himself/herself (6 per cent). Other character traits associated with positive appeal outcomes included grit, intelligence, maturity, and responsibility. Conversely, the following descriptions were correlated with high refusal rates (in brackets): "bad attitude" (100 per cent); "itinerant" (100 per cent); "dishonourable" (100 per cent); and made an "unfavourable impression" on or "did not impress" Department officials (77 per cent). Additionally, character traits like immaturity, foolishness, stupidity, laziness, and irresponsibility were strongly associated with appeal denials. Of particular note here is the degree to which potential deportees' *habitus*, or general comportment, was weighted in the decision, in the sense that nebulous good or bad "impressions" of a person in the eyes of a state actor carried weight.

While the deportation appeal cases are too numerous to describe each one in detail, it is worth quoting some records to illustrate how state actors drew on instrumental notions of meritorious actions (serving economic utility) and notions of merit associated with broader notions of deservingness (rooted in social and economic valuations) in deciding appeal cases. One example in which wealth and status trumped criminal activity as grounds for deportation is a 1956 case involving a Ukrainian immigrant, "Mr. Pr.," who was serving a one-year prison sentence for attempted rape at the time of appeal. Despite the conviction, both the judge in the case and the IAB felt that it would be wrong to deport him, due to his "excellent work record in Canada," which included establishing his own small contracting business and accumulating $6,000 worth of assets. In another case, from 1957, three members of the "D." family were ordered deported due to the violation of different mental and physical health-related clauses. The IAB was inclined to overlook these circumstances given the family's high socio-economic standing. It noted that the father was a superintendent at a Toronto carpet company, where he earned $8,000 per year and was considered "one of [their] most valued employees." Furthermore, the family had $15,000 equity in their Toronto house and an annuity fund established prior to immigration that would pay out $360 monthly to the father for ten years after he reached age sixty-five. Finally, a trust fund set up for the daughter, who had been "certified as an imbecile," would ensure that she never became a public charge.

Cases in which immigrants were ordered deported on similar charges, yet experienced divergent appeal outcomes, are particularly informative. Take, for example, three cases from 1956, all involving middle-aged, male German citizens ordered deported under section 19(1)(e)(iii), because mental health issues had led them to become inmates of an asylum or hospital for mental diseases. The IAB noted the following about the first, "Mr. J.," who was admitted to a mental hospital with a diagnosis of acute schizophrenia, and whose prognosis for recovery was considered "excellent":

> Prior to his breakdown, the appellant had an excellent work record. He remained in farm work for a full year after his arrival here at comparatively low rates and repaid in full his assisted passage loan before payments were actually due. After leaving the farm, he went into butter making and when this work failed, and he was unable to secure employment in the late autumn, he did chores for a farmer in the area without any remuneration except shelter which the farmer provided.

"Mr. J."'s resourcefulness (continuously seeking new employment when the previous opportunity fails), humbleness (willingness to take on menial work), sense of duty (repaying the assisted passage loan before it was due), and thriftiness (repaying the loan despite low levels of remuneration) resulted in his deportation order being reversed. While unsteady employment is more frequently associated with denied appeals, in this case the loan repayment appears to serve as an alternate indicator of reliability and commitment.

An opposite decision is reached in the second case, of "Mr. Wi.," who was admitted to hospital with a diagnosis of schizophrenia, and whose prognosis for recovery was noted as "unfavourable." The assessment of his case is as follows: "At the time of the examination, the appellant was very vague and did not impress the Special Inquiry Officer favourably. As well as can be ascertained, it would appear that he worked for a few months after his arrival on a farm and then a variety of manual jobs, although he could not be specific about his employment." Despite the similarly patchy employment records, the decision conveys the highly subjective perception of "Mr. Wi." as untrustworthy (he is reluctant to reveal details) and otherwise "did not impress" the officer in some unspecified way.

In the third case, "Mr. Wu" was admitted to a mental hospital due to a "paranoid condition" for which the prognosis for recovery was considered "poor" (as it was in the second case). Here the IAB notes:

> The appellant's own record, prior to his illness, was an excellent one. He worked steadily at his trade of wood carver for almost five years and, up to that time, had apparently purchased two homes, for he has jointly with his wife an equity of more than $3,000 in a home valued at $8,000 and a mortgage valued at $2,300 on the house they previously occupied.

Thus far, steady employment and achievement of middle-class status in terms of assets weighs against the poor prognosis for recovery and, hence, possibility that this achievement may not be sustained. At this point, the wife's position is taken into account:

> Since her husband's hospitalization, the wife has succeeded very well in looking after the family. She has steady employment as a machine operator earning $36.00 weekly. In addition, she receives $100.00 monthly from rented rooms, a $20.00 monthly payment on the mortgage the couple own, and $11.00 monthly in Family Allowance. She has managed to keep all mortgages and all other payments up to date.

His wife's relevant personal qualities like thrift, willingness to work hard, and reliability are accepted as evidence of merit in lieu of "Mr. Wu.'s" own uncertain ability to demonstrate them in the future.

In another pair of cases from 1959, two immigrants from Hungary, "Mr. O." and "Mr. Pa.," were ordered deported due to convictions on minor criminal charges related to theft. Both had previously been convicted on other minor charges. In the case of "Mr. O," the IAB upheld the deportation order, noting: "Although his convictions are not for offences of the more serious type, combined with a very spotty work record they present a picture of a young man who has so far given no indication that he is anxious to establish himself in Canada. He blames all his convictions on drunkenness." In contrast, "Mr. Pa.'s" deportation was stayed because, despite periods of unemployment, "his work record is fair and he has shown a willingness to take any job available," including working as a coal miner, at a cement company, and as a labourer at a grain company.

As with order-in-council admissions, it was not uncommon for assessments of individual merit in deportation appeals to be conducted from a more holistic perspective that included that person's immediate and extended families. Another trio of comparable cases, this time involving young persons of German origin, illustrates the power of family to affect individual admissibility. In one case from 1958, the deportation order for a young "Mr. H." was upheld due to the absence of a family support network. The man had been convicted under the Criminal Code for theft, which he admitted to engaging in as a response to hunger and homelessness. While the Department noted his "reasonably good" work record and was sympathetic to the motivation behind "Mr. H.'s" criminal activities, the inability of a brother living in Canada to support "Mr. H.'s" rehabilitation led to a negative outcome in the case.

In contrast, two cases from 1957 show the power of support from the "right" kind of family. In one, "Mr. L.," who had been convicted of automobile theft while on probation for another crime, was successful in his deportation appeal despite being described as "most difficult to work with" and as a young man who "showed open defiance of probation conditions and refused the guidance of all interested in him." The Department's decision to allow him to stay rested on the willingness of the man's sister (a nurse) and mother ("who appears to be a hardworking woman who became a widow during the war") to assist in his rehabilitation. Likewise, "Mr. P.," who had been convicted of twenty-one charges of fraud, was successful in his deportation appeal, due to the good standing of his family. He had started working for his father, who owned two homes worth a total of $23,000, who had $5,000 in savings, and who ran (along with "Mr. P.'s" brother) a contracting company. The Department noted that the family "appear to be a good, clear-cut type and are becoming well established in Canada"; importantly, they had also "accepted the young man back in the family [and] are doing their utmost to keep him away from his former companions."

Thus, while individual-level admissibility had become distinct from group-level admissibility, it was sometimes judged, in practice, in the broader context of family relations. As the following section shows, the contextual effect of family later became institutionalized in admissibility criteria for skilled workers.

Institutionalizing Implementation Practices

The admissions practices developed by high-level immigration bureaucrats in the course of case process activities were gradually systematized and ultimately institutionalized in the 1962 immigration regulations that universalized skilled worker admissions and the 1967 "points system" for selecting skilled workers. In 1954, instructions were issued to lower-level case processors that they were to refer applications from groups not considered admissible under section 20(1) of the immigration regulations to headquarters for order-in-council consideration. Specifically, the First Immigration Manual stated that "unsponsored applications from persons other than those in Section 20(1) who are (i) Professional and Technical, and (ii) Managers and Administrators" should be referred up to the deputy minister for consideration.[25] As outlined in chapter 2, section 20(1) of the immigration regulations referred at the time to the citizens of majority White European and settler colonial states (the United Kingdom, Australia, New Zealand, South Africa, Ireland, the United States, and France), meaning that this passage applied to individuals from countries named in sections 20(2) and (3) (China, Japan, India, Pakistan, and Ceylon) as well as those not named. Later, in 1960, immigration officers were instructed to forward applications made by Chinese students in Canada for permanent residence to headquarters for consideration.[26] Again, admissibility cannot be seen simply as a function of economic utility but as a means of creating a multicultural national status group. The first indication of this is the types of occupations emphasized early on, for example, in the exemptions systematized in the First Immigration Manual in the early 1950s: professional, technical, managerial, and administrative professions. While the desirability of these occupational groups appears commonsensical from a contemporary perspective (indeed, professional and managerial groups are still privileged in the Federal Skilled Worker Program today), their desirability in the 1950s cannot be attributed solely to labour market considerations. This is because, throughout the 1950s, Canadian economic growth was concentrated in natural resources, manufacturing, services and agriculture, not in management and the professions.[27]

As early as 1955, the admissions practices of immigration bureaucrats were understood to be established enough to constitute an unofficial admissions policy for individual workers from inadmissible national and racial groups. This policy is referenced in discussions of how to manage immigrants from the British West Indies, an immigrant group that other scholars propose was considered inadmissible well into the 1960s (see, e.g., Calliste 1993; FitzGerald and Cook-Martín 2014; Satzewich 1989). In 1955, the Director of Immigration stated, regarding a proposed immigration agreement with the British West Indies, that such a program was "now being carried out to a certain extent by our policy of admitting certain meritorious cases."[28] In the area of (temporary) student admissions, steps were taken in 1958 to create a general policy. In response to increasing requests from prospective nursing students from the British West Indies, foreign student admissions were formalized in an Operations Memorandum and opened to individuals from all national origins.[29] As illustrated earlier in the chapter, such students had been admitted experimentally via order-in-council for a number of years prior to this more formalized approach. That this student policy was a gateway to settlement is clear from another memorandum from the following year, in which it was estimated that nurses' aides from the British West Indies and British Guiana were being admitted permanently as "cases of exceptional merit" on a regular basis in the three years prior: 1956 (12 individuals), 1957 (27 individuals), and 1958 (33 individuals).[30] In 1961, the Department stated explicitly, in reference to individuals from majority non-White countries with training in psychiatric nursing and assurance of employment in a Canadian hospital that, "it was the practice of [the Admissions Division] to seek the authority of the Governor-in-Council for the [order-in-council] admission of persons not acceptable under Regulation 20."[31]

These de facto, but not public, policies for admitting skilled workers from diverse origins, as well as the selection criteria that emerged in case processing, became formally institutionalized in the 1962 immigration regulations. Section 31(a) of those regulations introduced Canada's first universal admissions policy for skilled workers. It was open to any person "who, by reason of his education, training, skills or other special qualifications, is likely to be able to establish himself successfully in Canada," including his/her spouse and unmarried children under twenty-one years of age. In the wake of the 1962 immigration regulations, the intersectional nature of the long-practised inclusion of these workers received full articulation in the accompanying First

Immigration Manual for lower-level case processors. The 1964 version of that manual states, with regard to the new regulations and their objectives:

> Over the years, Canada has endeavoured to select immigrants who were adaptable to Canadian life in terms of culture and political philosophy, as such persons, finding familiar institutions in Canada, feel more at home and this assists in their re-establishment in the new life they find here. This explains why Canada makes every effort to sustain the movement of immigrants from countries having like economic, social and political backgrounds. On the other hand, there is no reason why qualified people from other countries cannot integrate successfully into Canadian society and the existing Immigration Regulations recognize this principle.[32]

The foregoing analysis of order-in-council admissions shows that the statement about there being "no reason why" qualified individuals of all origins could not be successful in Canada was rooted in the Department's experimental practices over the previous eight years.

The terms in which the First Immigration Manual instructed immigration officers to adjudicate individual admissibility under section 31(a) underscores the underlying "recast" idea of race. This "recasting" had resulted from immigration bureaucrats' interpretations of individual immigration cases, in which the social class element of race came to take precedence over the biological element of race. In 1962, the manual stated that any person "regardless of citizenship and ethnic origin" was admissible if their "education, training, skills or other special qualifications taken together with his attributes of sincerity, determination, initiative and resourcefulness" indicated to the selecting officer that they could settle and become an "integral member of the Canadian community."[33] It furthermore added that "an immigrant must possess the qualities mentioned above to a high degree and must be a self-reliant, 'self-starting' person."[34] This quotation clearly shows that the admissibility of individuals, irrespective of their ascribed group membership, hinged on perceived social class in terms of both economic standing and utility as well as cultural resources and moral qualities (e.g., work ethic, ambition, taste for upward mobility).

A look at the original "points system" outlined in the 1967 immigration regulations makes it clear how strongly immigration bureaucrats' experimental implementation practices informed the institutionalization of this policy. Their influence was strong both in terms of the significance assigned to the moral dimension of economic admissibility they imputed into the "personal assessment" factor and in terms of the

Table 3.1. "Points system" for adjudicating independent (economic) immigrants under the 1967 Immigration Regulations (P.C. 1967–1616)

Criterion	Maximum points
Education and training	20
Personal assessment	15
Occupational demand	15
Occupational skill	10
Age	10
Arranged employment	10
Knowledge of English and/or French	10
Relative in Canada willing to assist in settlement	5
Employment opportunities in the area of destination	5
Intention to establish a business or retire (considered in lieu of occupational demand and occupational skill)	25

sheer number of people to whom this selection criterion would subsequently be applied. The "personal assessment" criterion was applied to "independent applicants," that is, skilled workers, and to "nominated relatives," who will be discussed in chapter 5. Table 3.1 provides an overview of the selection criteria used to adjudicate independent (economic) immigrants and the maximum number of points that could be awarded for each criterion. Fifteen points were allotted to the "personal assessment" factor, making it equal in worth to occupational demand and the third most highly weighted factor behind education and training and intent to establish a business or retire. It was more highly weighted than many factors that should have been given precedent if economic utility was the Department's primary concern. These included occupational skill, age, arranged employment, and knowledge of English or French (maximum of ten points each), as well as having relatives in Canada or employment opportunities in the immigrant's intended area of destination (maximum of five points each). The "units of assessment" to be used in performing the "personal assessment" read as though they were transposed directly from the language of immigration bureaucrats' adjudications of individual order-in-council admissions and deportation appeal cases. Here, immigration or visa officers were to assess "adaptability, motivation, initiative, resourcefulness and other similar qualities" based on their "judgment of the personal suitability of the applicant and his family to become successfully established in Canada."[35] Another notable aspect of this description is the mention of the independent immigrant's family, an institutionalization of the practice – demonstrated in order-in-council admissions and deportation appeals – of evaluating the individual in his/her family context as a "total package." In addition to the abovementioned criteria, twenty-five points could be awarded to independent immigrants who intended to establish a business, reflecting immigration bureaucrats' consistent respect for entrepreneurial spirit throughout the period. With a minimum total score of fifty points required for admission as an independent immigrant, the personal assessment – an admissions criterion derived from the aggregate practices of high-level immigration bureaucrats – may not have been sufficient for admission, but its relatively high weighting certainly made it consequential.

Interpreting Impulses from the Broader and International and Domestic Contexts

The interpretive practices of high-level immigration bureaucrats in postwar Canada were pragmatic and experimental responses to multiple macro- and meso-level pressures to develop a new immigration policy. Archival evidence suggests that these state actors came to recognize a certain logic in these responses over time. This logic emerged in reference to what existing scholarship has identified as two different institutional objectives informing the context in which immigration bureaucrats were working (see chapter 2 for more details).

The first objective related to foreign policy. Seeking parity with stronger and more prominent nations like the United Kingdom and the United States, Canadian immigration bureaucrats were attuned to what an increased presence of negatively racialized groups could mean for the national status group. Looking abroad, they saw that these groups were associated with poverty and social and political unrest in those countries. The United Kingdom and the United States are mentioned as places where the intersection of race and (low) social class had generated social problems that were damaging to those countries' international reputations. There are explicit references to social and economic unrest abroad, that is, of "social problems ... generated by mixing the problems of race and poverty, in places as far apart as Britain and California."[36] In the case of the United Kingdom, members of the Department perceived the country's long-standing history of "racial riots" as being directly linked to immigration by "unskilled persons" who settled in urban areas and fell victim to "poverty and squalor and created a social problem."[37] Canadian immigration bureaucrats viewed with concern the "generally depressed circumstances" of some non-White communities, including "Negro settlements such as we have in Halifax,"[38] and they were keen on avoiding "the tragic examples of Britain and the United States."[39] At the same time, they expressed the conviction that accommodating negatively racialized groups harmoniously in the national collective, while avoiding racialized poverty and social unrest, could be an opportunity. It could allow Canada to gain status in relation to other members of the club of rich, industrialized nations to which Canada was aspiring to belong. In their words, eliminating explicit racial discrimination in immigration policy had the potential to "enable Canada to give a striking example to the world and to adopt a position of leadership at this difficult time when racial problems are so pressing."[40]

In light of Canada's ambition to assume a stronger position in the global political and economic hierarchy, some previously undesirable origin countries began to appear more attractive in the eyes of the Department. This was the case for Japan, where country-level gains in economic and political status made it a perceived source of immigrants with the kind of middle-class traits that would help Canada elevate its own status. In 1965 Japan was described in Departmental correspondence as an "industrialized," "literate" country with a "well-developed society" and high "level of education," leading immigration bureaucrats to declare it to be "one obvious source of the skilled immigrants Canada needs."[41] In addition to socio-economic developments, they perceived Japan as harbouring ambitions on the geopolitical level that mirrored Canada's own, thereby further elevating the status of the country in their minds. As one memorandum stated, "While Japan's standard of living may indeed be lower than Canada's at present, it is rising much more rapidly than Canada's and is already comparable to that of some European nations."[42] In other words, being as good as, or better than, Canada at "what counts" in postwar nation-building transformed Japan, in the eyes of the Department, from an undesirable sending country into a desirable one, with subsequent effects on immigrant admissibility.

These foreign policy considerations pertaining to race and international status also involved comparisons with members of another club to which Canada belonged: the Commonwealth. Here the Department was concerned that Canada could be classified as similar in standing to other (non-White) Commonwealth countries, if racially diverse immigration led to an increase in poverty. The terms "under-developed" and "low living standard" were frequently used to classify the British West Indies as a sending country, and variations on the term "relatively low calibre" were regularly used to classify potential immigrants from there.[43] For immigration bureaucrats in 1958, the "problem of The West Indies" was viewed as "an economic and social one" in that "there is a vicious circle between unemployment, poverty, ignorance, indolence, high labour costs, low productivity, and back to unemployment and poverty."[44] As with classifications used to describe non-White immigrants in Canada, those applied to non-White Commonwealth countries went beyond material concerns about relative economic standing. The term "low calibre," used to describe the population of the West Indies, is defined in the dictionary as a "degree of mental capacity or moral quality" and as a "degree of excellence or importance."[45] Such terms are thus clearly moral evaluations of those countries' perceived capacity to create populations and economies that have "what it takes" to assume a leadership role in the Western world. If Canada was not to be seen as on par with the "poor" Commonwealth countries that were relatively low in the geopolitical status hierarchy, it had to avoid exhibiting the characteristics ascribed to those countries and their populations.

At the same time, shared colonial ties to the United Kingdom led immigration bureaucrats to see potential nation-building advantages in the recruitment of elites from India, Pakistan, and Ceylon. In 1963, they described subsets of the populations in these countries as good potential sources for "well qualified" and "high caliber" immigrants, despite the racialized inadmissibility of these groups in general.[46] This changing perception of individual-level admissibility appears to derive from the recognition that the legacy of British colonialism included the institutionalization of British educational standards for the native elite. One memorandum from the Immigration Attaché in New Delhi described the conditions in India, Pakistan, and Ceylon as follows:

> As an excellent example there are the Anglo-Indians in India, who because of their close ties with the British before Partition, were brought up with English as their mother tongue, and who were in a position to take advantage of opportunities for good education. Many of them are very well qualified in professional categories, but because of their mixed blood, Christian faith, and Westernized outlook, they are being deliberately squeezed out of the positions they should be entitled to hold in the new Indian social order ... I can see no reason why Canada should not gain by taking in a carefully selected number of those well-qualified people whose potentialities are being suppressed here.[47]

From this point of view, colonial institutions had socialized the native elite into bearers of the kind of socio-economic, cultural, and moral markers of middle-class status recognizable in the United Kingdom, a country which Canada wished to match in the postwar international political order. Any perceived deficiency in socio-economic attainment on the part of would-be elite immigrants from these countries was not attributed to putatively innate characteristics of their racial group, but to discrimination and "red tapism"[48] directed at elite status individuals as a result of domestic politics. At the same time, the reference to "mixed blood" in the quotation above shows that biological racialism had not faded from perceptions of racial groups; it was merely trumped by class and status markers in individual cases.

In addition to foreign-policy considerations, domestic social and political concerns informed immigration bureaucrats' development of admissions policies for skilled workers. Among these was the issue of perceived racism on the part of the Canadian general public, and how best to manage racial diversity arising through immigration in light of that. Here we can see one way in which gradual experimentation in case processing may have been an essential part of the policy formulation process that paved the way for the sweeping changes that appeared in the 1967 immigration regulations. From the Department's perspective, the pace of a policy change needed to be managed carefully in order to allow the general public to adapt and to prevent a racist, anti-immigrant backlash. Absent this gradual management of expectations, immigration bureaucrats felt that racial discrimination in the labour market would pose a barrier to settlement and ultimately stymie their efforts to manage demographic change. As the Director of Immigration stated, in 1958:

> Basically, of course, [racial discrimination] is at least partially a correct interpretation of our attitude, and I think that it would be wrong for us to pretend otherwise to the West Indians ... I have always followed the line that the Canadian Government is doing what it can to deal with the problem but it cannot go ahead of public opinion. However much we may deplore it, the fact remains that in a situation of unemployment in a great many communities in Canada the preference will still be given to a white person.[49]

Similar concerns were expressed regarding the employment prospects of nurses from the West Indies, who were applying not just for schooling in that profession but for permission to remain in the country permanently afterward. A memorandum from the acting officer in charge of the Toronto office to the central district superintendent in 1956 recounts a confidential remark made by the registrar of the Registered Nurses Association of Ontario to the effect that, while the association would register nurses irrespective of "race or creed," hospitals desired to "maintain a considerable majority of white nurses" among their staff.[50] In the meantime, they hoped that the gradual admission of non-White skilled workers would change public perceptions. As the director went on to state on that occasion, the "long term" solution to the "problem" of immigration from the British West Indies "would be to admit such coloured persons who, because of their qualifications, are likely to become exceptional citizens and thus render the Negro more generally acceptable in Canada."[51] An example of the kind of case they had in mind was that of a "Negro" telephone operator from Jamaica, who had a job offer from Bell Telephone and $700 in savings available to transfer to Canada, was granted admission as a permanent resident on the grounds that the case was "meritorious."[52] Later, in 1961, policymakers observed that Canada's domestic servant recruitment agreements with the British West Indies were "attracting a *higher class of girl* who will not stay in domestic service any longer than necessary, but will move out after a year into the occupation for which she is best suited, and be in the long run *a greater credit to herself, her race, and to Canada*"[53] (emphasis added). Note that references to "a higher class of girl" and individuals who would be a "credit" to themselves, their race, and the country construct individuals within this racialized group as admissible, while leaving the general inadmissibility of the group unaltered. This "recast" notion of race would become the basis of the middle-class multiculturalism that emerged from these practices: a shared socio-economic basis of community membership despite perceived incompatibilities between ascribed group memberships. Those phrases are also a reminder that this shared socio-economic basis of social cohesion goes beyond notions of economic utility, that is, an individual's class position and potential contributions to the economy, to include moral judgments of status and moral worth.

Conclusion

This chapter has illustrated how revisiting the historiography of Canada's postwar immigration policy change using the cultural sociology of immigration policy approach and data on order-in-council admissions and deportation appeals sheds new light on the role of micro-level mechanisms and their effects. First, the idea of race contained in the Canadian national cultural repertoire comprised two elements (biological racialism and status in the global economic and political order). Embedded within that cultural context, immigration bureaucrats' boundary work, which involved "recasting" of the idea of race to emphasize its socio-economic element, led to the emergence of the distinction between individual-level and group-level admissibility. Group-level racialization in intersectional (race/class) terms broadly supported the notion that immigrant groups from European and Western Hemisphere source countries were fundamentally preferable and admissible, and that immigrant groups from non-European and non-Western Hemisphere source countries were not. This perception persisted both in the letter of the law and in immigration bureaucrats' interpretative practices in relation to the groups they were tasked with managing on the ground. However, in immigration bureaucrats' implementation practices (order-in-council admissions and deportation appeals), membership in a positively racialized group was no longer automatically correlated with admissibility. Conversely, membership in a negatively racialized group no longer constituted automatic grounds for inadmissibility. Furthermore, the interpretive practices of immigration bureaucrats revealed that "merit" in individual admissibility did not refer only to instrumental notions of economic utility. It also referred to more immaterial, moral, and cultural terms attributed to the essential nature of persons. In other words, even at their inception, merit-based systems for selecting immigrants were not just about what people *did* but who they *were*, and the notion of "who people were" was constructed in fundamentally intersectional terms, in reference to race and class.

Turning to the final mechanism, this chapter showed how the micro-level interpretive practices of high-level immigration bureaucrats around the admissibility of skilled workers were subsequently institutionalized in the "points system" introduced in the 1967 immigration regulations. This is important because the institutionalization of the cumulative outcomes of boundary work during the policy formulation process amplifies its material and symbolic effects. Thus, the cumulative outcomes of the relatively small number of admissions practices examined here likely had a much broader impact on immigrant admissions than their numbers suggest. The long-term effect of this institutionalization (explored in greater detail in chapter 6) is that "admissible" multicultural skilled workers have become defined as middle-class multicultural workers. This is relevant not just to shaping the kind of human capital endowments that make skilled workers admissible to the Canadian nation but also Canadians' perceptions of the class and status attributes that make non-White individuals worthy of membership.

The findings presented in this chapter are also relevant to scholarly debates beyond the historical Canadian case. For one, they show that notions of moral deservingness played a strong role in high-level immigration bureaucrats' case processing of order-in-council admissions and deportation appeals, in ways that could both uphold or attenuate legal grounds for exclusion (barred entry or removal from the country). This echoes findings in contemporary studies of lower-level bureaucrats' deportation and border control practices, which likewise ascribe an important role to notions of deservingness (see, e.g., Ellermann 2006; Pratt 2005). What the historical Canadian case adds to these earlier insights is evidence that such dynamics can inform the creation of written policy, rather than just the subsequent application of that policy.

While generative in their own right, the micro-level interpretive practices of immigration bureaucrats did not operate in a vacuum, but rather within the macro-level and meso-level shifts in the idea of race that are given strong explanatory weighting in scholarly work on the link between race, state, and nation (e.g., Thompson 2016), and on immigration policy's role in defining that relationship (e.g., FitzGerald and Cook-Martín 2014; Triadafilopoulos 2012).[54] The postwar implementation practices described in this chapter are strikingly different from the ones used to ensure the inadmissibility of European Jews in the 1930s, which were described in chapter 2. One possible explanation for this is that macro-level ideational change in perceptions of race after the Second World War helped make these new practices thinkable. As Abella and Troper (1991) document, Jews seeking admission to Canada in the 1930s as agriculturalists – one of the few admissions categories available to anyone – were willing to transfer ever-increasing levels of funds to Canada in order to qualify, sometimes thousands more than were officially required. Monetary assets are one of the strongest signals of belonging to the desirable middle or upper-middle class, due to their connotation of a strong work ethic, taste for upward mobility, entrepreneurial spirit, occupational success, and so on. In the case of that strongly negatively racialized group at that time, immigration bureaucrats did not see those assets as grounds for differentiating between individual-level and group-level admissibility. This suggests that, compared to the postwar policy context examined here, the idea of race was less bifurcated and more reflective of biological racialism in the prewar policy context. This would have precluded the mechanism of "recasting" through which postwar immigration bureaucrats came to see individuals as admissible on class terms, despite their racialized group-level inadmissibility.

Paying attention to micro-level mechanisms of immigration policy change allows us to see how race came to operate in Canada's universal immigration policy for skilled workers. As the next chapter shows, similar dynamics were at play in the creation of the universalized family admissions policy that was formally established by the 1967 immigration regulations, alongside (and in relation to) Canada's "points system."

Chapter Five

Putting the "Class" in "Family Class"

In addition to selecting skilled workers based on meritorious individual traits, a core purpose of universal immigration policies as they emerged in the mid-twentieth century is to manage the admission of family members. Here policymakers speak of "family reunification" policies. According to Kofman (2010), this term refers to the process whereby a primary immigrant brings immediate family members (e.g., children, spouses) into the destination country. It also encompasses family-formation migration, which involves two phenomena. The first is second-generation immigrants (with or without receiving-country citizenship) bringing a spouse from their parents' homeland/ diasporic space into the receiving country. The second is permanent residents or citizens of a given country bringing in partners they have met while travelling abroad for work or on holiday.

Compared to universal skilled worker admissions policies, universal family reunification policies have been the subject of more sustained critique for perpetuating racialized exclusion, often along gendered lines. Two concurrent trends across Western immigrant-receiving countries are seen as evidence of persistent racialized selection in family reunification policies: the growth of restrictive admissions practices towards family immigrants amidst the increasing racial and ethnic diversity of permanent immigration flows. As Joppke (2005b, 68) notes with regard to Australia, increased calls for skills-based immigration have been paralleled by "attempts to restrict (usually low-skilled and heavily non-European) family migration [that are] denounced as proxies for opposing non-European immigrants." In Canada, the policy trends related to race and family also appear linked and negatively correlated: racial inclusion has gone hand in glove with the narrowing range of admissible family members since the 1960s. In the wake of the 1967 immigration regulations, the top origin countries of immigrants shifted steadily from mainly European ones prior to 1970 to mainly Asian ones from the 1990s onward (Reitz 2012). A simple glance at the range of admissible relatives in the early 1950s compared to 2015 – not taking into account changes in sponsorship requirements – reveals an equally striking shift. In the 1950s, individuals coming from Europe could enter as spouses, fiancé(e)s, children, parents, grandparents, adult children (along with their own families), and siblings (along with their own families). Today, only spouses (or common-law partners), fiancé(e)s, and dependent children remain in the admissible family categories.

In order to explain the exclusionary turn in family reunification policies, scholars have pointed to how macro-level (national) cultural conceptions of gender and family have been used by politicians and policymakers to interpret family relationships in narrow ways. Evidence of this has been furnished by studies carried out in a range of European contexts, including the Netherlands (Bonjour and de Hart 2013; van Walsum 2009), Norway (Eggebø 2013; Myrdahl 2010), and the United Kingdom (Wray 2006). The authors of these studies argue that normative ideas about the foundations of "real" marriages have exclusionary effects. Defining "real" marriages in "Western" terms as conjugal relationships based on love rather than economic utility, sometimes evidenced by a "male breadwinner" constellation within the family, can exclude individuals in marital or family constellations that are not rooted in such cultural ideals. Even when the "real" nature of marriage is assessed in reference to sending-country norms, stereotypical and homogenizing representations of such norms, as they are perceived within receiving-country institutions, can likewise lead to exclusion.

Gaucher (2018) has documented similar patterns in the contemporary Canadian case. She shows, in reference to the evolution of contemporary case law, that the legal and normative definition of family is firmly centred on conjugality, that is, (heterosexual) marriage. The Canadian legal understanding of conjugality, as it applies to full citizens outside of immigration law, has evolved through court decisions and been recognized as comprising multiple, complex levels of sexual, emotional, and economic interdependency between different types of individuals. For example, it has evolved to include spouses and partners of varying sexual orientations, with varying documentation requirements for accessing benefits and, in the case of polygamy,[1] varying numbers of persons involved. In contrast to the relatively expansive application of the law to what Gaucher calls "inside families" (56), that is, Canadian citizens, very little flexibility is accorded "outside [immigrant] families" when it comes to spousal sponsorship cases and refugee claims.

The purpose of this moral boundary-making is to protect the nation, both literally and figuratively. As the first institution involved in an individual's socialization, the family is accorded an immensely important role in the social reproduction of the physical and imagined national community (Yuval-Davis 1997). If the imagined community is a contingent "category of practice" (Brubaker 1996, 21), then reproduction of the imagined community depends on which practices are passed on to future generations. In Benedict Anderson's (1991, 6) terms, the "style" in which unknown fellow members of the national community are imagined, and thus become recognizable as members, must be learned. While Anderson points to the institutional basis of this learning – schools, administration, courts – the family precedes these institutions in the life trajectory of new community members. Arguably, a prerequisite for learning "traffic habits" (169) in an institutionalized setting is a socially acquired knowledge of, and belief in, those institutions.

In the interest of protecting national communities that are imagined in racial and gendered terms as White and patriarchal, normatively driven exclusion of inadmissible families widely functions along intersectional lines. As Korteweg and Triadafilopoulos (2013, 128) argue in reference to the Netherlands, "mobilizations of gender, religious, and ethnic differences at the highest level of policy making reinforce perceptions of the gendered practices of ethnic minority women and girls (and by extension, of ethnic minority men and boys) as obstacles to integration, enabling calls for strong forms of assimilation." In reference to family reunification policies in the United Kingdom, Yuval-Davis, Anthias, and Kofman (2005, 519) assert that intersecting notions of gender, ethnicity, and religion allow policymakers to see (predominantly female) family migrants as "introducing traditional practices, such as arranged marriage, authoritarian gender and generational relations, and religious practices into secular, modern and liberal societies." Myrdahl (2010, 106) goes further, calling political discourses embedded in immigration policymaking on "forced marriage" in Norway a "racial project" that serves to construct "Third World spaces" as "oppressive and subjugating," and their inhabitants as fundamentally incompatible with the Norwegian nation. These symbolic constructions, in turn, are used to justify exclusionary immigration measures that disproportionately affect Muslim women, in the interest of securing the reproduction of the liberal-democratic nation by individuals whose social group memberships make them compatible with that enterprise (see also Bassel 2010; Kilic, Saharso, and Sauer 2008; Korteweg and Yurdakul 2014; Muegge and de Jong 2013).

Beyond what Bassel (2010, 159) calls the now "routinized" attention to the intersection of gender, religion, and ethnicity in policy dynamics leading to family immigrant exclusion, researchers have been slower to turn their attention to social class. Where this is done, the focus is most often on class as market position, such as income and human capital, not on class in the broader sense of status and morality (Weber 2007a). Staver (2015, 1457) argues that the "economic logic of selection" emphasizing occupation, education, and other aspects of human capital as predictors of labour market success have been "drifting" from economic immigrant selection policies to family reunification policies. Likewise, Block (2015, 1441–5) notes that "socioeconomic membership (occupation, income, education)" determines a sponsor's access to family reunification, not just "ethnocultural membership (language, skills, civic knowledge [and] ethnicity)." Looking at marriage migration in Finland, Pellander (2019, 2) argues that income requirements and emotional attachment are taken into consideration (the former sometimes trumping the latter), "even in cases in which they are not officially requirements." When Wray (2009, 593) states that "class intersects with ethnicity" to stratify family reunification rights in the United Kingdom, disproportionately excluding Muslim South Asians, she is referring to indicators of market position, like income and employment status.

Picking up on the findings presented in chapter 4, this chapter illustrates that a focus on class as market position, denoting economic utility, limits our understanding of how the class distinction aligns with others in shaping immigrant family admissibility. An emphasis on market position overlooks how class-based social stratification plays out in nuanced ways at the intersection of economic and identity-related classifications in immigration policy, a phenomenon documented in reference to contemporary immigration policies in Germany, the United States, and Canada (Elrick and Winter 2018; Ellermann 2019; Tichenor and Jacobson 2020). Identity-related classifications can comprise a range of socio-economic distinctions (e.g., wealth, occupational prestige), cultural distinctions (e.g., educational attainment), and moral distinctions (e.g., personality traits like ambition, self-reliance, work ethic, and community-mindedness). As chapter 4 showed, these distinctions are implicated in group-level racialization (e.g., in the positive racialization of European-origin immigrant groups in socio-economic terms). They are also important for decoupling individual- and group-level admissibility (e.g., in the use of middle-class socio-economic traits to admit individuals from otherwise inadmissible, non-European-origin immigrant groups).

Seen through the lens of a cultural sociology of immigration policy, the interpretive practices of high-level immigration bureaucrats, which drew heavily on socio-economic distinctions, played a significant role in shaping family-related admissions in the postwar era. They were a means of universalizing existing family categories and generating new, racially inclusive ones, through experimentation. The four micro-level mechanisms of policy change posited by the cultural sociology of immigration policy framework are illustrated in this chapter in reference to three cases: Asian fiancé(e)s, adopted children, and the sponsored dependent/nominated relative distinction in general family admissions. Due to the limitations of working with archival data (see the Methodological Appendix), these mechanisms are not equally visible in each case.

Drawing on the Canadian national cultural repertoire and ascribed cultural repertoires of immigrant groups (foremost the Chinese), actors in the Department leveraged normative ideas about family and dependency in their boundary work around family immigration to make some categories of family immigration more racially inclusive. This was evident in the case of Asian fiancé(e)s, adopted children and sponsored dependents. At the same time, the bifurcated idea of race contained in the Canadian cultural repertoire (which defined race both biologically and in reference to socio-economic status) allowed immigration bureaucrats to "recast" that idea as it pertained to notions of who non-European family immigrants were. In the course of this "recasting," immigration bureaucrats racialized "the immigrant family" in general as a status group that was fundamentally inadmissible due to its low economic utility and socio-economic status. This is illustrated most clearly in the boundary work around the development of the sponsored dependent/nominated relative distinction, where contemporary perceptions of family immigration as inherently problematic appear to have emerged. At the same time, individual-level admissibility became decoupled from the group-level inadmissibility of this new status group, facilitating the emergence of selection procedures for admitting family members of diverse origins whose class and status made them compatible with the emergent middle-class Canadian nation. This was visible in the case of nominated relatives and, to a lesser extent, adopted children. The results of this boundary work were subsequently institutionalized in the family immigration provisions contained in the 1967 immigration regulations, ensuring that their material and symbolic effects would be replicated on a large scale.

Family Norms and the Inclusion of Asian Fiancé(e)s

A reading of Canadian immigration law and regulations in effect from 1952 to 1967 suggests that the contemporary exclusion of family immigrants on normative grounds, documented by Gaucher (2018), operated in a similar way in that historical period. Until 1967, the range of relatives who could be sponsored varied by country of origin. For Europeans, Americans, and select other origins, "family" comprised spouses, children, siblings (and their respective spouses and children), fiancé(e)s, grandparents, and unmarried nieces and nephews. For those of "Asian" (e.g., Japanese or Chinese) origin, "family" included only spouses and unmarried children under twenty-one years of age. Until 1957, the right to have an extended immigrant family was furthermore limited for all but the most privileged origin groups to Canadian citizen (not permanent resident) sponsors. Additionally, in 1954, an order-in-council (P.C. 1954–973) was used to codify Eurocentric definitions of particular family members in law, including "child," "unmarried," and "wife or husband."[2] It defined a "child" in exceedingly limited terms as "the issue of lawful wedlock and who would possess the status of legitimacy if his father had been domiciled in Canada at the time of his birth." The term "unmarried" was to apply to someone who was not – and never had been – married. The terms, "wife and husband" were defined as meaning "a man and a woman who have entered into a marriage within the meaning given thereto in the law of any province of Canada." The preclusion of non-Western notions of marriage and child legitimacy make this regulation a particularly strong example of how norms embedded in historical family reunification policies in Canada had the potential to exclude immigrant families from non-European, non-Western Hemisphere countries.

However, when implementation practices and internal policy deliberations are taken into account, the role of norms in determining family immigrant inclusion and exclusion is less straightforward. At the outset of the period under consideration, the idea that family life was an undisputed cornerstone of Canadian society was firmly anchored in the national cultural repertoire. Immigration bureaucrats drew on this normative stance, in some circumstances, to be more inclusive toward immigrant families of diverse racial and national origins than the letter of the law suggests. The First Immigration Manual issued to immigration officers defined the "family unit," for the purpose of case processing, as including "the head of family with his/her spouse and dependent unmarried children under 21, and in addition any other relatives who are dependent on the head of family for support and who normally reside with the family (e.g. aged parents, children over 21 attending school, etc.)."[3] The loose phrase "any other relatives" hints at a pragmatic and flexible delineation of core family membership. Additionally, in 1954, immigration officers were given "discretion to maintain the family unit" by admitting common-law partners, who were otherwise considered inadmissible on moral grounds:

The official attitude of the Department is that marriage is an institution based on religious beliefs and conventional morality. To look with tolerance upon common-law relationships may, in a very real sense, be interpreted as condoning immorality … None the less it will be borne in mind that the Government of Canada recognizes common-law relationships by paying pensions to common-law wives and allowances to children … Moreover, experience shows that due to circumstances, highly respectable and responsible persons do live in common-law relationships.[4]

As this quotation indicates, the flexible interpretation of family norms that benefited citizens and residents (e.g., common-law wives receiving pensions) were extended, in practice, to immigrants, and not solely used as a basis for exclusion. Likewise, although the 1953 immigration regulations allowed lower-level immigration officers to require a literacy test (in the immigrant's own language), they were not to use this test to break up families. The First Immigration Manual instructed immigration officers to "prevent the temporary breaking up of a family" by admitting any members of a family unit who were unable to pass the literacy test (if ordered to take it).[5]

Despite narrow, Eurocentric legal definitions of family and strong limitations on the range of relatives who could be sponsored, Asian-origin family members did at times benefit from high-level immigration bureaucrats' flexible interpretations of family norms and interest in maintaining the family unit. This was the case with the gradually emerging admissibility, in practice, of Asian fiancé(e)s in the 1950s. As will be shown in greater detail in the discussion of adopted child admissions, Canadian immigration bureaucrats ascribed to Chinese people an innate commitment to family life and saw it as the one redeeming feature of a group that had historically been negatively racialized and excluded. Although fiancé(e)s of Asian origin were not legally admissible under family reunification provisions until the 1962 immigration regulations, Chinese and Japanese fiancé(e)s and their children were admitted on an "experimental basis" from 1956 and 1957 onward, respectively.[6] This experimental practice began with Chinese fiancé(e)s and their "illegitimate" children, in recognition of what high-level immigration bureaucrats perceived to be culturally ingrained family norms in China. The Department's commitment to keeping families intact led it to interpret the laws pertaining to Chinese families flexibly and inclusively. As the head of the Admissions Division stated in 1958:

We were aware of the Chinese custom whereby most males marry before their 19th birthday, and suspected that most if not all of the Chinese between 18 and 25 years admitted to Canada since then as single were actually married, and many with children. It was expected, therefore, that the fiancée provision would be used by these young men to bring forward their wives (and children) in the guise of fiancées with or without children.[7]

One interesting thing about this practice, aside from its inclusivity towards family members from one of most inadmissible groups under Canadian immigration policy, is that it amounted to a de facto legalization of what the Department believed was ongoing immigration fraud. In other words, it recognized that Chinese families had been circumventing restrictions on sponsoring married sons and daughters with children (a privilege officially enjoyed only by European immigrants until 1962). It also relativized the illegality of their practices based on their perceived understanding of Chinese family structures, on a case-by-case basis, without explicitly extending the admissions policy laid out in the Immigration Act and regulations.[8] This practice towards fiancé(e)s was extended to Japanese-Canadian sponsors in 1957, in the spirit of fair treatment within provisions for the admission of "Asians."[9] Among the different types of immigrants admitted by order-in-council notwithstanding their group-level inadmissibility on racial grounds, these two – Chinese fiancé(e)s and "illegitimate" children – were among the most frequently admitted. Between 1956 (when they were made admissible in practice) and 1962 (when they were included in the immigration regulations), 104 Chinese fiancées and thirty-six "illegitimate" children were admitted as permanent residents.

Creating a Universal Family Category from the Bottom Up: Adopted Children

Prior to the 1967 immigration regulations, there was no legal provision for the admission of children adopted abroad or for bringing foreign children to Canada for the purposes of adoption. Nevertheless, adoption cases surfaced regularly in immigration applications forwarded to the minister for consideration, from at least 1953 onward.[10] In total, eighty-one such cases (twenty-eight of them described in detail) came to light in the archival records I reviewed on adopted children and on order-in-council admissions in general, mainly spanning the years 1953 to 1964. The records suggest, however, that this number under-represents the volume of adoption-related cases sent to the minister's office for approval. In 1961, the Canadian Welfare Council reported having received ninety-three inquiries in the preceding twelve-month period from families looking to adopt children from Asia.[11] A letter sent in 1961 from the deputy minister to the solicitor representing a family in the case of an immigration application for a child to be adopted – which was refused – states that the case is "not a unique and isolated request, but one of several hundred similar ones received each year."[12] The incomplete nature of archival records thus limits the analysis here to those cases that happened to be saved for posterity.

Irrespective of quantity, the adjudication of adoption-related cases outside the provisions of immigration law had a strong qualitative impact on the policy formulation process. In the course of processing these cases, state actors in the Department created a new category of admissible family member from the bottom up. The routine of practice they developed in reference to these cases generated the principles according to which an entry category for adopted children could be established within the broader context of managing an inevitable increase in racial diversity. The analysis of adoption-related immigration cases shows how immigration bureaucrats drew on normative ideas of family contained in the Canadian national cultural repertoire and ascribed to the national cultural repertories of other immigrant groups (foremost the Chinese) to make this type of family immigration racially inclusive. This occurred despite their ongoing perceptions of some immigrant groups, particularly the Chinese, as fundamentally inadmissible. To a more limited extent, it shows how individual-level and group-level admissibility diverged, as the "recast" idea of race allowed immigration bureaucrats to see children from legally inadmissible racial groups being admitted in cases where the prospective adoptive parents displayed middle-class attributes.

Emergent Principles of Policy Formulation: Control, Consistency, and "Bona Fide" Cases

From at least 1953 onwards, the Department responded to adoption-related cases by developing what Lipsky ([1980] 2010) calls a "routine of practice." In general, routines of practice are used by bureaucrats to simplify their clientele and their environment, and they "effectively *become* the public policies they carry out" (Lipsky [1980] 2010, xii–xiii, emphasis in the original).[13] In this case, the emergent routine comprised three principles: control, consistency, and the need for cases to be "bona fide." Its application set the parameters for generating a new admissions category that was universal from the outset, in the sense that children from any country could be – and were – admitted as adoptees. As with skilled workers, the key to this transformation was the emerging distinction in implementation practices between individuals and groups: while racialized notions of admissibility were maintained at the group level (e.g., in perceptions of Chinese immigrants as innately inadmissible), exceptions were occasionally made for individual members of these groups.

The principle of control centred largely on whether the child to be adopted had living relatives in the country of origin. This was due to the racialized concern that applicants were circumventing restrictive family reunification clauses, or that the child would one day sponsor its birth parents and other family members. I describe the control principle as racialized because it operated at the group level to exclude Asian-origin adoptees. In the eighteen cases I reviewed involving adoptees with living relatives, ten involved Asian children, and seven of those ten were refused. The three remaining cases were approved only because details of the case assured the Department that no precedents for extended family sponsorship would be set, or because the Department added provisos to ensure this would not happen. As the Director of Immigration stated with regard to the case of a Japanese couple seeking the admission of two children from Japan whose parents were still alive, "children who are not orphans would … in due time … seek the admission of their natural parents, when aged, as dependents."[14] In another case, the principle of control as avoidance of precedent setting led to the refusal of a case involving the adoption of two Chinese boys by a childless Chinese-Canadian couple in Victoria. The issue in the case was that the boys' mother was still alive, albeit in ill health. While the Director of Immigration acknowledged that this was "no doubt a compassionate case," he nevertheless recommended that it be refused, since there was also "no doubt that if we were to approve this case, we would be faced with many others of an equally compassionate nature."[15] In a case involving an application by a Chinese-Canadian couple to adopt a related Chinese girl whose parents were still alive, the Department stated that "the child's admission, by itself, would certainly not do Canada any harm," but that "approval … would definitely be used as a precedent by the Chinese [and we would] soon be faced with many similar applications for the admission of nephews, nieces, cousins of both sexes and all ages."[16]

Where applications by Chinese-Canadians to adopt Chinese children with living relatives were approved (as happened in three cases), it was because the Department added provisos to ensure that no precedent for further Chinese family migration was being set, or because it felt the case rested on conditions that were not easily replicable. In two of these cases, the Department approved the couples' applications under the stipulation that International Social Services (ISS) select a child for adoption, in order to ensure that the couples were not selecting relatives.[17] In another case, the doctor-attested inability of the prospective Chinese-Canadian adoptive mother to conceive her own children was regarded as a safeguard against copycat applications. The Director of Immigration stated, "As this couple are childless, it is doubtful if this case could be used as a precedent by persons seeking the admission of inadmissible relatives [as adopted children]."[18] Medically attested childlessness was only an acceptable proviso, however, as long as the Department was sure that the children being adopted were in no way already related to the couple. As the deputy minister stated, "If we are going to permit childless Chinese couples in Canada to bring forward nieces, nephews, and similar minor close relatives for adoption in Canada, even though their parents are still living with them as a complete family unit in Hong Kong, this will open the door to a lot more opportunities for abuse and evasion than we are encountering now."[19]

The maintenance of Chinese group-level inadmissibility via the principle of control becomes even more apparent when compared to the handling of cases involving families who were not uniformly of Asian origin. Examples include cases in which potential adoptees with living relatives (grounds for exclusion in the case of Asian families) were either non-Asian or to be adopted by non-Asian Canadians. Eight out of nine applications for such adoptions, involving children from Jamaica, Lebanon, Korea, Japan, the United Kingdom, Yugoslavia, Barbados, and Poland, were approved. In one such case, involving a child from Lebanon who was the distant relative of the potential adoptive father and had living relatives in Lebanon, the Director of Immigration wrote to the minister, stating, "I don't think the world will be turned upside down if you decide to exercise your Ministerial prerogative to over-ride the Departmental position which I have felt obliged to take in this matter."[20] In another case, the Department had no problem approving the admission of three children from Barbados whose living parents had remarried and "had no plans for [the children] in their new lives."[21] The applications by non-Asian Canadian missionaries abroad to admit adopted Asian children with living relatives in the country of origin were also approved without any expression of concern on the part of the Department.[22] Read in contrast to cases in which Asian-Canadian parents were seeking the admission of Asian children with living relatives for adoption, these cases show that the principle of maintaining control by not setting precedents for expansive family admissions reinforced the racialized group-level inadmissibility ascribed to Asian immigrant groups. This group-level inadmissibility was rooted in immigration bureaucrats' perceptions of Asians – particularly Chinese – as innately untrustworthy and disrespectful of official rules. As the deputy minister stated in 1964, there is a "Chinese disregard for authority [such that] beyond self-interest and possibly the Chinese family structure, the Chinese are not bound by the ethical demands of the European way of life."[23] It is not that members of other racialized groups could not exploit order-in-council admissions in adoption-related cases; it is that they were not considered innately likely to do so.

The second principle underlying high-level bureaucrats' routine of practice was consistency. As the deputy minister stated, with "several hundred" adoption-related cases being received each year, it was important to deal with them "on some basis of consistency and uniformity."[24] The principle of consistency was used in both expansive and restrictive ways, depending on the likelihood that an uncontrollable precedent would be set, by introducing a decision that would need to be consistently adhered to in the future. This was the case with the childless Chinese-Canadian couple from Victoria introduced in chapter 1, who were permitted to adopt two children with living relatives from China, in part because the Director of Immigration pointed out that an order-in-council admission had been issued "under identical circumstances" to a childless Chinese couple the previous year.[25] This made subsequent admissions hard to refuse. In another case, a moneyed Chinese-Canadian resident applied for the admission of his nephew in Hong Kong so that the nephew could inherit his estate and carry on his business. When the minister indicated a willingness to approve the application, the deputy minister intervened, stating:

> [A] Minister should not put himself in the position of doing for the rich what he will not do for the poor [since] the poor are far more numerous than the rich [and] Chinese with [inadmissible] sons over age 21 would feel doubly aggrieved if other Chinese were allowed to sponsor nephews for reasons which pertain not so much to close family ties as to the disposition of estates.[26]

These quotations illustrate that the principle of consistency helped to make adopted children a slightly more inclusive entry category on the individual level while leaving pre-existing racialized notions of the group-level inadmissibility of Chinese persons untouched.

The simultaneous emergence of universal individual-level admissibility for adopted children and maintenance of racialized notions of group-level inadmissibility can also be seen in the final principle inherent in high-level bureaucrats' routine of practice: the need for a case to be "bona fide." A bona fide case was understood as one in which "the adoption was undertaken in good faith, [and in which] the child would be received in the home of the parents and would be reared by them."[27] Elsewhere the term bona fide is described as denoting a case in which "a child has been adopted as a means of satisfying the adoptive parents' natural desire for children of their own, and not as a device to secure the admission of an otherwise inadmissible person."[28] Thus one of the cases involving a childless Canadian-Chinese couple is assessed as a "bona fide application, which would be morally justified," due to the couple's natural inability to satisfy their desire for children.[29]

As with the principles of control and consistency, the need for a case to be bona fide was developed with reference to group-level perceptions of Chinese. As the acting deputy minister stated in 1963, "The Asian cases, mainly Chinese, have always been a source of trouble [and] the main difficulty is the question of identifying the adopted child and in determining whether the case is bona fide."[30] Perhaps more than the others, however, the bona fide principle facilitated the admission of Chinese individuals due to high-level bureaucrats' essentialized notions of the Chinese family. As the acting deputy minister stated clearly, "Because of the Chinese view of family life, children are essential, and if a marriage does not produce offspring, adoption is the normal recourse."[31] According to this racialized logic, the Department saw itself in the position to approve the application submitted by a Chinese-Canadian couple for the adoption and admission of an orphaned niece in Hong Kong. Because the woman's own child had recently been killed, the woman – now childless – was considered "in danger of nervous collapse" and would find "solace" in having a child again.[32]

The routine of practice developed by high-level immigration bureaucrats was strong enough by 1959 to be institutionalized in the First Immigration Manual. In that year, section 4.54 of the manual advised immigration officers of the following for the first time:

Applications for the permanent admission of children adopted by Canadian residents abroad may be dealt with without reference to BHQ [Branch Headquarters] when the children are citizens of countries included in Regulation 20(a) or (b). Applications for children who are citizens of all other countries are to be referred to the Chief, Admissions Division, BHQ for consideration on their individual merits. Order-in-Council authority is required when the child is a citizen of a country included in Regulation 20(d) or Regulation 21.[33]

This early policy articulation formalized the distinction, in practice, between individual-level and group-level admissibility. At the group level, admissibility continued to be defined in terms of ascribed group membership. Children who were British subjects by birth or by naturalization in the United Kingdom, Australia, New Zealand, or the Union of South Africa; citizens of Ireland and the United States; and French citizens by birth or naturalization in France or in the Saint-Pierre and Miquelon Islands (i.e., those covered under regulation 20(a) or (b)) were declared eligible in principle for admission. Children of Asian origin and those who were citizens of India, Pakistan, and Ceylon (i.e., those covered under regulation 20(d) or regulation 21) were not declared eligible in principle but could be considered on an individual basis. In other words, while the manual reaffirmed group-level differences in admissibility, it also explicitly laid the foundations for individual-level admissibility notwithstanding ascribed group membership.

Also in 1959, a Department representative described the new policy in more detail to a member of the Senate. He stated plainly that "immigration regulations do not provide for the admission of children for adoption, or even of adopted children,"[34] before proceeding to outline four broad categories of cases and the Department's stance regarding each. These four categories were differentiated according to two main criteria: (a) whether the adoption took place abroad or in Canada; and (b) whether the nationality of the child in question fell under the admissible nationalities outlined in the immigration regulations. The most straightforward of the four categories, which generally led to admission by order-in-council, was the one involving the adoption abroad by Canadian residents or immigrants preparing to enter Canada of a child who belonged to one of the following groups: British subjects by birth or naturalization in the United Kingdom, Australia, New Zealand, or the Union of South Africa; citizens of Ireland; citizens of France born or naturalized in France or in St. Pierre and Miquelon Islands; citizens of the United States; citizens by birth or naturalization in Austria, Belgium, Denmark, the Federal Republic of Germany, Finland, Greece, Iceland, Italy, Luxembourg, Netherlands, Norway, Portugal, Spain, Sweden, or Switzerland; or refugees from a European country. If the child to be adopted abroad did not belong to one of these abovementioned national categories (the second broad category of adoptees), the application was "very carefully and sympathetically considered" and "special authority" was sought to allow entry in cases involving "exceptionally compassionate or humanitarian reasons for approval." Finally, the Department did "not encourage" applications for the adoption of children in Canada (the third and fourth broad categories), either of a favoured nationality or not (although the latter were viewed particularly unfavourably), due in part to the complicated overlap in jurisdiction with the provinces.

Although the routine of practice developed to deal with these applications was institutionalized in the First Immigration Manual in 1959, the general public was not to know that it existed until the publication of the 1967 immigration regulations. From 1962 to 1966, the First Immigration Manual imparted on immigration officers, increasingly emphatically, that "Departmental policy with respect to adopted children and children to be adopted in Canada will not be publicized in any way," and that immigration officers were to "ensure that their correspondence does not give the impression that a special adoption program is in effect."[35] Instead, officers were to emphasize that "there is no provision in the Regulations for the admission of adopted children or children to be adopted."[36] The fact that this public stance did not actually match what was happening at the case processing level is a strong reminder of how important the micro-level practices of state actors are to assessing the kinds of inclusion and exclusion that actually occur under immigration laws and regulations. It also illustrates how experimental admissions practices over a sustained period of time helped pave the way for what otherwise appears, on the surface, to be an abrupt, paradigmatic policy shift in 1967.

Interpreting Impulses from Broader International and Domestic Contexts

The micro-level interpretive practices of immigration bureaucrats, while generative in their own right, were also shaped by the macro-level (geopolitical) and meso-level (governmental) contexts in which they were embedded. In 1960, Prime Minister Diefenbaker announced a plan to bring orphaned refugee children to Canada. This was billed as Canada's contribution to World Refugee Year.[37] The only clearly stated parameter of the program was that it was to target orphaned children who were recognized as refugees by the United Nations High Commissioner for Refugees (UNHCR).[38] The lack of further specifications, and the immediate emergence of unforeseen problems, put members of the Department in the situation of having to adapt and expand their routine of practice to accommodate a new situation. The first problem emerged with the revelation that few refugee children registered by the UNHCR appeared to be available for adoption. At the same time, migration from Mainland China to Hong Kong in the wake of the Cultural Revolution had prompted applications to admit children to Canada who were not recognized by UNHCR. Additionally, as the effects of the Cultural Revolution created political and economic turmoil in Hong Kong, a growing number of Hong Kong Chinese began looking to international migration for relief (Madokoro 2016). Flooded with applications in the wake of the program's public announcement, the Department quickly moved to interpret the newly announced program's two main qualifiers – that it apply to "orphans" who are recognized "refugees" – less literally and more "within the spirit of the programme."[39] This meant that a child who was not a refugee under the auspices of UNHCR but "living in a refugee situation such as exist[ed] in Hong Kong" was to be considered for admission under the scheme.[40] Furthermore, "foundlings" (children not proven to be full orphans, but whose parents could not be identified) and "illegitimate children whose mothers were living but who had been released for adoption" came to be considered alongside the "full orphans" originally envisaged in the program announcement.[41]

By 1963, following these geopolitical developments, the Department was able to articulate a finer-grained and more expansive version of its adoption-related policies, while continuing to emphasize that "neither policy [was] covered by the … Immigration Regulations."[42] For adoptions in Canada, the general rule of the Department was to admit any orphan if (a) the province approved; (b) the child was young and had no family ties; and (c) the case was "otherwise bona fide," that is, if "the child [had] been adopted as a means of satisfying the adoptive parents' natural desire for children of their own, and not as a device to secure the admission of an otherwise inadmissible person, who [would] not be raised as the adopting parents' own child." For adoptions abroad, the general policy of the Department was that (a) the child be legally adopted according to the laws in place in the country of origin; (b) the provincial authorities recognize the adoption; and (c) the case was bona fide (according to the definition above).

Despite the assertion that their adoption-related policies were "basically quite reasonable [and] should go a long way toward meeting complaints," there was great reluctance to codify it in law, as it was felt that "it would be quite difficult to devise a regulation … in view of the many 'ifs and buts.'"[43] Some of these "ifs and buts" included the cases of illegitimate children whose mothers were living, Chinese couples (who were to be scrutinized with regard to previous involvement in "illegal immigration activity"), and the occasional overaged child or child who was neither an orphan, nor a foundling, nor an illegitimate child. In considering how to formulate new immigration regulations, as eventually happened in 1967, the Department determined that control over three elements would need to be codified, all of which are recognizable from the foregoing overview of case-processing activities: age, provincial approval (not just recognition of the adoption), and the stipulation that the child in question must be an orphan, a foundling, or illegitimate. Should the codification of its adoption-related policy violate Departmental principles, after all, it would always be possible to "deal with the additional cases as exceptions and secure Orders-in-Council authorizing admission,"[44] as it had always done.

Institutionalizing Adoptees as Family Immigrants

The routine of practice developed by high-level bureaucrats to adjudicate adoption cases, which was subsequently modified in reference to geopolitical events, created the parameters for the universal admissions category for adopted individuals that eventually became sections 31(f) and (g) of the 1967 immigration regulations. According to these sections, an adopted son or daughter from any country of origin could be sponsored for admission to Canada as a permanent resident if they had been adopted while under the age of eighteen, were unmarried, and under the age of twenty-one at the time of admission. Furthermore, any child under the age of thirteen could be admitted to Canada for adoption from any country in the world provided they were an orphan, abandoned child of undetermined parentage, a child born out of wedlock and given up for adoption, or the child of parents who were separated and who had given the child up for adoption.[45] The wording of this universal provision clearly owes its existence to both the routine of practice developed by immigration bureaucrats, which evolved in the course of processing individual applications, and subsequent responses to geopolitical events beyond the control of that bureaucracy. The announcement of an adoption program in honour of World Refugee Year in 1960 and concurrent refugee movements in Asia pushed immigration bureaucrats to adapt their routine to new circumstances. Specifically, these events warranted the reconsideration of the tight controls they had placed in their routine of practice on admissible forms of relationships within the adoption category, particularly illegitimate children and children with living relatives.

Continued group-level racialization around perceived family norms played an interesting role in the evolution of the adopted children category. One aspect of the racialized perception of Chinese family norms – the essentialness of children – facilitated the creation an individual-level admissions category that benefited, rather than excluded, Chinese immigrants. On the other hand, the racialization of the Chinese as a group that was inherently untrustworthy and disrespectful of rules also resulted in the focus on controllable, bona fide cases that initially limited admissible forms of relationships within the adopted children category.

Intersectional Admissibility in Individual Adoption Cases

Because there are fewer records of individual adoption cases available, there is little evidence in this family category of how the perceived class and status of individuals mediated group-level concerns about admissibility. Nevertheless, available evidence suggests that intersectional selection dynamics were relevant, particularly moral distinctions denoting middle-class status, such as community-mindedness, occupational prestige, self-reliance, perseverance, and entrepreneurial spirit (Lamont 1992).

In two cases, a prospective adoptive parent's membership in the clergy, a relatively high-status and community-oriented occupation, led to approval. In the first, from 1953, the deputy minister intervened in the impending rejection by a lower-level immigration officer of a case in which missionaries (a respected, community-oriented occupation) in Japan had applied to adopt and bring to Canada the "illegitimate child" of a Japanese mother and a Scottish father. While the immigration officer responsible wished to refuse the case on the grounds that "an adopted Asiatic child is not admissible to Canada as an immigrant,"[46] the deputy minister overrode the decision with the justification that the adoptive father was a "prominent missionary in Japan [who is] very anxious that his adopted son be a Canadian citizen."[47] In the second case, a reverend and his wife successfully obtained the admission via order-in-council of a Korean child they had adopted in Korea, a decision forwarded to the family with the following words by the executive assistant to the deputy minister: "If there had been any doubts about the validity of your application, they were certainly dispelled, as far as I was concerned, when I saw her photograph! She appears to be a most charming and sweet little girl!"[48]

Other markers of appropriate class and status facilitated adoption-related admissions as well. In one case, the fact that extended members of the prospective Chinese-Canadian adoptive family in Manitoba had served in the Canadian armed forces (a strong indicator of commitment to the national community) led the Department to approve a couple's application to adopt the woman's orphaned niece from Hong Kong, notwithstanding the niece's inadmissibility under the immigration regulations.[49] One immigrant Chinese couple in Victoria, who had applied to adopt a child from Hong Kong, was given favourable consideration in part because the husband was "a partner in a travel agency [and] prominent in donating his services to community projects in Victoria."[50] Being a partner (not just employee) in the travel agency suggested not only that the husband earned a sufficient amount to support a family but also had a certain entrepreneurial spirit; his community activities alluded, furthermore, to a willingness to contribute actively to community-building and social cohesion. In yet another example, the decision to allow a British-born couple to adopt their niece from England hinged on their income and debt situation, that is, their class and status. Immigration bureaucrats were concerned that the husband, an employee at an aluminum factory who earned $4,400 per year, might not be able to support another child in addition to his wife and the three children they already had. However, the family's subsequent display of desirable moral traits, like self-reliance, perseverance, and determination to elevate themselves financially through hard work, changed the Department's mind. Following the initial application, the husband negotiated a pay raise and the wife entered the labour market as a supply teacher. This "impressed" representatives of the Department and made the Acting Director of Immigration "believe that circumstances in the home will improve."[51] The case was decided in the applicants' favour.

Creating Sponsored Dependents and Nominated Relatives

The third example of how high-level immigration bureaucrats' interpretive practices shaped Canada's universal provisions for family immigration is their role in generating two new general entry categories for family immigrants: sponsored dependents and nominated relatives. The boundary work preceding the creation of these categories "recast" the idea of race, as it pertained to immigrant families from non-European countries, resulting in the emergence of "the immigrant family" as a new status group. This racially diverse group was framed as fundamentally incompatible with the Canadian nation, due to its low economic utility and socio-economic status. Against this backdrop, individual-level and group-level admissibility diverged. Selection instruments were developed to admit extended family members who had a high probability of participating in the labour market (labelled nominated relatives), based on markers of economic utility and socio-economic status. At the same time, normative conceptions of legitimate forms of dependency within Canadian families were applied inclusively, to admit individuals (labelled sponsored dependents) whose likelihood of labour market participation was deemed to be low. The boundary work around the admissibility of these two new family categories was subsequently institutionalized in family selection criteria contained in the 1967 immigration regulations.

Family Immigration as an Intersectional Policy Problem

Given the wide range of family members that Canadian citizens and permanent residents could sponsor from European countries, the Department anticipated that a sharp rise in all types of family immigrants would occur if and when those sponsorship provisions were universalized, that is, opened to immigrants of all national and racial origins. Additionally, they recognized that the universalization of skilled worker admissions from 1962 onward would lead to the rise of non-European immigrants who could subsequently apply for family sponsorship.

Concerns about increasing family immigration from non-European origin countries were rooted in immigration bureaucrats' perceptions of these groups as inadmissible in intersectional terms. As illustrated in chapter 4, the negative racialization of non-European groups derived from both their perceived inferiority in terms of their innate biological characteristics and inferior socio-economic status. Immigration bureaucrats expected the increased presence of non-European family immigrants to amplify the traits that made these groups inadmissible, as new arrivals subsequently sponsored others of the same background. What concerned members of the Department is what sociologists call the homophily principle. This principle states that "contact between similar people occurs at a higher rate than among dissimilar people" (McPherson et al. 2001, 416). Individuals tend to associate with others of similar education, occupation, and occupational prestige. Especially in the case of marriage, relationships tend to be homophilous on educational and other class characteristics, although intergenerational mobility means that kinship ties introduce some heterogeneity in educational attainment and class (e.g., through the presence to less-educated parents and parents-in-law; see McPherson et al. 2001, 426–7). The Department's concern that family immigration from non-European countries could rapidly expand the presence of biologically and socio-economically "inferior" groups, due to the homophily principle, was articulated during the policy formulation process. With regard to domestic servants from the British West Indies, who had the right to sponsor relatives and fiancés after settlement, it was assumed that women "from the lower classes in their own countries" would, in turn, sponsor people who would become "unskilled workers."[52] Likewise, in 1961 it was noted of sponsored family immigrants from India that "the majority of our applications are sponsored by Sikhs who originally come from the poverty stricken Punjab area, who are in turn sponsoring semi-literate, unskilled disease-ridden relatives who can contribute little or nothing to the Canadian economy or culture."[53] The Department's perceptions of Italian family immigrants echoed this belief. In reference to an interview the minister himself conducted with an Italian couple in Rome in 1965, he reported:

> [The couple was] in their forties with Grade IV education, no skills and several children who were coming to Canada under the sponsorship of the woman's brother. The man himself had five brothers and sisters similarly without qualifications, who also wanted to come to Canada, and could do so once the man was here and could act as a lateral sponsor.[54]

This process, dubbed by policymakers the "seed effect of sponsored immigration" had been of perpetual concern with regard to southern Europeans (e.g., Italians, Portuguese) since the late 1950s. The "seed immigrant" diagram of exponential family chain migration became a recurring attachment in reports, memoranda, and the 1966 White Paper on Immigration (see figure 5.1).[55] This metaphor carried over to descriptions of other family groups. For example, in 1965, the Department expressed concern about the "dangerous combination" of wide-open sponsorship provisions and a substantial movement of relatively "low-calibre," unsponsored West Indian "seed migrants."[56]

The racialization of family immigrants as a group, in class terms, helps shed light on how sponsored Italian family members emerged as one of the most inadmissible immigrant groups in the 1950s.[57] As outlined in chapter 3, Italians in general – and southern Italians in particular – occupied relatively low position in the hierarchy of preferred racial and ethnic groups in the Canadian national cultural repertoire. Nevertheless, as Europeans, Italians had been given more expansive family sponsorship provisions than non-European groups, particularly Chinese, Japanese, East Indians, and immigrants from the British West Indies. These broader provisions were anchored in Order-in-Council P.C. 1956–785, which amended the 1953 immigration regulations. They included the ability to sponsor not just "core dependents" like spouses, unmarried children under the age of twenty-one and aged parents, but extended relatives, including brothers and sisters (along with their spouses and children) and married children (including their spouses and dependents). As a result of these relatively generous

Figure 5.1. "Seed immigrants" and family sponsorship

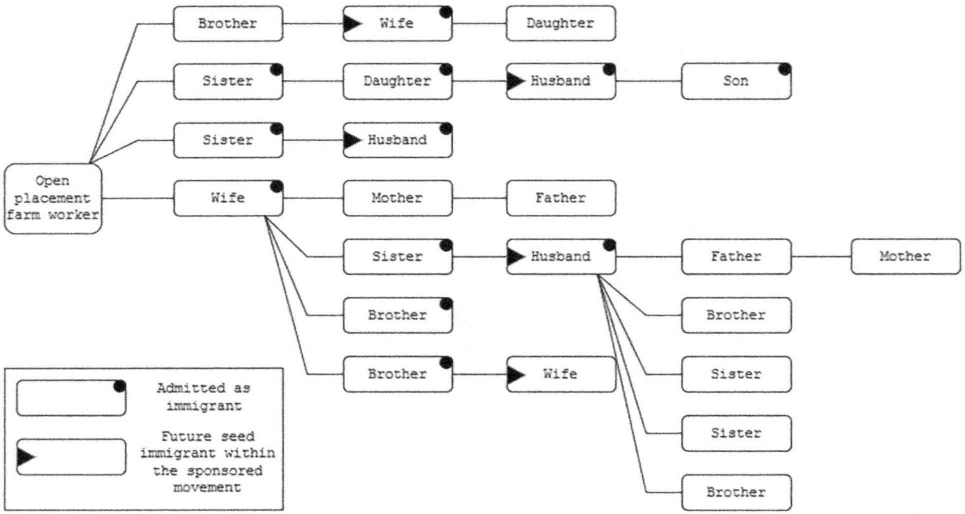

Source: The original figure appears in RG76, Vol. 723-25-2, Part 2. It is accompanied by the following text: "This illustrates the 'chain reaction' movement of sponsored immigrants resulting from the selection of one open placement farm worker from the Portuguese Azores [in 1934]. Up to 1950, 23 persons have been nominated. In the process 5 immigrants with no blood relationship within this family were admitted who will be in a position to sponsor their own blood relatives." The version of the figure presented here has been modified. The original contains the names of each immigrant and their year of immigration, and this personal information has been removed. Different symbols are also used to denote sponsored immigrants and "future seed immigrants," for the sake of optical clarity.

provisions and the large size of Italian extended families, members of this group were arriving in relatively large numbers. By the late 1950s, the Department was observing with "concern" the "large scale movement of sponsored immigrants to Canada, many of whom have poor qualifications in relation to the immediate needs of the Canadian economy."[58] They increasingly described sponsored family immigrants as "low quality," "unskilled," "semi-skilled," "uneducated," having "no particular academic background," and being prone to "employment difficulties."[59] Later, these descriptors expanded to include "untrainable," which denoted "those whose level of education was so low that there was little prospect, within their lifetime, of their being trained to undertake skilled employment in the labour force."[60] By 1963, the link between sponsored family immigrants and deficits in education and training had become generalized to the extent that the Acting Director of Immigration declared, "virtually all the unskilled workers now come into Canada as sponsored immigrants."[61]

It is important to note that concerns about family immigrants were not related exclusively to their perceived economic utility, that is, their ability to fulfill a need in the labour market. Descriptors such as "low quality," "uneducated," and lacking in "academic background" evoke judgments about their socio-economic, cultural, and moral worth. Just as non-White immigrant groups, like the Chinese, were racialized in intersectional terms, in relation to both putative biological traits and the perceived socio-economic position of the group in the global international hierarchy, so too were family immigrants as an emergent status group. Spanning multiple origins, including visibly White (northern) Italians, family immigrants became negatively racialized as innately deficient in socio-economic, cultural, and moral terms.

The knock-on effect of this racializing "immigrant family" status was the modification of perceived hierarchies of national group worth. By the 1960s, the negative racialization of Italians, spurred by the strong association of that national group with "immigrant family," contrasted markedly with the increasingly positive racialization described in chapter 4 of the Japanese, who had long been considered one of the most inadmissible racial and national groups. A European and an Asian immigrant group had effectively "traded places" in the moral hierarchy of immigrant groups that was part of Canada's cultural repertoire at the beginning of the postwar era (see chapter 3). Here we can see a group-level effect of the "recasting" mechanism in the course of boundary work around immigrant admissibility.

Managing and Institutionalizing Universal Family Admissions
in Terms of Class, Status, and Family Norms

Against the backdrop of emergent characterizations of the "immigrant family" as a racialized status group, one important step taken by immigration bureaucrats in the bottom-up creation of a new general family admissions policy was to explore ways of managing the class and status composition of this group. This was eventually accomplished through the distinction, in the 1967 immigration regulations, between sponsored dependents and nominated relatives (see table 5.1). Nominated relatives, a category that comprised a large range of extended family members, became subject to selection criteria similar to those applied to skilled workers. As with so many features of the 1967 immigration regulations, this distinction between categories of family members did not appear abruptly but emerged over time in the course of bureaucrats' interpretive practices, which were also a response to meso-level institutional pressures like case processing backlogs. Table 5.1 provides an overview of the types of relatives included under each of these categories.

Over the course of the 1950s and 1960s, the Department began dividing family members, initially referred to as "close relatives," into two broad categories, based on their perceived likelihood of participating in the labour market. In 1952, at a time when family immigration from non-European source countries as severely restricted in immigration law and regulations, "close relatives" encompassed a large range of individuals: spouses; fiancé(e)s; children and (step-)siblings, along with their spouses and unmarried children; parents; grandparents; and orphaned nephews and nieces under the age of twenty-one.[62] With such a wide range of individuals eligible for admission, it is perhaps unsurprising that many of the Department's immigration offices abroad were facing unwieldy numbers of applications that transformed quickly into insurmountable backlogs. While backlogs had been documented for southern European-origin countries throughout the period, the Department expressed concern when the total backlog of applications from Italy, Greece, and Portugal reached 38,500 in September 1965.[63] Combined with the perception of family immigrants as "low skilled" or "low calibre," these strong family inflows were a particular worry in the context of immigration bureaucrats' efforts to build a national middle-class status group befitting of Canada's ascendency to the club of rich, powerful nations (see chapter 4).

In figuring out how to resolve the problem of high volume, "low quality" family immigration, high-level bureaucrats increasingly sorted

Table 5.1. Types of family members considered to be nominated relatives and sponsored dependents under the 1967 Immigration Regulations (P.C. 1967–1616)

Nominated relatives (including immediate family of persons listed)	Sponsored dependents
• Children aged 21 and over • Married children under age 21 • Siblings • Parents under age 60 • Grandparents under age 60 • Nieces/nephews • Uncles/aunts • Grandchildren	• Spouses • Fiancé(e)s • Unmarried children under age 21 • Parents aged 60 and over, including accompanying immediate family members of that person • Grandparents aged 60 and over, including accompanying immediate family members of that person • Parents and grandparents under age 60 if widowed and/or otherwise unable to care for themselves, including accompanying immediate family members of that person • Siblings, nieces/nephews, and grandchildren under age 18 • Unmarried adopted children under age 21 • Children to be adopted who are aged 13 and under, and who are orphans, abandoned, born out of wedlock and placed for adoption, or placed for adoption because the parents are separated with no prospect of reconciliation • Relatives other than the ones listed, if these are the sponsor's only closest living relatives, including any accompanying immediate family members of that person

close relatives into "priorities" for processing. In doing so, they made potential labour market participation a key distinction. In 1957, all departmental offices abroad were ordered to prioritize applications from "close relatives" as follows. Priorities A to C comprised, in order of descending priority: (A) spouses and unmarried children; (B) parents, grandparents, and unmarried orphaned nephews and nieces under the age of twenty-one; and (C) fiancé(e)s. Priority D was reserved for married children and their spouses/children. Siblings and their spouses/children were assigned to Priority E. Notably, it was specified that applications under Priorities A to C were to be "accepted without regard to their occupational categories," whereas applications under Priorities D and E were to be approved only if "the occupation

the proposed immigrant intends to follow in Canada is in short sup-
ply or when employment has been pre-arranged."[64] Thus, while still
under the umbrella of "close relatives," family members became differentiated into two categories: those destined for the labour market,
and those likely to remain outside it. When it was proposed in 1960 that
Canada's immigration policy for close relatives should also be selective, but that this could apply "only to those who are to engage in the
labour market,"[65] it was understood within the Department which relatives would be affected.

Throughout the course of the 1960s, the term "close relatives" was
replaced by ones that made the anticipated relationship of family members to the labour market more explicit: "true dependents" (later "sponsored dependents") and "sponsored immigrants" (later "nominated
relatives"). From 1962 onwards, the Department kept statistics on the
relative proportion of these two groups, documenting a roughly equal
proportion of each type of family in 1962 (64,139 "dependents" in total,
compared to 55,547 "others," that is, "sponsored immigrants").[66]

Terms such as "true dependents"[67] or the "basic dependent family
unit"[68] came to describe relatives who were not expected to enter the
labour market. Regardless which exact term was used, members of the
Department shared the implicit understanding that "dependency" was
the basis on which relatives in this category were deserving of membership. This often tacit understanding was stated most clearly in the process of drafting the 1966 White Paper on Immigration: "The minimum
sponsorship group should be those who pose no economic problem to
Canada and who have a moral (and perhaps even a legal) claim on the
sponsor by virtue of *dependency (not relationship)*" (emphasis added).[69]
The distinction between dependency and relationship as a basis for
admissibility allowed for the inclusion of a broad range of relatives
under the umbrella of "true dependents," such as spouses, fiancé(e)s,
unmarried children, parents, and grandparents. Some within the
Department saw "dependency" as trumping any alleged hierarchy of
proximity in familial relations and pushed to include "wholly dependent other relatives who by virtue of age, youth or infirmity are incapable of self-support, [who] will not need to enter the labour force and
[who] have a valid claim on the sponsor, e.g. an aged aunt or uncle, a
spinster sister past marriageable age, etc."[70] The extent of this inclusive tendency was already evident in the Department's case processing activities. For example, from 1954 to 1959, orders-in-council were
used to admit at least 105 individuals who were classified as aged or
widowed parents as well as 666 overage children, notwithstanding
theses individuals' legal inadmissibility due to racialized restrictions

on family admissions. In one order-in-council admission from 1963, a Chinese-Canadian resident had applied to sponsor his Chinese daughter-in-law in Hong Kong, who was described in the case summary thus: "She has had only the most elementary schooling – three years primary education – and speaks no English. She has no qualifications of any kind, except for housework, is unemployed and dependent for support on [the would-be sponsor]."[71] The case – one of many – was approved, apparently without further correspondence on the matter. The lack of debate illustrates the unquestioned acceptance of dependency as a basis of membership, as long as the prospective immigrant's labour market participation was out of the question. Given the group-level racialization of the "immigrant family" as fundamentally "low-skilled" and "low-calibre," the admissibility of dependents rested on the Department's confidence that their presence would not pose a socio-economic threat.

Equally unquestioned by high-level bureaucrats in the Department was the tacit understanding that family immigrants likely to engage in labour market activities needed to have their admissibility considered in terms of their potential contribution to the socio-economic base of the Canadian national status group. The increased prevalence of terms like "sponsored immigrants,"[72] "sponsored immigrant workers,"[73] and "unskilled workers in the sponsored movement"[74] marked the transformation of these relatives into the equivalent of independent immigrant worker applicants well in advance of the institutionalization of this shift in 1967. Included in the ranks of "sponsored immigrants" were all relatives who were not truly dependent, particularly the siblings and adult children with their families who had been of growing concern in the case of sponsored immigration from Italy.

In the run-up to the 1967 immigration regulations, relationship went from being the only criterion for evaluating the admissibility of sponsored family members now called "nominated relatives" to being one criterion alongside others. As Prime Minister Pearson would state at the end of this process, in 1967, Canada's new immigration policy "should recognize the value of relationship just as fully as it recognizes any other factor in immigration," and there should be "a genuine trade-off between personal qualifications and relationship."[75] For selection purposes, relationship came to denote the social capital perceived as resting in family ties. Thus relationship to a sponsor replaced "expected speed and ease of initial settlement," arranged employment, knowledge of Canada's official languages, and the general employment situation in the place of destination as factors affecting immigration bureaucrats' perceptions of admissibility.[76] Relationship was to be considered alongside education, "personal qualities," strength of demand for one's intended occupation, age, and the "skill factor" of one's occupation.

As a factor in the selection of nominated relatives, relationship was not treated as a simple binary (i.e., as existing or not) but was transformed into a scale based on the sponsor's financial ability to assist with settlement. To this end, elaborate means of evaluating settlement arrangements replaced the practice of "eyeballing" the financial position of immigrants and sponsors. This is evident in the proliferation of questions on immigration forms pertaining to financial matters.[77] A 1966 Operations Memorandum on the processing of sponsored cases provided three full pages of instructions on how to perform the seven steps required to calculate a sponsor's financial position. Lower-level immigration bureaucrats were then to weigh that information against a chart outlining minimum financial requirements based on intended place of residence and total family size. The numbers on the chart were based on "a median between maximum welfare benefits for indigent Canadians and minimum expenditures incurred by the average Canadian family for living expenses."[78] Recognizing that "an immigrant family probably lives at a lower standard," the thresholds for acceptable settlement arrangements were set at "two-thirds of those required for an average Canadian family of the same size."[79] According to one example given in the memorandum, a married sponsor with one child wishing to sponsor his married brother with two children would need to have a minimum monthly income[80] of $340 if everyone was to be accommodated at the sponsor's place of residence. This place of residence, in turn, would need to have a minimum of five rooms. In the absence of sufficient accommodation, the sponsor would need to have a monthly income of $430 in order to help finance the immigrants' accommodation elsewhere. The existence of a relationship sufficient for immigration purposes was determined to exist or not based on the sponsor's ability to meet these financial thresholds. Thus, building on Prime Minister Pearson's assertion in 1966 that Canadian immigration policy "should recognize the value of relationship just as fully as it recognizes any other factor in immigration,"[81] this value became a numerical one.

As relationship was quantified and institutionalized in reference to material wealth as a selection criterion for nominated relatives, further markers of class position and status (also newly quantified and institutionalized) came to define their admissibility. The institutionalization of skill measurements was already underway by the time the 1953 immigration regulations were issued. Section 17 of these regulations gave the minister the discretionary power to subject immigrant workers and family members (except "true dependents") to literacy tests prior to admission. These aforementioned tests were to ensure that individuals selected to take them could read, a skill that was to be demonstrated by reading cards printed in capital letters "in such person's own language or in the language he wishes the test to be made."[82] Without clearly articulated benchmarks for literacy – if/when it was tested – this early approach reflects a tendency until the 1960s to "eyeball" the class and status positions of sponsored immigrants.

From 1962 onwards the Immigration Branch used a "skill digit" to quantify immigrants' skills and education and began tracking and comparing sponsored and unsponsored groups by country of origin (see table 5.2). For immigration purposes, codes 1 and 2 denoted "unskilled," code 3 "semi-skilled," and codes 4 to 9 "skilled" persons; codes 7 to 9 were defined as covering professionals with a university education. On this basis, the department was able to quantify its long-held perception of sponsored family immigrants as being relatively low skilled and thus a danger to the socio-economic base of the Canadian national status group. In 1963, this quantification revealed the following portrait of the relative skill levels of sponsored versus unsponsored immigrants from selected sending regions whose citizens had access to extended sponsorship privileges prior to 1967 (see table 5.3).

At a time when the Canadian government was under pressure to eliminate explicit racial discrimination from its immigration policy, this quantification of economic merit also allowed group-level racialization to be reconceptualized in terms of socio-economic metrics. In other words, the intersectional terms in which immigration bureaucrats had come to assess immigrant origin groups in practice became quantified and systematized. For example, table 5.3 shows that the group-level admissibility of American and British immigrants was now clearly justified in terms of their ability to contribute to the economic base of the Canadian national status group due to their high skill levels. In contrast, more racially suspect European groups, particularly Italians, were now demonstrably incompatible, due to their low skill levels. Noting that 35–45 per cent of sponsored immigrants (average skill level of 2.7) would enter the labour market, and that 92 per cent of all Italian immigrants were sponsored (average skill level of 1.9), the Department had numerical proof that sponsored immigrants – and Italians in general – were a threat to the nation and needed tighter regulation.[83]

The modified version of the "points system" that appeared in the 1967 immigration regulations to assess the admissibility of nominated relatives can be seen as emerging from the interpretive practices that marketized a wide range of family relationships. Table 5.4 provides an

Table 5.2. Immigrant skill levels (1963 survey) "skill digit" code*

Skill code level	Description of skill level
9	Senior professional, entrepreneurial or managerial skills
8	Intermediate professional, entrepreneurial or managerial skills
7	Junior professional, entrepreneurial or managerial skills
6	Junior technologist or senior technical skills or independent tradesmen
5	Mastership or supervisory skills
4	Journeyman or equivalent junior foreman skills
3	Apprentice or equivalent semi-skilled worker skills
2	Minor labour skills
1	Unskilled labour
0	Skill irrelevant
–	Occupation and training not stated

Table 5.3. Average skill levels by sending country and type of immigrant*

Sending country	Skill level by type of immigrant		
	All workers	Unsponsored	Sponsored
All countries	4.0	4.6	2.7
British Isles	4.8	4.9	3.5
United States	6.0	6.0	4.2
S. Europe	2.6	3.5	2.3
Italy	2.1	3.0	1.9
Greece	3.7	3.8	3.6
Portugal	2.5	4.0	2.3

* Source for tables 5.2 and 5.3: Reproduced from Appendix "E." Confidential memorandum to Cabinet, "Immigration White Paper – Sponsored Immigration to Canada," Cabinet Document 561–65, 24 November 1965. In RG 76, Vol. 723 File 551–25–2 Part 1.

Table 5.4. "Points system" for adjudicating nominated relatives under the 1967 Immigration Regulations (P.C. 1967–1616)

Criterion	Maximum points
Education and training	20
Personal assessment	15
Occupational demand	15
Occupational skill	10
Age	10

overview of criteria used to adjudicate nominated relatives as well as the maximum number of points allotted to each criterion. Like independent immigrants (i.e., skilled workers), nominated relatives were to be assessed according to their education and training (maximum twenty points), "personal assessment" and occupational demand (maximum of fifteen points each), and occupational skill and age (maximum of ten points each). In contrast to independent immigrants, nominated relatives were not to be assessed for knowledge of English or French or for employment opportunities in the area of destination. The threshold for selection also differed and was set at between 20 and 35 of a possible 70 points, depending on the type of relative.

As with independent immigrants, the assessment criteria for nominated relatives reveal that selection was not motivated purely by economic utility but also by concerns about status and moral worthiness. The absence of two assessment criteria directly related to labour market integration – language skills and employment opportunities – illustrates the importance of class and status beyond economic utility. The same is true for the strong weighting given to the "personal assessment," which, as chapter 4 illustrated, institutionalized moral and status-based perceptions of worth as selection principles after they had emerged in the course of both policy deliberations and case processing during the postwar era.

Parliamentary Influence on the Formulation of Family Sponsorship Policy

As this chapter has argued, high-level immigration bureaucrats' interpretive implementation practices fundamentally shaped the process whereby the 1967 family sponsorship policy was formulated as well as the entry categories and selection criteria contained in that policy. However, as other scholars have noted, family sponsorship is also the only area in which Parliament played a role in influencing immigration policy formulation in the postwar era (Hawkins 1988; Kelley and Trebilcock 2010; Triadafilopoulos 2012). This occurred at two points in time: in 1959, in response to an order-in-council restricting family sponsorship; and in 1966, in response to the government's White Paper on Immigration, which outlined plans to limit the sponsorship privileges of noncitizens. Since these attempts at restricting family sponsorship occurred under a Conservative government (1959) and a Liberal one (1966), they cannot simply be attributed to policy preferences rooted in party politics. As Hawkins (1988, 124) states, "whichever party was in power was obliged to do something about the escalation of the sponsored movement." Instead, scholars argue that parliamentary interference in the normally executive domain of immigration policymaking occurred around the issue of family sponsorship for two related reasons (Ellermann 2021; Hawkins 1988). First, the issue of family sponsorship itself was unique in that it directly affected immigrants and citizens across a wide range of ethnic communities and thus provided a rare incentive to act collectively as interest groups, for example, by lobbying the Department and Members of Parliament. Second, the involvement of Parliament meant that government actions became susceptible to domestic and international political pressures from which the Department of Citizenship and Immigration was normally insulated. As Boucher (2013) points out, the interference in executive policymaking that can follow from public scrutiny and pressure in the parliamentary arena is something that high-level immigration bureaucrats prefer to avoid, though it is not always possible to keep a policy issue inside the policymaking venue that they control.

In 1959 and 1966, parliamentary influence over policy formulation both emerged from, and was a response to, the Department's strong discretionary powers. In 1959, Minister of Citizenship and Immigration Ellen Fairclough issued Order-in-Council P.C. 1959–310. This limited family sponsorship as part of the Conservative government's efforts, under Prime Minister John Diefenbaker, to address the perennial issue of large-scale inflows of unskilled family members from southern Europe, particularly Italy. The order-in-council did this by excluding married children and siblings from the range of relatives who could be sponsored from Europe (except the British Isles and France), the Americas, Egypt, Israel, Lebanon, and Turkey. The change drew the ire of immigrant communities, particularly Italians, who correctly deduced that it was primarily directed towards them. Former Minister of Citizenship and Immigration J.W. Pickersgill (the Opposition's immigration critic in 1959) was one of several Members of Parliament to criticize the order-in-council in the House of Commons. The combination of parliamentary and media backlash against the indirect discrimination on grounds of national origin directed towards a large and well-represented immigrant constituency led to the order-in-council being revoked within months (Hawkins 1988).

While the revocation of the order-in-council represented an example of Parliament limiting the discretionary policy formulation powers of the Department of Citizenship and Immigration, the entire debacle was also a result of those discretionary powers (Kelley and Trebilcock 2010, 331). A previous order-in-council (P.C. 1956–785),[84] had effectively limited immigration from Europe (except the British Isles, France, and some types of workers from Europe), the Americas, Israel, Lebanon, and Turkey to sponsored family members. This had amplified the family component of what was already large-scale immigration from southern Europe and thereby contributed to a policy problem that had yet to be solved.

Departmental discretion also prompted parliamentary scrutiny in the wake of the 1966 White Paper on Immigration,[85] which was tabled in the House of Commons by Jean Marchand, Minister of Manpower and Immigration.[86] The Liberal government under Lester B. Pearson had been elected in 1963 on a platform that included a promise to end racial discrimination in immigration policy. Political pressure to fulfil this promise was mounting both domestically and internationally.[87] Reflecting the internal deliberations described in this chapter, the White Paper situated proposals to augment and systematize the admission of skilled workers while managing family sponsorship in the context of intersecting economic and social concerns. The ability to sponsor extended family, including adult children and siblings, was depicted as having the "potential for explosive growth" in immigrants who "do not have to meet any standards of education or skill" (Canada, Department of Manpower and Immigration 1966, 14). This was framed not just as an economic but as a social concern, with the concentration of low-skilled, family immigrants of the same ethnic origin having the potential to create "ghetto-like slums" in large cities like Toronto and Montreal (15).

The proposed solution was to allow Canadian citizens to sponsor extended family members, subject to admissibility criteria like education and work-related skills, while limiting the family sponsorship privileges of non-citizen immigrants to immediate dependents, that is, spouses and underage children. The assumption was that the five-year time lag required to acquire Canadian citizenship would slow down the entry of unskilled family members: "If each successive link in the chain requires five years to forge – while the immigrant becomes a citizen before he becomes a sponsor – we will not continue to face the dilemma that unskilled workers may be an increasing part of the immigration movement although the proportion of jobs that require little education or skill is declining" (Canada, Department of Manpower and Immigration 1966, 20). By differentiating family sponsorship rights according to citizenship, a legal status open to all landed immigrants, the Department felt that a non-discriminatory solution had been found to manage the problem of harmful racialized class dynamics in immigration and settlement.

As was the case in 1959, the political backlash in Parliament was in part generated by the bureaucratic discretion it ended up limiting.[88]

Ministerial control over implementation had made the petitioning of Members of Parliament one of the most effective ways for members of the public to ensure that an immigration case was processed. This state of affairs had generated a "contentious relationship between members of parliament and the Department"; Members of Parliament in urban ridings with large immigrant populations were "inundated with cases" that were "burdensome" and "time consuming" to manage (Hawkins 1988, 106–7). In the wake of this backlash, an internal taskforce was appointed to amend the proposed policy. This included dividing family immigrants into sponsored dependents and nominated relatives, as outlined in the White Paper, and universalizing sponsorship privileges by treating citizen and non-citizen sponsors equally. The taskforce was also to ensure that selection criteria for workers and extended family members were standardized (Triadafilopoulos 2012). As published, the White Paper lacked details on how selection policies would be implemented that had been emerging through deliberative processes within the Department, as illustrated in this chapter.

While the response to the White Paper provided a further impetus for finalizing the immigrant selection instrument that would become known as the "points system," parliamentary pressure ultimately had a limited effect on policy formulation. This is because the interpretive implementation practices described in this chapter had already generated major elements of policy as it would appear in the 1967 immigration regulations, including the distinction between sponsored dependents and nominated relatives, the idea of assigning points to determine admissibility, and the use of selection criteria like "merit" and the "personal assessment." However, parliamentary intervention in the wake of the 1966 White Paper did lead to a minor tempering of bureaucratic discretion with the passing of the 1967 Immigration Appeal Board Act, which gave Canadian citizens the right to have rejected sponsorship applications reviewed in an independent administrative process (Kelley and Trebilcock 2010).[89]

Conclusion

High-level immigration bureaucrats played a significant role in shaping family-related provisions in Canada's postwar universal immigration policy. This role included experimenting with admissions practices that ultimately paved the way for the paradigmatic policy shift that was reflected in the 1967 immigration regulations. This shift comprised the universalization of admissions criteria for established categories of family immigrants as well as the creation of new categories.

Drawing on existing cultural repertoires, high-level bureaucrats leveraged normative ideas about family and dependency in the course
of boundary work around universalizing family admissions to make
some aspects of this policy area more racially inclusive. This was
shown in reference to Asian fiancé(e)s, adopted children, and sponsored dependents. At the same time, immigration bureaucrats drew
on the bifurcated idea of race (as a concept denoting innate biological characteristics and socio-economic status) in the Canadian national
cultural repertoire in their boundary work around family admissions.
In "recasting" this idea (privileging its class and status element over
its biological one), immigration bureaucrats created a new racialized
group – "the immigrant family" in general – which was seen as fundamentally inadmissible due to its low economic utility and socio-
economic status. This was illustrated in reference to the boundary
work that generated the distinction between sponsored dependents
and nominated relatives. At the same time, individual-level and group-
level admissibility diverged in the interpretive practices of immigration bureaucrats. This facilitated the creation of selection principles
and procedures for admitting family members from diverse racial and
national origins who displayed appropriate markers of class and status. This was demonstrated using the case of nominated relatives and,
to a lesser extent, adopted children.

The results of this boundary work were subsequently institutionalized
in the family immigration provisions contained in the 1967 immigration
regulations. The institutionalization of immigration bureaucrats' interpretive practices made them widely applicable to future admissions
of different types of immigrant family members: adopted children (a
new type of admissible family member from 1967 onward); nominated
relatives (particularly the adjudication of their "personal assessment"
under the points system); and sponsored dependents. The material
effect of this institutionalization was to make immigrant family admissions demographically multicultural along middle-class lines. Symbolically, it helped create a lasting association between middle-class status
and belonging in the officially multicultural Canadian nation.

The findings presented in this chapter are relevant beyond the historical Canadian case. They speak to the broader scholarly debate about
the nature and origins of the racialized immigrant family exclusion documented in the contemporary implementation practices of lower-level
immigration bureaucrats in a range of national contexts.[90] The centrality of class and status in explaining the interpretive practices of postwar
Canadian immigration bureaucrats suggests that contemporary studies
that emphasize intersectional exclusion along racial and gender lines

should direct more attention to the role of this third, related distinction. Where scholarship on contemporary family reunification policy implementation has done so, it tends to attribute class-based exclusionary tendencies to the rise of neoliberal thought currents in the 1980s and 1990s (see, e.g., Dauvergne 2016). However, the historical Canadian case suggests that class-based distinctions in boundary work around family admissibility pre-date that ideological shift.

Furthermore, this chapter's findings lend support to, and historicize, recent scholarship that points to the *inclusive* potential of intersectional boundary work in immigration policy implementation (Ellermann 2006; Satzewich 2015). This is not to deny that implementation practices in the area of family reunification can lead to exclusions along the lines of race, gender, sexuality, and other social distinctions. However, it suggests that the characterization of such practices as inclusive or exclusionary should be an empirical question in a field that often presumes exclusionary tendencies.

The concluding chapter of this book offers some thoughts on how the institutionalization of Canadian immigration bureaucrats' interpretive practices in the postwar era – and the demographic and symbolic multiculturalism that resulted from this institutionalization – has influenced the material and symbolic effects of Canada's merit-based immigration and policy. In doing so, it considers how aspects of the 1967 institutionalization of admissions criteria for nominated relatives and sponsored dependents set these groups up for ever greater exclusion. The legacy of the policy created by immigration bureaucrats is ultimately Janus-faced. One the one hand, it liberalized immigrant admissions in a way that was more racially inclusive; however, the intersectional nature of this inclusion brought with it limitations. These limitations have had material consequences, in the sense that they have affected immigrant eligibility for entry to Canada in, perhaps, unanticipated ways. They have also, I argue, had symbolic consequences. The middle-class nature of the multiculturalism created by immigration bureaucrats has informed Canadians' idea of who can and cannot be a member of the nation, that is, ideas of multicultural citizenship. In light of this, the final chapter of the book considers the potential limitations of the "Canadian model" of merit-based immigration and middle-class multiculturalism, including on its successful diffusion to other national contexts.

Chapter Six

Conclusion: The Legacy
of Middle-Class Multiculturalism

Previous scholarship on the transition from explicitly racist to universal immigration policies in Global North countries in the mid-twentieth century has emphasized the role of macro- and meso-level economic, cultural, and political factors in explaining that transition. These factors include economic change and the need to select individuals whose skills could contribute to an emergent knowledge economy; the establishment of global human rights norms; foreign policy objectives related to maintaining state legitimacy in this new cultural context; and domestic political pressures from groups in favour of a more inclusive immigration policy (e.g., ethnic community organizations) and some against it (e.g., trade unions).

This book has demonstrated that micro-level actions – the interpretive practices of state actors – also played an important role in immigration policy formulation in the postwar Canadian case. Interpretive practices pertaining to the adjudication of individual order-in-council admissions and deportation appeals were especially relevant. As international and domestic political and economic pressures caused a breakdown in the routine practices of White nation-building through immigration, high-level immigration bureaucrats began using their discretionary power over implementation to experiment with new ways of managing immigration from a diverse range of source countries. They developed new practices that distinguished between individual-level and group-level admissibility and, simultaneously, new ways of seeing race in relation to nation-building. Culturally informed notions of who people were – in racial, ethnic, socio-economic, moral, and other terms – were key to immigration bureaucrats' emerging sense of what kind of immigrants from "non-preferred" (non-European, non-Western hemisphere) source countries could become part of the Canadian nation.

Examined through the lens of a cultural sociology of immigration policy, the process whereby cultural understandings shaped immigration policy formulation at the micro level of policy formulation involved four mechanisms. First, the cultural repertoires that high-level immigration bureaucrats were embedded in contained shared ideas of who immigrants were in racial, socio-economic, and moral terms. Second, these state actors drew on these cultural repertoires while conducting "boundary work" around the admissibility of individuals and groups from "preferred" (European, Western Hemisphere) and "non-preferred" countries. Third, the idea of race in the Canadian national cultural repertoire, which comprised two elements (one biological and one denoting socio-economic status), was "recast" in the course of boundary work to emphasize middle-class markers of class and status as a new common basis for nation-building through immigration. This allowed immigration bureaucrats to admit individuals with appropriate class and status traits irrespective of their racial and national group memberships. Finally, the cumulative results of this boundary work were institutionalized in the 1967 immigration regulations, in the form of selection criteria for skilled workers and extended family members. While the individual order-in-council admissions and deportation appeal cases analyzed here comprised a relatively small proportion of overall admissions in the postwar era, they nevertheless had powerful implications for immigration policy reform in postwar Canada.

The adjudication of order-in-council admissions and deportation appeals added not only an experimental process to postwar immigration policy formulation but also shaped policy content in distinctive ways. These adjudication practices did not eliminate race as a social distinction that influenced perceived admissibility; instead, they made the effect of race on admissibility contingent on other social distinctions, foremost class. Social class in this context meant more than just market position, economic attainment, or utility. It also encompassed status-based perceptions of deservingness that privileged middle-class traits, like the pursuit of higher education, entrepreneurial spirit, self-sufficiency, a strong work ethic, and civic-mindedness. The multiculturalism that emerged in the implementation aspect of postwar policy formulation was thus, in demographic and policy terms, a middle-class multiculturalism.

In highlighting the generative nature of immigration bureaucrats' interpretive actions during Canada's postwar transition to a merit-based immigration policy, this book does not discount the importance of macro- and meso-level forces that previous scholarship has identified as integral to this paradigmatic policy change. The interpretive implementation practices of immigration bureaucrats represent a pragmatic and experimental response to those forces, and the logic of the relationship between the two became apparent to immigration bureaucrats over time. These actors were faced with international and domestic imperatives to eliminate explicitly racial discrimination while avoiding the racialized poverty and social unrest that they perceived to be the result of poorly diversified immigration policies elsewhere. They came to recognize that admitting individuals whose economic, social, and cultural capital made them a "credit to [their] race"[1] could help build multicultural social cohesion on a shared middle-class identity. They also realized that, if successful, the resultant policy could transform Canada into a "striking example to the world"[2] and aid its global foreign policy ambitions.

Whether the role of bureaucratic implementation practices in shaping Canada's merit-based immigration policy, and the mechanisms through which this occurred, are unique to the Canadian case remains an open empirical question. Insofar as relevant data on historical implementation practices are available, this question could be answered through a series of comparisons across different institutional configurations of immigration management, using the cultural sociology of immigration policy lens. One potentially fruitful line of comparison would be across countries with both high immigrant intakes and Westminster-style systems (e.g., Canada, Australia,[3] the United Kingdom), in which the executive branch of government plays a central role in policymaking. Another line of inquiry could compare and contrast these countries with ones in which the institutional configuration of migration management is more decentralized, allowing for greater influence of local and state-level practices (e.g., the United States and Germany). This could provide insights into whether and how the degree of centralization in policy formulation (including implementation) matters for the relationship between culture, meaning-making, and immigration policy.

Given the empirical focus on the policymaking function of immigration bureaucracies, the findings presented in this book have implications beyond the narrower scholarly debate about the emergence of Canada's merit-based immigration policy. First, they demonstrate that immigration policy *implementation* can be a part of immigration policy *formulation*. Existing scholarship on immigration policy implementation emphasizes the capacity of lower-level bureaucrats to shape policies substantively in ways that are not explicit in legal and policy documents. However, the shaping of policy content through implementation is viewed as occurring *after* policy formulation processes have generated immigration laws and regulations, in the course of efforts to interpret and reconcile discrepancies between written policy and the complexities of real life. In contrast, this book highlights how such interpretive moments in immigration policy implementation can occur prior to the creation of legal and policy documents, and can influence both the *process* leading to their generation and their *substance*. Kang (2017) makes a similar point in reference to the practices of lower-level agents in the Immigration and Nationalization Service (INS) operating at the United States border to Mexico. However, she does not examine implementation at the level of case adjudication. By taking individual cases – in which qualifications for admissibility are articulated in concrete racial, ethnic, socio-economic, and moral terms – into account, this book is able to illustrate the role of implementation in policy formulation at a more fundamental level. This is important for illuminating its effect on the substantive content of policy. The findings in the historical Canadian case suggest that studies of immigration policy formulation need to incorporate implementation practices that occur prior to the announcement of new laws or regulations in order to achieve a fuller understanding of the nature of immigrant inclusion and exclusion that unfolds under those legal frameworks.

Second, the book demonstrates that the theoretical framework of a cultural sociology of immigration policy can serve as a tool for systematically historicizing and expanding recent intersectional analyses of immigration policies and their implementation (see, e.g., Abu-Laban 1998a; Banerjee 2019; Boucher 2020; Ellermann 2019; Elrick and Winter 2018; Romero 2008; Tichenor and Jacobson 2020; Tungohan et al. 2015). Given the strong potential of state policies to generate – and perhaps rectify – complex social inequalities, Hankivsky and Jordan-Zachery (2019, 2) identify a "pressing need" for "methodological approaches and empirical work that demonstrates the value added of intersectionality to public policy." The cultural sociology of immigration policy framework provides a tool for guiding qualitative work on immigration policy formulation from an intersectional perspective. In particular, the inclusion of boundary work as a mechanism linking cultural repertoires to policy formulation makes this framework well suited to detecting how intersecting social distinctions influence notions of immigrant admissibility. The boundary work mechanism lends itself to this endeavour because it directs empirical attention to whether and how multiple, potentially overlapping principles of classification that refer to economic, moral, and cultural social distinctions are deployed in concrete situations by state actors. It also allows scholars to work deductively, to assess the empirical relevance of social distinctions that have previously been identified as relevant (e.g., race, class, and gender), as well as inductively, to capture the emergence of a relevant social distinction that may not have been anticipated in a particular social context (e.g., age, ability).

Any future use of a cultural sociology of immigration policy to compare and contrast the intersectional nature of social distinctions informing immigrant selection policies and their implementation would do well to address one limitation of the present study: its relative inattention to gender. The focus in this book on the evolving relationship between race and class in notions of immigrant admissibility can be seen as an artefact of the scholarly debates to which it is responding. These debates focus on explaining the paradigmatic postwar shift in immigration policies in Canada and elsewhere, which is generally characterized as a shift away from race and towards economic utility in defining immigrant admissibility. In the first instance, this framing directs attention to race and class, insofar as the admission of skilled workers involves assessing qualities such as "skill," a concept tied to socio-economic status. Nevertheless, there are clearly gendered dimensions to this book's object of study, that is, the emergence of new immigrant selection criteria for skilled workers and family members. "Skilled workers" as denoted by entry categories in immigration policies have long been male, because their occupational, work, and income criteria generally favour male breadwinner applicants (see, e.g., Boucher 2016). As a result, women tend to be over-represented in entry categories for family immigrants (see, e.g., Kofman 2014). By not exploring this gendered aspect and its intersection with race and class, this study replicates a tendency in intersectional scholarship in general not to focus on all three "core" social positions implicated in social stratification (i.e., race, gender, class) simultaneously but to foreground singular axes or particular pairings (Anthias and Yuval-Davis 1992; Choo and Ferree 2010). But this need not remain the status quo, and there is room within the historical Canadian case to further examine and theorize the intersection of gender with race and class in shaping notions of immigrant admissibility, particularly with regard to some of the immigrant groups discussed in this book, like Asian fiancé(e)s, domestic workers from the British West Indies, and Jamaican nurses.

Systematizing and expanding intersectional analyses of immigration policy formulation and implementation is not just desirable from an academic perspective but is also essential from a policy perspective. This book shows that the emergence of merit-based immigration policies in countries of the Global North in the mid-twentieth century – like their legacy thereafter – is not a story about social positions like race, gender, and class becoming irrelevant as distinctions that inform ideas of immigrant admissibility. Rather, it is about the *transformation* of how these distinctions inform immigrant admissibility in practice. Whenever social distinctions inform how public policies are applied to large numbers of people, they have the potential to create and perpetuate significant social inequalities. Inattention to the effects that policies that appear to be neutral have on groups defined by one or more social distinctions (e.g., male, White immigrant workers or female, non-White family immigrants) can create the impression that there are no such effects. This is generally the case when national governments or international organizations use qualitative or quantitative methodologies that do not incorporate an intersectional perspective to assess the costs and benefits of immigration policies. For example, the most recent OECD report on labour migration to Canada describes that country's skilled worker recruitment framework as the "most elaborate and longest-standing" one in the OECD and a "role model for successful migration management" (OECD 2019, 13). At the same time, the words "gender" and "gendered" are used once each, and the word "race" is used once, to describe immigration policies prior to the 1967 immigration regulations. More contributions to historicizing the intersectional selection and settlement effects of Canada's merit-based immigration policy, and policies modelled after it, could help change a historical narrative that downplays the social inequalities generated by selection effects that shape populations along middle-class multicultural lines.

The remainder of this chapter considers both the material and normative legacies of the middle-class multiculturalism that was created by immigration bureaucrats and institutionalized in the 1967 immigration regulations. It also offers thoughts on how these legacies challenge the widely held perception of Canadian immigration and multiculturalism policies as exceptional cases of best practice, given the ongoing social inequalities they helped create.

The Material Legacy of Middle-Class Multiculturalism: Exclusionary Selection Effects

A number of scholars have identified the rise of neoliberalism since the 1990s, with its emphasis on self-sufficiency and economic instrumentalism, as a cultural shift that drove governments in Canada and elsewhere to restrict the entry of individuals who were perceived as not economically useful and/or potential burdens on welfare systems (see, e.g., Abu-Laban 1998b; Kymlicka 2017; Winter 2015). For example, Dauvergne (2016, 9) argues that the late twentieth and early twenty-first centuries ushered in a "new politics of immigration" that is marked by the "loss of settlement and society as immigration values." The loss of settlement as a core value manifests in a growing preference for temporary or circular categories of admission, which do not permit immigrants to stay in a receiving country on a permanent basis and build their futures there. It also manifests in the watering down of permanent admission categories through conditional or probationary clauses. The move away from society as a value, that is the idea that immigration contributes to the building of a new social collective that is "something more than a mere economy" (141), is reflected in the privatization of settlement and support services that were previously seen as state responsibilities. Because settlement and society are no longer valued, the argument continues, immigration policies have become hyperselective along economic lines, dividing potential immigrants into rich and poor, and "rob[bing] migration of a human face" (179).

The findings presented in this book do not contradict this assessment, but they do point to the 1950s and 1960s, not the 1990s, as the period in which the foundations for these more exclusionary politics were laid. The interpretive practices of immigration bureaucrats institutionalized intersectional selectivity in Canadian immigration policy in the postwar era. This institutionalization provided the framing, vocabulary, and policy instruments (e.g., the "points system") that made it easy to narrow the range of admissible economic and family immigrants over time. This is because the selection criteria that were institutionalized in 1967 for economic and family immigrants alike defined individuals to a large degree in marketized terms that made them vulnerable to broader social and economic shifts over the following decades, including the emergence of the knowledge economy and the neoliberal ethos of the 1990s.

Socio-economic Selectivity

In the 1967 immigration regulations, the admissibility of independent economic immigrants and nominated relatives – two groups defined in terms of their anticipated labour market participation – became institutionalized in terms of economic utility (e.g., education and training) and markers of membership in the emergent middle-class status group (as determined in the personal assessment). This, in turn, made them vulnerable to exclusion over time due to economic restructuring and changing ideas about what kind of workers were needed. Throughout the 1950s and early 1960s, Canada recruited immigrants to fill both blue-collar and white-collar occupations. However, looking to build an advanced, industrialized society that would rank favourably with world powers such as the United Kingdom and the United States (see chapter 2), policymakers in the 1960s were sensing major shifts in the national economy. In 1964 there was a feeling among members of the Department that "a modern industrial revolution is in progress"[4] and that immigration policy would have to be attuned to it. This meant that there would be successive changes to the desirable occupational groups and educational levels to be demonstrated by applicants. Members of the Department forecasted that there would be a static, and eventually declining, number of jobs available in the Canadian economy for unskilled workers. Looking at labour market data from 1931 to 1961, they noted in 1965 that service, manufacturing and construction, transportation and communication, commercial and financial, managerial, professional, and clerical occupations were increasing as a share of total employment. Fishing and hunting, logging, mining and quarrying, general labour, and agricultural occupations, on the other hand, were on the decline. In other words, the occupations in which "a relatively large proportion of the workers have advanced formal education" were on the rise, while ones "requiring the lowest levels of formal education [were] declining."[5] In light of these observations, the Department planned periodically to "review and redefine" from year to year the educational standards required by "native Canadians" entering the labour market and adjust immigrant selection accordingly.[6]

The selection tools that the Department created for ranking immigrants according to educational attainment, language, occupational demand, and so on, lent themselves to increasing socio-economic selectivity. Since the "points system" was incorporated into immigration regulations rather than the Immigration Act, it could be altered by the minister without consulting Parliament. This means that it was easy from the outset to increase socio-economic selectivity without drawing political attention, limiting not just the kinds of workers who were considered admissible but also the ability of the wide range of extended family members who fell under the nominated relative category to qualify for sponsorship.[7] The eventual impact of such changes on family admissibility can be seen in the occupations listed for admissible family members who required order-in-council admission due to passport or visa issues in 1963 and 1964. Records show that the skilled trades (e.g., welding, carpentry, dressmaking) were the second most common occupation – behind "housewife" – in each of those years, with 82 and 238 skilled tradespersons documented for those years, respectively.[8] Large numbers of would-be immigrant workers were increasingly vulnerable to exclusion from immigration programs as selection principles evolved to favour white-collar occupations.

While Department officials were already predicting a shift towards white-collar occupations in the 1960s, it was the emergence of the "knowledge economy" from the 1970s onward that made Canadian immigration policy hyper-selective in socio-economic terms. An individual applying under the Federal Skilled Worker program (subsumed under the Express Entry system in January 2015) now needs to have an occupational skill level of O, A, or B under the National Occupational Classification (NOC) system. These skill levels designate managerial, professional, and technical jobs, respectively, which require a minimum of a college diploma (for the technical/skilled trade level).[9] Approximately 21 per cent of all permanent residents admitted in 1994 had at least a bachelor's degree, including 21 per cent of spouses/dependents accompanying skilled workers and 12 per cent of individuals admitted as sponsored family members. By 2009, those figures were considerably higher: 44 per cent of all immigrants had a bachelor's degree or higher, including 39 per cent of spouses/dependents accompanying skilled workers and 33 per cent of sponsored family members (Reitz, Curtis, and Elrick 2014).

Increasing socio-economic selectivity due to economic change was also destined to affect admissibility under the other category of family immigrants created by immigration bureaucrats: sponsored dependents.[10] In contrast to nominated relatives, who were treated as potential labour market participants, sponsored dependents' admissibility was based on their presumed absence from the labour market and financial dependence on a Canadian citizen or permanent resident sponsor. For them (as well as for nominated relatives insofar as they were also sponsored), economic restructuring had the potential from the very beginning to affect the sponsors' ability to meet minimum income thresholds, housing, and other commitments. While sponsors of spouses and underage children have remained exempt from income requirements (and the category of spouse has been extended to include common-law and same-sex partnerships), this is not the case for other family members originally included under the sponsored dependent category, including siblings, nieces/nephews, and grandparents. As the right to have an extended family became defined in terms of socio-economic standing, structural economic changes in the remuneration and status of occupations made access to that right more exclusive.

Now there are clearly circumscribed class positions from which a Canadian citizen or resident may sponsor extended family members that were not thinkable in the 1950s and 1960s. This is arguably due in part to middle-class assumptions underpinning the calculation of income cut-offs used to gauge sponsors' financial eligibility. Since the

1976 Immigration Act, sponsors' income must meet or exceed the Low-Income Cut-Off (LICO) amount set each year by number of persons in the family unit. The LICO is defined by Statistics Canada (2015, 5) as the threshold "below which a family will likely devote a larger share of its income to the necessities of food, shelter and clothing than the average family"; specifically, the income levels calculated represent the "threshold at which families are expected to spend 20 percentage points more than the average family on food, shelter and clothing." It is thus a relative – not absolute – measure of the resources "needed" to live life according to the normative parameters set by the spending habits of an "average" Canadian family of the same size. Let us consider for a moment the LICO for a three-person family in 2015, which was $37,234. Perhaps it would be a challenge for a three-person family to live the life of an "average" Canadian family on that sum, if the "average" Canadian family is imagined as a middle-class family that aspires to own a single-family home, operate at least one vehicle, and so on. Certainly, one might argue, there is scope for a three-person family to live on less than that if its members are not determined to inhabit a spacious dwelling, have sole use of one or more vehicles, and indulge in Canada's consumer culture at the same level as an "average" family. By putting a dollar sign on the right of a Canadian citizen or permanent resident sponsor to have an extended immigrant family, postwar immigration bureaucrats created a selection instrument that may one day make the right to (extended) family life the preserve of middle- and upper-classes.

The Neoliberal Turn and the Delegitimization of Dependency

Postwar immigration bureaucrats' conceptualization of sponsored dependents' admissibility also made this group of immigrants vulnerable to exclusion in the wake of the neoliberal ethos that emerged in the late twentieth century.[11] With its insistence on individualism and reduced state interventions to mitigate the effects of free-market capitalism, this ethos led to the stigmatization of dependency as a valid form of relationship and, with that, increasing sponsorship obligations and greater restrictions on the range of potentially dependent relatives who could be admitted as a matter of course.

While postwar immigration bureaucrats anticipated, to some extent, the increasing socio-economic selectivity of worker admissions, the same cannot be said for the circumscription of dependent family admissions in light of changing societal norms about dependency. From a contemporary viewpoint, one remarkable aspect of the postwar period was the strong sense of moral obligation and collective responsibility towards family that underpinned immigration policymaking. As chapter 5 argued, this moral commitment to the family facilitated transformations in the racial inclusivity of family admissions categories and even created a new legally admissible type of family member (adopted children). From the mid-1960s onward, as the introduction of new immigration regulations was imminent, the consensus among immigration bureaucrats was that the admission of "true dependents" was a "matter of right."[12] This right was based on the notion that there were "human reasons for exempting [true dependents] from normal selection criteria."[13] Elsewhere, the obligation is referred to as a "moral obligation"[14] towards dependents that the Department's immigration policy would honour without question.

In terms of admissions practices, this moral obligation towards dependents led immigration bureaucrats to agree that no financial or other conditions should be placed on the admission of spouses and minor children, and that only very limited conditions should apply in the case of other dependents. Regarding the admission of spouses and unmarried children, they were adamant that these relatives should be "admissible without any investigation of the sponsor's financial position and without any question as to his ability to support these relatives."[15] For other dependents, admission was to be "virtually a right" and "almost unconditional."[16] Furthermore, no thresholds for settlement arrangements were to be applied, except in cases of "grave criminality," "active subversion," and "contagious illness (pending a cure or arrest of contagion)."[17] Some members of the Department were also in favour of ensuring that the sponsor was not in hospital, in jail, receiving public assistance, or "unable for other similar reasons to make adequate reception arrangements for the immigrant."[18] Regardless of the conditions under discussion, however, they were in agreement that any sponsor unable to meet the minimum criteria would not have his or her application refused; rather, the application would be "deferred until such time as the sponsor can overcome the difficulty."[19]

Although the conditions discussed by members of the Department were minimal and not designed to lead to any exclusions, Prime Minister Pearson was adamant that placing any conditions at all on the sponsorship of dependents was a violation of the moral responsibility Canada had towards them. He made this stance explicit in a 1967 "verbalization" of the government's immigration policy vision, which is worth quoting at length:

Moreover, I do not think that we should require, for this kind of sponsorship, any financial evidence of ability to support the sponsored immigrant. To impose financial standards smacks of paternalism. If a man wants to take his old grandmother into his house, it is not for government to say that he doesn't have room or can't afford it. Admittedly, the result of lifting such rules may be that in some cases social assistance will be required. But that is a price I think we should be prepared to pay ... [I]n my view the unity of the dependent family ought not to be set aside because it can result, in a few cases, in the community having to bear extra welfare costs.[20]

This statement illustrates the degree to which dependency was a legitimate and respected form of relationship in Canadian society in the postwar era. Moreover, it underlines the notion that responsibility towards dependents was not an individual matter but one that concerned the national community, even in the case of newcomers. This was not just posturing on the part of the prime minster, but a sentiment that was included, almost verbatim, in the revised introduction to the First Immigration Manual used by case processors in 1970. The manual states that "when an immigrant is accepted to come and work in Canada, an obligation is automatically accepted toward his dependents, normally his wife and children [but also] toward others who, in the normal course of family relationships, become dependent on him or would have become part of his household had he not migrated."[21] This passage also references the example of an "aged grandmother" and reiterates the prime minister's characterization of financial tests as "paternalistic."[22] These amendments followed a 1966 Operations Memorandum on the processing of sponsored applications, which freed sponsors of dependents from evaluation on any settlement criteria, financial or otherwise. It stated that "applications for spouses, dependent children and fiancées are to be approved regardless of settlement arrangements," and that only if "extreme hardship" were immanent was the application to be deferred, but never rejected.[23] In Dauvergne's (2016) terms, this stance indicates a solid commitment on the Canadian state's part to settlement and society as core immigration values when it came to dependent family members.

The notion of collective responsibility for dependents can also be seen as part of the organizational culture of perceived collective responsibility towards immigrants in general that was evident in the Department during the period under consideration. Throughout the 1950s, the Department was running, in effect, a one-stop immigration shop. It surveyed industries within each province to determine the number of immigrants they needed and the occupational profiles that were to be filled. This information was then transmitted to immigration offices abroad, where recruiters vetted potential immigrants. Those selected were given assisted passage to Canada, temporary accommodation at their place of destination, and – if employment was not completely pre-arranged – assistance in finding and securing a job.[24] Even in 1966, the Department was prepared to provide food and shelter for unsponsored workers until they were self-supporting.[25] Thus the collective moral obligation to support dependents continued to be mirrored at the orga-nizational level, in the Department's sense of collective responsibility towards immigrants in general who, throughout the migration process, were in a way dependent on assistance for becoming self-sufficient.

Insofar as the unconditional acceptance of dependents was rooted in a sense of collective moral obligation towards them, contemporary restrictions on, and exclusions of, such family members must be seen as resting, at least in part, on an absence of that sense of collective moral obligation. There appears to have been a shift in national values towards disdaining dependency. At the very least, dependency is now considered a matter of individual responsibility, as indicated by income thresholds and other conditions designed to ensure that extended fam-ily sponsorship does not end up being supported, financially, by the national collective. Dependency may be, under certain circumstances, acceptable at an individual level, but the collective is no longer pre-pared to absorb the risk associated with it.

Perhaps the starkest example for this shift is the admissibility of immigrant parents and grandparents. The right to sponsor these fam-ily members has been severely curtailed. It is no longer a right but a privilege reserved for middle-class and upper-class Canadian citizen and permanent resident sponsors. From 2011 to 2014, parents and grandparents were ineligible for admission as permanent residents. During that time, they could only be sponsored to "visit" Canada for a period of two years, under the so-called parent and grandparent super visa. This super visa comes with high financial requirements for spon-sors, including the ability to pay for private medical insurance for the sponsored parent or grandparent (Alboim and Cohl 2012). In January 2014, the Conservative government reopened the permanent admis-sions category for parents and grandparents but capped the number of applications it would consider that year at 5,000 (CBC 2014). While the subsequent Liberal government increased the number of applications it would accept in a given year to 10,000 in 2016, admissions under this category are restrictive relative to demand for parent and grandparent admissions: 14,000 applications were received within five days of the opening of the 2016 program (CBC 2016). The financial requirements placed on sponsors are high, as they need to demonstrate an income equivalent to or greater than the LICO plus 30 per cent for each of the three tax years preceding the sponsorship application. At the time of writing, this means that a sponsor in a four-person household (two adults and two children) looking to sponsor a parent or grandparent needs to have had an annual income of at least $60,271 for each of the last three years (Immigration, Refugees, and Citizenship Canada [IRCC] 2020). Parents and grandparents who are not admitted under the quota are still eligible for temporary entry under the super visa, which has been maintained as an alternative pathway to (temporary) entry. When it comes to this group of dependents who used to be admissible as a matter of principle, Canada now exemplifies the paternalism that Pearson detested: it is now unquestionably the right of the government to tell a person who wishes to take in their aging grandmother whether that person has room and can afford it. It is also unquestionably the right of the government to set aside the unity of the dependent family if there is any risk of additional welfare costs accruing to the national collective. In short, Canada's moral stance on dependency, at least in the case of immigrant families, has changed completely in less than fifty years.

Intersectional Selection and Settlement Effects since 1980

Socio-economic selectivity and changing social norms surrounding dependency are exclusionary trends that were facilitated by how immigration bureaucrats defined the admissibility of workers and family members in the postwar era. But what has become of the inclusivity – foremost racial inclusivity – that immigration bureaucrats worked so hard to manage?

Studies of the distribution of immigrants across legal entry categories and their subsequent economic outcomes provide some answers to this question. The entry category under which an immigrant is admitted matters because these categories offer different levels of legal security (in terms of duration of stay and/or dependency on a spouse or employer), access to settlement services, and labour market flexibility.[26] In order to gain a comprehensive picture of how race and other social positions matter under immigration policies that are socio-economically selective, it is instructive to compare and contrast selection patterns and economic outcomes for immigrants admitted under a wide range of entry categories, including ones that are not explicitly reserved for skilled workers. One recent study does this for over three million immigrants to Canada from 1980 to 2016 in the following categories: the Federal Skilled Worker Program (FSWP); the Canadian

Experience Class (CEC); the Family Class (FC); and the Live-In Care-giver Program (LIC) (Lightman and Elrick 2021).[27]

The findings show that immigrants admitted under all of the afore-mentioned entry categories were from diverse origins. India, China, and the Philippines were among the top five birth countries of immigrants in each category. However, the LIC category is racialized, with 82.8 per cent coming from the Philippines. It is also a highly feminized category, with 85.8 per cent being female. These racialized, skilled women are deskilled and forced by virtue of the terms of entry under the LIC into a mandatory period of precarious work in a socially devalued occupa-tion (care work). Despite the fact that the same percentage (40 per cent) of people in the LIC and the FSWP categories have bachelor's degrees, the lack of recognition of nursing and care work as skilled occupations under the FSWP has excluded these racialized women from entering under that category, which does not tie immigrants to particular occu-pations or employers.[28]

Strong gender dynamics are visible in the allocation of women from diverse origins to family-related – rather than employment-related – entry categories, despite their high levels of human capital. Only 31.1 per cent of workers who entered under the FSWP and 33.5 per cent of workers who entered under the CEC were female. Aggregated over time, the proportion of immigrants with tertiary education who enter under the FC or as spouses/dependents of FSWP workers (28.9 per cent) is slightly lower than the proportion of FSWP workers (40.8 per cent). It is also slightly lower than for spouses and workers in the CEC (36.7 per cent for spouses and 42.8 per cent for workers). In terms of language ability, spouses/partners in the FC and those accompany-ing workers in the FSWP or CEC have the same, or a higher, level of proficiency compared to the workers themselves. Skilled individuals are not equal before the law but sorted along racial and gender lines into very different entry categories, with attendant advantages and disadvantages.

Perhaps the unequal distribution of skilled workers across entry categories by gender and race would be less concerning if returns on human capital were equal across those categories. This is not the case. Controlling for factors like age at arrival, time since arrival, mari-tal status, and number of children, workers (predominantly male) in the FSWP have the second highest economic returns over time, after workers in the CEC (who are also disproportionately male). However, their skilled accompanying spouses/partners and spouses/partners in the FC do not see favourable returns on their human capital over time. These gendered economic outcomes are worst under the entry category where gender intersects strongly with race: the racialized and predominantly female skilled workers who enter under the LIC fare worst economically over time.

Broader gendered dynamics in institutions like the family and the labour market certainly affect these outcomes, as they affect outcomes in the Canadian population more generally (see, e.g., Walby 2011). Nevertheless, immigration policy clearly places some skilled women – especially racialized women – in subordinate legal positions in terms of labour market entry (e.g., requiring two years of work in the severely undervalued care sectors for LICs). It also places these women in a subordinate legal position within their families; as secondary applicants on immigration applications, their labour market success is less strategically important from a household perspective (Banerjee and Phan 2015; Cooke 2007). This subordinate status likely amplifies, or at least facilitates, the disadvantageous gendered dynamics these women encounter in their family and work life.

The gendered selection dynamics operating in contemporary Canadian immigration policy can be seen as a path-dependent outcome of male-centric definitions of skilled occupation developed in the 1960s, at a time when women were largely presumed to be dependents and thus outside the labour market. In archival records reviewed for this book, Department members consistently framed dependent family members in feminized terms, as seen in the Department's response in 1953 to a request by the provinces for improved efforts to recruit female immigrants from the United Kingdom. This response stated that "in all stories and articles prepared for publicity abroad every attempt is made to refer to the women's side of settlement [and] almost invariably photos are included showing women in their kitchens."[29] The assumption that female spousal dependents would not aspire to engage in the labour market – implied in the suggestion that female immigrants could be enticed to move to Canada based on pictures of kitchens – was expressed most explicitly in a Cabinet document prepared in 1958, which stated that, "the majority of [immigrant] women are housewives."[30] The Department's framing of dependents as feminine continued until revisions to the First Immigration Manual were completed in 1971. In the discussion in Appendix "B" of the manual's use of the term "head of the family," the Department articulated reluctance to define women in this way:

> There may, of course, be some cases where the wife, because of particular circumstances is, in fact, the main support of the family. In such cases she could properly be considered the head of the family and could accordingly

be assessed rather than her husband. However, the fact that a married
female applicant in Canada is employed here at a greater salary than that
of her husband in their homeland is not reason, in itself, to designate the
woman as the family head. This will be determined on the basis of who
would be responsible for the support of the family, considering the circumstances of the husband and wife, as if they were living together in
their own country.[31]

This quotation suggests that, irrespective of women's potential engagement in the labour market, the Department held fast throughout the
postwar era to notions of women as dependent, financially and/or
symbolically, on their husbands, in line with the traditional male breadwinner model of family. The origins of what are now well documented
gender biases in skilled worker selection criteria (see, e.g., Boucher
2016) can thus be traced back to the gendered assumptions of those
tasked with inventing Canada's "points system."

From Immigrant Selection to Naturalization

When Canadian immigration policy grants an immigrant permanent
residence, it places them in a legal position to naturalize at a later date,
that is, to become a full legal citizen. Immigration policy is therefore the
first step in a two-step process of nation-building through immigration.
Naturalization is the important second step, because citizenship as a
legal status gives immigrants access to important political rights, like
the right to vote, diplomatic support when abroad, as well as the firmest
possible protection against deportation (Hansen 2009). It also removes
any potential legal barriers to participating fully in the institutions that
underpin social and political life in the country and promises a sense
of membership and belonging in the national community (Bloemraad,
Korteweg, and Yurdakul 2008). Canada has one of the highest naturalization rates in the world and touts this fact as evidence of its successful
immigration system: approximately 85 per cent of the total immigrant
population eligible for naturalization have acquired Canadian citizenship (Government of Canada 2020). This is a higher rate than in other
countries with long-standing mass immigration programs, including
Australia (74 per cent) and the United States (44 per cent) (Statistics
Canada 2013).

However, naturalization rates among more recent cohorts of
immigrants have been declining, raising concerns that citizenship is
becoming less accessible (Korteweg and Elrick 2014). Recent research
suggests that naturalization policy changes since 2006, which augment

the middle-class selectivity in immigration policy, are at least partly responsible for the trend. These changes include measures that can make naturalization more difficult for low-income individuals with poor language skills and low levels of education, like the "Knowledge of Canada" test (i.e., the citizenship test), mandatory language testing in French or English, and higher application fees (Hou and Picot 2020; Winter 2014a). Statistical analyses of naturalization trends among recent immigrants across five censuses between 1996 and 2016 by Hou and Picot (2020) show that, although naturalization rates have decreased for all recent immigrants, they have decreased most sharply among particular types of individuals. These include individuals who are members of low-income families, who have low proficiency in English or French, and who have a high school diploma or less education. The likelihood of an individual displaying all three of those characteristics becoming a Canadian citizen fell from 77.2 per cent to 51.7 per cent from 1996 to 2016. Two-thirds of that decline occurred between 2006 and 2016, when more stringent knowledge and language testing as well as higher fees were introduced (17). Winter's (2021) qualitative study of the naturalization experiences of thirty-seven highly educated recent immigrants to Canada shows how selectively focusing on human capital – which is formal and explicit at the immigration stage for skilled workers – is applied to all permanent residents at the naturalization stage. Most of Winter's respondents were able to navigate the paperwork as well as the knowledge and language tests with relative ease due to attributes denoting upper-middle-class status, like "talent, creativeness, self-sufficiency, and entrepreneurship" (17).

Ultimately, the material legacy of Canada's first universal immigration policy is one of wide-reaching intersectional inequalities in immigrant selection, economic attainment, and citizenship acquisition. Thus, the Canadian model of mass, merit-based immigration and middle-class multiculturalism comes with high economic and social costs that are distributed unequally across the hundreds of thousands of immigrants accepted for admission as permanent residents each year. Ellermann (2019) uses the term "human-capital citizenship" to denote how contemporary Canadian immigration policy, applied to skilled workers, family, and refugees alike, shapes future members of Canadian society. According to her, this version of membership "imagines citizens as bearers of human capital, and human capital as the skills and psychological attributes associated with high-status and highly paid positions in the global knowledge economy" (3). The findings presented in this book both confirm this assessment and point to its deeper historical roots.

The Normative Legacy of Middle-Class Multiculturalism

The normative legacy of middle-class multiculturalism in Canada is likewise one of simultaneous inclusion and exclusion along intersectional lines. This becomes clear when a key finding presented in this book – that postwar immigration bureaucrats managed racial inclusion by creating a new middle-class basis for a shared national identity – is applied to discussions of the symbolic and normative aspect of immigrant inclusion in the imagined national community.

Reassessing Multicultural Citizenship

The term "multiculturalism" denotes many things. It refers to a demographic description, government policies designed to recognize and accommodate the integration of racially and ethnically diverse groups, public discourse used to signal recognition of diversity, and a normative claim about the equal worth and dignity of all human beings (Bloemraad and Wright 2012). According to Kymlicka (1995), Canadian multiculturalism (as both a political theory and a policy) is designed to make citizenship accessible to members of racial and ethnic minority groups. Bloemraad (2006) specifies two related processes through which this occurs. First, Canada's multiculturalism policy allocates government resources to organizations that foster the inclusion of racially and ethnically defined groups in political processes and institutions. This ensures that members of these communities emerge as political and community leaders who can work to increase participation in political processes. Second, it makes citizenship more inclusive on a symbolic level, by officially reimagining the national community as one that acknowledges multiple racial and ethnic backgrounds. This gives native-born citizens and immigrants alike a common ground on which to develop a shared sense of national solidarity. This symbolic aspect of multicultural citizenship is no less important than providing material support for institutional participation. As discussed in chapter 3, the state is a superordinate classifier that plays a strong role in defining the cultural context in which people inside its borders interact. When a state signals that racial and ethnic minorities have an equal claim to membership in the national community and backs this signal institutionally (e.g., through changes to the historical narrative presented in educational textbooks), it takes a symbolic step towards levelling the racial hierarchies that frame social interactions. Strong evidence from public opinion polls, government surveys and studies of employment outcomes indicates that Canada is far from eliminating racialized hierarchical distinctions and their attendant social effects (see, e.g., Environics 2019; Oreopoulos 2011). Nevertheless, the symbolic reimagining of national identity in the Canadian case is thought to play an important role in generating higher levels of support for diversity relative to other national contexts that have not included efforts to redefine the nation into their more pragmatic, integration-oriented multiculturalism policies (Bloemraad and Wright 2012).

Beyond creating solidarity across racial and ethnic lines, Kymlicka (2017) argues that an important symbolic aspect of multicultural citizenship as it emerged in Canada in the 1960s and 1970s was its conceptual link to Marshall's ([1950] 1965) notion of citizenship as a tool for redressing market-generated inequalities through the extension of civil, political, and social rights. In other words, the solidarity generated by early formulations of multicultural citizenship as a new national identity had the potential to encourage all citizens to band together against not just racial and ethnic injustices, but socio-economic ones as well.

A number of scholars have diagnosed Canadian multicultural citizenship as being under threat since the 1980s and 1990s, in part due to the emergence of "neoliberal multiculturalism" (see, e.g., Kymlicka 2017; Winter 2014b). What distinguishes this version of multiculturalism from its predecessor is a reframing of the social value of racial and ethnic diversity in terms of its economic utility. According to Kymlicka (2017), neoliberal multiculturalism represented a modification to what he calls the horizontal dimension of multicultural citizenship. This horizontal dimension denotes the capacity – built into Canada's original multiculturalism policy in the 1970s – for building a shared national identity among immigrants and citizens that recognizes and respects racial and ethnic differences. Neoliberal multiculturalism modified this shared sense of national belonging by reframing ties to racial and ethnic identities as particularly useful economic assets in a globalized economy, insofar as they facilitate transnational economic cooperation, multilingualism, intercultural communication, and insofar as they increase the level of comfort people have working in racially diverse settings. As Kymlicka states, "Multiculturalism, as reimagined by neoliberals, was about enabling minorities to use their cultural markers as a source of market inclusion." (146). From his perspective, economic utility comes at the expense of fostering a shared sense of full national citizenship. While still inclusive of racial and ethnic diversity, neoliberal multiculturalism's emphasis on worker-citizenship erodes symbolic solidarity across socio-economic lines, excluding those who are not seen as valuable contributors to a globalized economy from the shared national community.

The findings presented in this book offer an alternative understanding of the quality and trajectory of multicultural citizenship in Canada. In terms of trajectory, this book argues that middle-class multiculturalism emerged as a way of managing racial inclusion in the Canadian nation in the course of immigration policy formulation in the 1950s and 1960s. The symbolic aspect of multicultural citizenship was thus not just a political response to racial diversity generated by immigration, but a notion that shaped the selection of those racially diverse immigrants in the first place. This finding is important for understanding why Canada's approach to multicultural citizenship has led to greater support for racial diversity than is the case elsewhere. Much as postwar immigration bureaucrats had hoped (see chapter 2), building middle-class multiculturalism into the policy instruments that managed mass immigration helped link visible racial difference with acceptable middle-class and status markers in the eyes of Canadian citizens.

This brings us to important substantive differences between the middle-class multiculturalism identified in this book and the neoliberal multiculturalism described by other scholars. First, conceptualizations of neoliberal multiculturalism focus narrowly on the reframing of multicultural citizenship in terms of economic utility. In contrast, middle-class multiculturalism embodies both the dimension of economic utility as well as broader moral and cultural distinctions that define both immigrants and the Canadian nation in terms of shared middle-class status. Second, and relatedly, neoliberal multiculturalism is seen as abandoning multicultural citizenship's commitment to building a shared sense of nationhood and social solidarity. This is not the case with middle-class multiculturalism, which immigration bureaucrats came to recognize as a solution to incorporating racial diversity into the Canadian nation-building project. Middle-class multiculturalism is thus very much about reimagining the nation and about building a shared sense of solidarity along intersectional (racial and class) lines.

Domestically, shifting the lens from neoliberal to middle-class multiculturalism modifies, but does not contradict, Kymlicka's (2017) diagnosis of increasing socio-economic social closure and disregard for social inequality in multicultural citizenship as it is experienced in Canada today. Middle-class multiculturalism results in social closure along class and status lines (not just in terms of economic utility). It also creates a sense of national solidarity that is contingent on membership in a multicultural middle class. This means that concerns about social inequality are not so much deflected as directed at fellow members of the middle-class multicultural in-group. Prime Minister Justin Trudeau's creation of a new ministerial post in December 2019 – the Minister of

Middle-Class Prosperity and Associate Minister of Finance – can be seen as a striking manifestation of the long-term effects of how postwar immigration bureaucrats reimagined national identity. The office grew out of his Liberal Party's platform, outlined in a 2019 document entitled *Forward: A Real Plan for the Middle Class*. Alongside a strong continuing commitment to ethnocultural diversity, the platform promises to build "a strong middle class," help "working Canadians get ahead," support entrepreneurs' efforts to "succeed and grow," and to make "life more affordable" for middle-class Canadians (Liberal Party of Canada 2019, 6, 11, 19, 7). The fact that middle-class Canadians are identified as the main beneficiaries of measures proposed in the platform but that the term "middle class" is never defined speaks to the degree to which the concept has become internalized as a marker of Canadian national identity in general. Yet while signalling inclusivity, the solidarity attached to the citizenship envisioned in middle-class multiculturalism is highly socio-economically selective and symbolically excludes the most vulnerable in Canadian society.

If middle-class multiculturalism has the potential to exacerbate social inequalities across the Canadian population, does it at least pave the way for middle-class visible minorities to feel a full sense of belonging in the Canadian nation? Theoretically, it should be especially effective at removing symbolic barriers to belonging for visible minority immigrants who have achieved middle-class status, as marked by tertiary education, employment in a professional occupation, assets, the ability to partake of middle-class leisure activities, and so on. This goes especially for second-generation descendants of visible minority immigrants. Having been born in the country and socialized by its institutions, the second generation should face fewer barriers to both structural and symbolic integration into the nation than their parents (Gordon 1964).

Yet there is evidence to suggest that middle-class multiculturalism has not levelled the symbolic playing field for second-generation descendants of visible-minority immigrants to Canada (Reitz and Banerjee 2007; Reitz, Simon, and Laxer 2017).[32] The promise of equal ability to claim full membership, and to be recognized as full members, has not been fulfilled. Based on an analysis of Statistics Canada's Ethnic Diversity Survey, Reitz and Banerjee (2007) show that more children of visible minority immigrants report experiencing discrimination (42.2 per cent) compared to first-generation visible-minority immigrants (33.6 per cent). Within the second generation, perceived discrimination varies by group: 34.5 per cent for Chinese, 43.4 per cent for South Asians, and 60.9 per cent for Blacks. As Reitz, Simon, and

Laxer (2017, 2480) show in a comparative analysis of data from France and Canada, reports of discrimination increase for second-generation Muslims by 25 per cent compared with first-generation Muslim immigrants. Despite middle-class multiculturalism, Canada appears to be doing little better than France at making some structurally integrated visible minority populations feel like equal members of mainstream society. This is a sobering finding when one considers that France has taken a stance towards racial and ethnic inclusion in the nation that is the opposite of Canada's multiculturalism approach. As Reitz, Simon, and Laxer point out, France's "Republican model" enforces an "assimilationist" framing of immigration, integration and citizenship that emphasizes "secularism and the exclusion of religion from the public sphere" rather than officially recognizing minority cultures. To this end, the French state even takes a "colour blind" approach to population statistics, eschewing racial and ethnic categories in its census that could provide the government and social scientists with the basic tools for detecting discrimination (see, e.g., Simon 2008).

Such findings suggest that, despite having created and fostered a very different institutional and symbolic context of reception since the Second World War, Canada has created what Beaman (2017) calls, in reference to the French context, "citizen outsiders." The term "citizen outsider" denotes the condition of being a legal citizen and structurally well integrated while hitting a "glass ceiling" when it comes to achieving the status of (and being recognized as) full members of the nation. Symbolic exclusion, despite socio-economic inclusion, results in experiences of discrimination that curtail citizen outsiders' ability to participate in society as full citizens compared to other native-born citizens who have experienced similar processes of socialization and achieved similar socio-economic status.

Public Support for Immigrant Selection Policies

The symbolic socio-economic selectivity of Canada's imagined multicultural nation also has the potential to shape ideas of who is or who is not admissible to Canada as an immigrant or refugee in the eyes of the general public. As Blinder (2015) argues in reference to the United Kingdom, members of the general public formulate opinions on immigration policy based on "imagined immigration," that is, the picture people have in their heads of who immigrants are. Insofar as public opinion influences immigration policymaking, public perceptions of who immigrants are can affect the kinds of immigrants a government admits.

There is reason to believe that the Canadian public's traditionally high level of support for immigration is tied, at least in part, to the fact that "imagined immigration" in the eyes of the Canadian public is highly selective in socio-economic terms. In his analysis of how immigration policy is depicted in Canadian media, Bauder (2011) shows that the immigration and settlement of highly skilled and affluent foreigners is generally taken for granted. Public opinion surveys, like the one conducted regularly by Environics (2019), consistently reveal that Canadians' positive overall attitude towards immigration rests, in part, on the widely held belief that immigrants are good for the Canadian economy. The findings presented in this book suggest that the historical origins of these perceptions lie in the middle-class multiculturalism that has affected immigrant demographics over the past several decades.

If support for immigration among the Canadian general public presumes socio-economic selectivity and economic utility, it seems logical that any entry categories not associated with these qualities are vulnerable to losing public support. Entry categories that are formally "non-economic" (e.g., for family members, recognized refugees, and asylum applicants) select individuals for admission to Canada based on their presumed *lack* of the kinds of traits that made non-White immigrants part of the imagined nation: entrepreneurial spirit, self-sufficiency, high levels of education, occupational status, and so on. The same perceptions apply to temporary foreign workers, whose perceived "low-skilled" status (compared to immigrants in the Federal Skilled Worker Program or Canadian Experience Class) makes their exclusion from the rights associated with permanent resident status politically and socially acceptable. When it comes to public support for limiting asylum-seekers and potentially "fraudulent" marriage migrants, the perception that these groups are somehow "jumping the queue" also places them outside middle-class rules of socially acceptable behaviour. Since acceptable multiculturalism was created as middle-class multiculturalism, the general public increasingly has little trouble accepting restrictions on categories that connote a lack of appropriate middle-class attributes.

Insofar as public perceptions about the compatibility of different, legally defined immigrant groups influence policymaking, any restrictions resulting from public calls to reduce family, low-skilled worker, and asylum-related admissions produce higher costs for those immigrant groups without protecting the middle-class nation in the way the public imagines. This is because the key assumption underlying restrictive opinions on family, low-skilled worker, and asylum-seeker admissions – that these state categories accurately describe real, pre-existing differences between these groups – does not hold. Scholars have shown that the admission criteria for family and refugee-related entry categories do not holistically reflect the traits of individuals entering the country; indeed, family immigrants and refugees often possess levels of education, work experience and occupational status that are comparable to those who enter the country as skilled workers (see, e.g., Elrick and Lightman 2016; Lightman and Elrick 2021; Stewart 2008). Instead, these categories represent a way of "seeing like a state" (Scott 1998) that is necessarily reductionist. They create clear distinctions between immigrants, for administrative purposes, that are less clear in real life (Richmond 1988). But the general public is not sensitive to nuance on an increasingly politically contentious topic; seeing immigrants through the state's eyes as either possessing economic utility and middle-class characteristics (skilled workers) or lacking both of those (family, refugees) makes expedient judgments of moral worth possible. Claims to worthiness based on middle-class worker citizenship are more appealing than those based on rights enshrined in the *Universal Declaration of Human Rights*, like the right to family life, the right to freedom from persecution, and the right to enjoy a reasonable level of social and economic security. This broader normative effect of entry categories on public perceptions of worthiness and admissibility has particularly strong potential for furthering racialized exclusion because those accorded refugee status by UNHCR and those who enter Canada to seek asylum under its laws are disproportionately non-White individuals from the Global South, whose access to mobility across international borders in the face of economic, political, and environmental pressures is all but blocked.

Conclusion

What do the material and normative legacies of middle-class multiculturalism identified here mean beyond the Canadian context, in countries that wish to replicate its perceived successes in immigration and multiculturalism? The socio-economic selectivity aspect of managing large-scale, demographically diverse immigrant inflows appears desirable to governments of OECD countries looking to Canada as an example of international best practice. A key assumption underpinning political and popular support for such policies is that a high degree of selectivity, achieved through instruments like a "points system," ensures the entry of immigrants who can easily integrate into the receiving country, that is, immigrants who have high "integration potential" (Helbling, Simon, and Schmid 2020, 3; see also Borjas 1990).

Yet a "points system" is not in itself a model for migration management. It is a policy instrument used to execute a model. As this book has shown, the Canadian model is the result, in part, of the *longue durée* of institutionalized habits of thought that frame "good" multicultural-ism as *middle-class multiculturalism*. Establishing and maintaining the model entails a long-term political commitment to large-scale immigra-tion and multicultural nation-building, which presumes a willingness to embrace demographic change. The same result cannot be achieved by reducing individuals to their university diplomas and bank account balances and treating them as suspect outsiders by demanding they pass tests to demonstrate compliance with set receiving-society "val-ues."[33] If it is replicable at all, adopting a Canadian model of immigra-tion requires time and the committed support of multiple institutions beyond the branch of the state responsible for immigration policymak-ing and implementation.

Replicability issues aside, policymakers elsewhere must recognize that the Canadian model comes with its own long-term threats to equal-ity and social cohesion. This is because it exacerbates the effects of neo-liberal dynamics that have shaped the economic, social, and political spheres in Canada and elsewhere since the 1980s. Under a mass immi-gration program like Canada's, these social inequalities can affect a large proportion of the country's population over time. In this sense, a regret-table and under-recognized aspect of the Canadian model is the broad intersectional exclusions that its immigration policy has generated.

Methodological Appendix

Working with primary historical sources, which comprise the main data source for this book, carries with it advantages and disadvantages. Like all sources of qualitative data, archival records have the important advantage of being extremely rich and descriptive, particularly for the time period under consideration, when carefully written and detailed memoranda were the norm in office communication. In this sense, they can be seen as "fossilized" articulations of the boundary work that immigration bureaucrats carried out in the course of redefining immigrant admissibility. Additionally, in contrast to interview data, the language of archived documents cannot be filtered through present-day norms of communication. This is particularly important given the book's focus on the evolving nature of boundary work, that is, how immigration bureaucrats talked about people in racial, ethnic, socio-economic, and moral terms, over time. It is hard to imagine an interview participant recruited to speak as a former government representative using language to describe individuals and groups that may have been commonplace in the 1950s but is completely unacceptable now (e.g., references to members of the "Negro race"). Yet it is precisely the presence, then absence, of such terminology, as well as how it was used, that is part of the story.

Foremost among the disadvantages of basing a qualitative study on archival documents is the incomplete nature of archival collections. This incompleteness can result from gaps (intentional or otherwise) in document transfers from ministries to archives, idiosyncratic document management and retrieval systems, and declining resources for refining and adding to existing collections. All three factors lead Calavita (2010) to describe her historical work on the Bracero guest worker program for agricultural workers in the United States as somewhat "archaeological." In other words, the process of finding relevant material in wide-ranging but often incomplete collections can be exploratory and remain incomplete. The researcher may fail to uncover some records pertaining to a particular subject and thereby leave aspects of that subject unexplored. Additionally, records may remain inaccessible due to access to information provisions or, if released, be heavily redacted. Since it is impossible to avoid these pitfalls of archival research, all the researcher can do is attempt to ensure that data of sufficient volume, quality, and diversity are collected in order to detect a patterns that are repeatedly confirmed during qualitative data analysis.

Finding Files

A variety of documents from the period spanning the years 1952 to 1967 were analysed for this book. They range from draft versions of immigration policy documents (speeches, reports, legislation, etc.) to correspondence among immigration bureaucrats regarding (1) how to interpret general statements of political purpose made by elected politicians; (2) how to formulate written regulations; (3) descriptions of, and thoughts on, individual immigration applications referred to the minister and his/her advisers for admission via order-in-council; (4) demands made on the Department of Citizenship and Immigration by other Canadian government departments, representatives of other governments, and organized interests (particularly ethnic organizations like the Chinese Benevolent Association); (5) individual immigration cases referred up the hierarchy for reconsideration; and (6) deportation appeals.

The majority of files are located in two Record Groups held by Library and Archives Canada: (1) RG 26, which contains the files from the Department of Citizenship and Immigration, with a strong focus on records from the deputy minister's office; and (2) RG 76, which contains records from the Immigration Branch. Library and Archives Canada identifies the deputy minister's files (RG 26) as being a particularly rich source of information on policymaking and immigration programs, and the majority of files I reviewed are from that group. Some records pertaining to order-in-council admissions were retrieved from RG 2 (Privy Council), while others were found distributed throughout files from the two aforementioned record groups. Deportation appeal records were concentrated in two volumes from RG 82 (General Board of Immigration Appeals).

I adopted a six-pronged approach to data collection. First, I collected the files referenced by other scholars who have looked at race and post-war immigration policy change in Canada (especially FitzGerald and

Cook-Martín 2014; Hawkins 1988; Triadafilopoulos 2012). I did this in order to ensure that my empirical data would allow me to engage with their analyses and findings directly. These records tend to focus on immigration policymaking and planning. They contain correspondence pertaining to – and draft versions of – Cabinet documents that formed the bases of orders-in-council to alter immigration regulations, the 1962 and 1967 immigration regulations themselves, the Sedgewick Report,[1] and the 1966 White Paper. They also contain internal reports on the Department's operations and performance, and minutes of the meetings of the Departmental Advisory Committee on Immigration (DACI) and the Senate Standing Committee on Immigration. The files referenced by other scholars did not address order-in-council admissions, deportation appeals, and other aspects of policy implementation that are featured in this book (see chapter 2 for a discussion of reasons behind this).

Second, I expanded my search to include records with titles that explicitly referred to immigration from majority White and majority non-White countries of origin. For example, I reviewed files on immigration from the United Kingdom, "France and French-speaking countries," Japan, Italy, China, and the British West Indies. I also took into account records referencing groups rather than countries of origin, like "coloured immigration" and "Asiatic immigration." Where records were explicitly dedicated to the recruitment of skilled workers of particular origins – for example, "coloured nurses" – these were also reviewed.

Third, I expanded the range of my search to focus on family admissions, for theoretical and empirical reasons. Theoretically, the family is an immensely important site for the reproduction of the imagined and physical national community that is defined practically and symbolically by immigration policy (Lee 2013, 2015). Families contribute, physically, to settlement, social reproduction, and labour within the nation state. As explained in chapter 5, they are also integral to the reproduction of the imagined national community. Given the family's vital position in maintaining the nation, I expected it to be the policy object around which the most substantial boundary work around race and admissibility would take place.

Empirically, in the Canadian case, the postwar policy "problem" of eliminating explicit racial discrimination in immigration policy was absolutely inseparable from the issue of sponsored family immigration. In 1965, the Minister of Citizenship and Immigration was quoted as saying that the "sponsored [family] immigration was the most difficult aspect of immigration policy."[2] In that same year, a secret working paper explicitly linked the issue of family sponsorship with the elimination of racial discrimination in its articulation of the four main objectives to be achieved in reforming family sponsorship policies. According to this paper, the "problem" was to "reconcile the following sometimes conflicting objectives" in a sponsorship policy:

No. 1 The complete elimination of discrimination between sponsors or their relatives on the basis of race, religion, ethnic origin, or geographic or national origins.

No. 2 No reduction in existing sponsorship classes.

No. 3 Development of a policy which will gain approval and support among ethnic groups.

No. 4 Reduction or control of the economically dangerous inflow of the unskilled worker so characteristic of the sponsored movement.[3]

The mixture of race-related and family-related objectives listed here clearly shows that, from the perspective of the policymakers themselves, managing racial inclusion was not just about adapting worker admissions but family admissions as well.

In practical terms, including records on family admissions involved collecting files officially labelled as pertaining to topics like "sponsored movements," "processing of sponsored cases," "adoption of children," "admission of close relatives and dependents of immigrants," and "servicemen's dependents and fiancées." Correspondence on the admission of family members was also distributed throughout the general files on different racial, ethnic, and national origin groups mentioned previously. To these I added files that explicitly linked national origins and family movements, for example, "children from the United Kingdom (orphans and refugees)."

The fourth data collection strategy reflects this study's innovative contribution to analyses of the emergence of universal immigration policies. Having conceptualized the adjudication of individual cases, that is, immigration policy *implementation*, as part of immigration policy *formulation*, I searched for cases considered by the minister and his/her advisers for admission by order-in-council. Those discussed by immigration bureaucrats in greatest detail, often in a series of memoranda, were scattered throughout the group-specific and policy-specific records described previously. However, there were also summaries of large batches of order-in-council admissions approved between the years 1954 and 1964. These were much less detailed and held in a single box in RG 26 (Volume 89). I conducted a qualitative content analysis on the 1,731 order-in-council admissions recorded in this box that were used to admit someone from a "non-preferred" (i.e., non-European, non-Western Hemisphere) origin country (see next section for details). While incomplete, these records provide insights into the scope and scale of these admissions, as well as the characteristics of individual applicants, that cannot be derived from the richer, but less frequently occurring, documents found in other files.

While it is beyond the scope of this investigation to account systematically for the boundary work engaged in by lower-level immigration officers, as Satzewich (2015) does in his study of contemporary family admissions practices, I did analyze records pertaining to the First Immigration Manual during the 1952 to 1967 period. The manual provided detailed instructions to immigration officers on how to interpret applications in reference to the Immigration Act and regulations. The records related to the manual are, unfortunately, incomplete. This is because it was revised piecemeal over the 1953–67 period, with individual pages being replaced at irregular intervals. No full copies of the manual as it was in force at any one particular point in time are on file. However, even the incomplete version of the manual – which was considered so confidential that immigration officers were instructed to carry it on their person in the event of a move[4] – provides insights into how high-level bureaucrats instructed their street-level colleagues to interpret individual-level and group-level admissibility.

Since immigrants from "preferred" (i.e., European, Western Hemisphere) origin countries were less affected by the kind of admissions restrictions that needed to be circumvented via order-in-council, I turned to another source of information on these immigrants: deportation appeals. While admissions and deportations are different aspects of immigration law, they are both sites in which state actors decide to include individuals in (or exclude them from) the territory and nation. Held in RG 82 (General Board of Immigration Appeals), there are two boxes of records (Volumes 11 and 12) containing 961 appeal decisions made between 1956 and 1967. In each case, there is a two- to four-page overview of the case as reviewed, on the order of the minister, which details the grounds for deportation as well as the background of the immigrant in question and prospects for remaining in Canada. The main countries of origin represented are Germany, the United Kingdom, and the United States. In combination with documents on order-in-council admission cases, these deportation appeals make it possible to compare and contrast how immigration bureaucrats assessed the admissibility of White and non-White individuals alike. This allows for a more balanced examination of how notions of race and admissibility evolved over the period in question. It also generates deeper insights into how individual-level assessments fundamentally shaped Canada's first universal immigration policy.

Finally, since secondary sources had suggested that the power of the provinces relative to the federal government had begun to grow during the 1950s (see, e.g., Kilbourn 1968), I reviewed files dedicated to correspondence between the federal and provincial governments on immigration matters. The purpose here was to evaluate the extent to which the subnational level of immigration policymaking contributed to boundary work around race and admissibility. I reviewed files of correspondence with the provinces in general, and with British Columbia and Ontario in particular, as well as ones containing correspondence with municipal authorities in Ontario. In the end, however, these files had little bearing on the analysis presented here, as I found no evidence of provincial involvement in the boundary work of defining immigrant admissibility.

Data collection took place gradually over the seven-year period from 2012 to 2019. The first phase (2012–16) occurred in the context of field-work for my PhD dissertation at the University of Toronto (Elrick 2017), during multiple short-term visits to Library and Archives Canada. The second phase (2017–19) took place during my first years as a faculty member at McGill University, as part of a research project undertaken to extend the original study. In total, fifty-nine boxes of relevant material (containing 500–2,000 pages each) were reviewed. During the second phase of data collection, I was aided by a student research assistant. Extensive notes were taken on site of all relevant documents in those boxes, including summaries of, and quotations from, those documents. All documents referenced in field notes were also photographed for future reference.

Analytical Approach

This book uses the discovery of an empirical anomaly as an occasion to question and extend existing theoretical explanations of a social phenomenon, namely the emergence of Canada's postwar universal immigration policy. As chapters 2 and 3 outline in detail, existing theories of how and why universal immigration policies emerged in the postwar era – and, more generally, of how the place of race in ideas of nation shifted during the same period – overwhelmingly emphasize macro-level and meso-level factors such as global normative contexts and organizational interests within states. Against this theoretical backdrop, the interpretive practices applied by immigration bureaucrats in the course of admitting non-White immigrants notwithstanding immigration regulations prohibiting their entry challenged these existing theoretical explanations and pointed to the need to include micro-level processes alongside macro-level and meso-level ones.

The qualitative data analysis conducted on the archival records described in the previous section followed what Deterding and Waters (2021) call "flexible coding." I began deductively, with a start list of codes that reflected the main principles of classification identified by other scholars as being particularly relevant to the boundary work that distinguishes national "selves" from immigrant "others." These included references to visible difference, language, culture, religion, morality, social class, and status (Bail 2008; Hall and Lamont 2013; Lamont 1992, Lamont 2000; Zolberg and Long 1999). The start list of codes was then adjusted inductively, while coding by hand, as new aspects were revealed in the data or codes became irrelevant. This approach allows the researcher to ask theoretically informed questions of the data without precluding the possibility that themes can emerge from the data that were not anticipated by theory.

In addition to coding field notes and excerpts from the archival records by hand, qualitative data analysis software (MaxQDA) was used to analyse two sets of archival records: the 1,731 order-in-council admissions from 1954 to 1964 found in RG 26 (Volume 89), and the 961 deportation appeal cases from 1956 to 1967 held in RG 82 (Volumes 11 and 12). This was done with the help of two student research assistants. The purpose behind using the software was to capture the frequency and consistency over time of the terms used by immigration bureaucrats to justify the admissibility or (in the case of deportation appeals) inadmissibility of individuals. The software also makes it possible, through its code relations browser, to chart the co-occurrence of codes in single excerpts and documents.

Coding was initially oriented toward mapping the terms that could be related to the concept, in Canadian immigration law, of "cases of exceptional merit." As explained in chapter 4, this was one of the concepts that guided the interpretive practices that immigration bureaucrats used to define admissibility outside the confines of the Immigration Act and regulations. The First Immigration Manual from 1954 defines "cases of exceptional merit" as follows:

a case which is being dealt with (i) on humanitarian grounds when rigid application of the regulations would result in personal or financial hardship to the prospective immigrant or the applicant, or (ii) by executive direction, or *(iii) for public benefit, which includes cases where, in view of the special qualifications or achievements of prospective immigrants, their admission*

is in the public interest; i.e., they will contribute appreciably to the social, econo-
mic or cultural life of Canada.[5] (emphasis added)

Picking up on the third component of that definition in particular, counts were generated for mentions of economic capital (e.g., salary, savings, assets), social capital (e.g., community and family ties), and cultural capital (e.g., educational or occupational status). Where the admissibility of one individual was clearly being considered in relation to the economic, social, and/or cultural capital of another (e.g., a family member), the ascribed attributes of that other person were noted as well. As with the hand coding of other documents, codes were also created to capture moral distinctions (e.g., work ethic). In the case of both deportation appeals and order-in-council admissions, additional codes captured the section and subsection of the Immigration Act or regulations from which an individual needed an exemption, or under which a person had been ordered deported. The coding techniques employed here generated a unique and systematic account of the economic, social, cultural, and moral terms in which state actors judged immigrants' eligibility for membership in the national community, both symbolically and concretely, in individual cases.

While particular individuals and political parties are attributed an important role in other accounts of postwar immigration policy formulation (see, e.g., Triadafilopoulos 2012), these were not coded for in the analysis. This choice reflects the book's theoretical emphasis on the cumulative outcomes of boundary work (i.e., how individuals and groups are talked about) as a cultural factor that shaped the policy formulation process and its outcomes. In the period under consideration (1952 to 1967), the country was led by two prime ministers from the Liberal Party: Louis St. Laurent (1949–57) and Lester B. Pearson (1963–8). It was also led by Conservative Prime Minster John Diefenbaker (1957–63). The Department of Citizenship and Immigration (Manpower and Immigration from 1966 onward) was presided over by seven ministers and five deputy ministers (Hawkins 1988, 407). The fact that the patterns of boundary work illustrated in the analysis covered the tenures of many different individuals and both main political parties can be seen as evidence that cultural elements above the level of individuals play a role in policy formulation.

Notes

1 Introduction

1 Some scholars argue that this transition was not fully complete until the passing of the 1976 Immigration Act. In 1970 the Assisted Passage Loan Scheme – a vehicle for defraying the costs of travelling to Canada that was reserved for European-origin immigrants – was made available to immigrants of all nationalities. This removed the last instance of positive discrimination by national origins. Furthermore, the 1976 Immigration Act stated for the first time that admission standards "do not discriminate on grounds of race, national or ethnic origin, colour, religion or sex" (quoted in FitzGerald and Cook-Martín 2014, 145). However, as discussed in chapter 2, focusing on implementation practices, instead of laws, can tell a different story. For example, the description of the general principles of immigrant selection articulated in the 1964 version of the First Immigration Manual issued to Canadian immigration officers states that officers should "ensure the universal application of uniform standards of selection without regard to race, colour or creed" (see RG 76, Vol. 932, Binder 3). The 1976 statement may be more inclusive, but it is not the first explicit articulation of an anti-discriminatory mandate in Canadian immigration policy.
2 Statistics Canada includes the Middle East in its Asian origin category.
3 While admissibility was defined in reference to national origin categories, these are widely acknowledged to have functioned as proxies for race. The most broadly admissible national origins were ones with majority White populations, and the least admissible ones had majority non-White populations. Hence the claim here that national-origin provisions served racialized – and racist – nation-building projects. For a general discussion of the historical link between race and national identity in immigration policy, see chapter 2 of Triadafilopoulos (2012).

4 Memorandum from the Director of Immigration, C.E.S. Smith, to the
  Deputy Minister of Immigration, Laval Fortier, Re: Application of Mr. and
  Mrs. P., Victoria BC for the admission of two Chinese children for adoption,
  18.12.1959. In RG 26, Vol. 120, File 3–26–1 Part 2.
5 Memorandum from the Minister to the Assistant to the Deputy Minister,
  24 May 1960. In RG 26, Vol. 133, File 3–35–2 Part 8.
6 As Hawkins (1991) notes, Australia's 1958 Migration Act gave similarly
  vast discretionary powers over admission and deportation to high-level
  immigration bureaucrats. To the best of my knowledge, whether and/or
  how the exercise of discretion shaped Australia's 1973 universal admissions
  policy remains an open question to be addressed empirically.

2 Bureaucratic Discretion in the Historical Canadian Context

1 Organizational details presented in this paragraph, the following one, and
  figure 2.1 are from documents prepared for the Meeting on Immigration
  Matters between Canadian Government Officials and Government of
  Ontario Officials, 8 June 1953. In RG 26, Vol. 134, File 3–36–1 Part 1.
2 The United Kingdom was the biggest source of immigrants to Canada well
  into the twentieth century. The move was attractive for Britons because it
  represented an opportunity to escape harsher economic conditions and a
  rigid class system. While Canada could (and did) draw immigrants from
  numerous source countries to build its economy and settle the west, those
  from Britain were considered preferable because they were "of the same
  stock as most Canadian-born citizens" and could therefore be expected to
  have fewer problems adapting to Canadian society (Kelley and Trebilcock
  2010, 122). By the late 1950s, immigration from the United Kingdom
  was dropping significantly, in part due to improved postwar economic
  circumstances in that country. See Kelley and Trebilcock (2010) for a
  comprehensive overview of Canada's immigration policies and patterns
  prior to the period examined in this book.
3 See the discussion of these in chapter 5.
4 The First Immigration Manual was issued in 1952 and consolidated existing
  policy statements, circulars, and instructions. It comprised thirty chapters,
  each of which contained formal instructions on a particular topic. These
  topics included the interpretation of immigration laws and regulations,
  administrative procedures, admissibility criteria for selecting immigrants,
  required documentation, and how to manage cases in which admissibility is
  questioned (inquiries, appeals, deportations). Entire chapters, or subsections
  therein, were modified regularly through operational memoranda, which
  could be inserted as individual sheets into the binders. The First Immigration
  Manual, including revisions up to 1973, is held in RG 76, Vol. 932–9.

5 First Immigration Manual: "Manual for the Guidance of Immigration and Visa Officers," Amend. No. 2363 (27–11–62). In RG 76, Vol. 932, Binder 1.

6 First Immigration Manual, chapter 4, Section 4.58, "Applications for fiancé(e)s," revision from 1962. In RG 76, Vol. 933, Binder 5.

7 First Immigration Manual, "Personal Qualities," Amend. No. 2494 13–5-63. In RG 76, Vol. 932, Binder 3.

8 These were also clearly articulated in the First Immigration Manual, by at least 1964. They may have appeared earlier, but the lack of availability of all amendments to the manual in sequence makes this unclear. One of the objectives of Canadian immigration policy listed in the 1964 description of the general principles of immigrant selection is "to ensure the universal application of uniform standards of selection without regard to race, colour or creed." In RG 76, Vol. 932, Binder 3.

9 Notes on Canadian Immigration Policy, Deputy Minister's Copy, Revised January 1961. In RG 26, Vol. 133, File 3–35–2 Part 8.

10 Operations Memoranda (renamed "Immigration Directives" in 1959) were used to update the First Immigration Manual and are thus interfiled with relevant chapters of the manual.

11 Operations Memorandum to all Immigration Offices, No. 4–8, 3 September 1957, Subj: Requests to the Governor in Council. In RG76, Vol. 933, Binder 4.

12 First Immigration Manual, "Admissibility," 1962 Amendment #2152 (13–3-62). In RG76, Vol. 933, Binder 4.

13 Examples of these briefs can be found in RG26, Vol. 128, File 3–33–19 Part 1 (from the National Japanese Canadian Citizens Association) and RG26, Vol. 125, File 3–33–7 Part 2 (from the Chinese Benevolent Association).

14 Memorandum from J.E. Duggan, Registrar of Canadian Citizenship, to the Deputy Minister, 11 May 1953. In RG 26, Vol. 128, File 3–33–19 Part 1.

15 Canada, Parliament, *House of Commons Debates*, 21st Parl., 6th Sess., Vol. IV (1952), 4270-1. See chapter 4 for further discussion of admissions based on "merit."

16 Confidential memorandum from L.H. Nicholson, Commissioner, Royal Canadian Mounted Police, Officer of the Commissioner, Ottawa, to Laval Fortier, Deputy Minister, Department of Citizenship and Immigration, 15.1952. In RG 26, Vol. 98, File 3-15-1 Part 1. As Kelley and Trebilcock (2010, 498) point out, Doukhobors – along with Mennonites and Hutterites – were pacifist farmers whose refusal to participate in the First and Second World Wars caused a lot of resentment among the general public. The added fact that the Doukhobors were of Russian origin would have made them especially unpopular during the Cold War.

17 Hawkins (1988, 26) calls the lack of "accurate and detailed information on which to base policy decisions" a "universal feature" of the postwar era.

The lack was noticeable to the extent that it was remarked upon by the Special Joint Committee of the Senate and the House of Commons that was appointed in 1966 to examine the White Paper on Canadian Immigration Policy (see chapter 5).

18 All quotations in this paragraph are taken from Notes on Canadian Immigration Policy, Deputy Minister's Copy, Revised January 1961. In RG 26, Vol. 133, File 3–35–2, Part 8.

19 According to Library and Archives Canada, the files they have are a small sample, held for the purpose of "illustrating procedure and legal precedent": http://www.lac-bac.gc.ca/005/005-1142.25-e.html, accessed 7 November 2019.

20 Offences were counted by the section of the Immigration Act or regulations named in the record of the appeal. Some individuals were deemed deportable due to multiple violations. The most frequent violations were of section 19 (1)(e)(iii), referring to non-Canadian citizens who had become the inmate of a penitentiary, jail, reformatory, or prison, or of an asylum or hospital for mental illness (653 cases); section 19(1)(e)(ii), covering persons convicted of offenses under the Criminal Code (198 cases); section 19(1)(d), referring to narcotics-related offenses (133 cases); and section 19(1)(iv), referring to persons who were members of a "prohibited class" at the time of entry (98 cases).

3 State Actors Shaping the Nation

1 Theoretically, the claim that macro-level cultural factors can affect policy is rooted in the "world society" institutionalist perspective. This perspective emphasizes the power of worldwide cultural constructs in shaping institutions and actions through "cognitive and ontological models of reality that specify the nature, purposes, technology, sovereignty, control, and resources of nation-states and other actors" (Meyer et al. 1997, 149).

2 See chapter 2 for details.

3 See Delgado and Stefancic (2017) for a general discussion of the key tenets of critical race theory.

4 The section entitled "Explaining the Absence of Implementation from Historical Analyses" in chapter 2 outlines empirical reasons for this, which complement the theoretical reasons discussed here.

5 Pragmatist theories of social action have regained popularity in sociology in recent years. See Schneiderhan (2011) and Whitford (2002) for overviews of this development.

6 Memorandum from the Deputy Minister to the Director of Immigration, Re: Stability in Immigration Programming, 5 May 1959. In RG 26, Vol. 133, File 3–35–2 Part 8.

7 Memorandum from the Deputy Minister to the Director of Immigration, 29 August 1961. In RG 26, Vol. 124, File 3–33–6 Part 2.

8 Confidential memorandum from the Deputy General Executive Assistant to the Director of Immigration, Re: East Indian Immigration, 17 November 1961. In RG 76, Vol. 823, File 552–1-567 Part 2.

9 Memorandum from the Deputy Minister to the Acting Director of Immigration, 1 September 1961. In RG 76, Vol. 823, File 552–1-567 Part 2.

10 Memorandum from the Director of Technical Services to the Deputy Minister, Re: Immigration in 1957, 3 April 1957. In RG 26, Vol. 133, File 3–35–2.

11 On Chinese fiancé(e)s, see: Confidential memorandum from the Acting Director of Immigration to the Minister, Re: Chinese Immigration, 25 February 1963. In RG 26, Vol. 125, File 3–33–7 Part 3. On Japanese fiancé(e)s, see: Operational memorandum from the Acting Chief, Operations Division, to the five Canadian District Superintendents and all overseas offices Re: Admission of Japanese fiancées, 27 March 1957. In RG 26, Vol. 128, File 3–33–19 Part 1.

12 Memorandum from the Minister to the Deputy Minister, 24 May 1960. In RG 26, Vol. 133, File 3–35–2 Part 8.

13 Identifying cultural repertoires as the first mechanism diverges from Steensland (2006), who refers instead to "cultural schemas." The difference between cultural repertoires and cultural schemas is somewhat contested in the field of cultural sociology. "Schema" arguably denotes a relatively fixed, dominant narrative embedded in our thinking structures, which could be considered as part of a cultural repertoire. This rigidity is implied in Mohr et al.'s (2020, 32) definition of a "cognitvie schema" as "a set of associations between concepts in memory acquired from experience and used for the purposes of categorization, recognition, and filling-in of missing information." Cultural sociologists conceive of cognitive schemas as being shared by groups and as organizing their thinking within a particular domain (25). From this perspective, immigration bureaucrats could be seen as an occupationally defined group whose shared experiences of performing tasks related to policy formulation, including implementation, generate associations between concepts over time (e.g., racial or national groups and moral or socio-economic characteristics), which then continue to inform those practices. If we accept this distinction between schemas and repertoires, a focus here on schemas would draw attention to more established patterns of association rather than state actors' creative engagement with (elements of) such established patterns. This potential for creative usage is more clearly denoted by the concept of cultural repertoires as used by scholars like Swidler (1986) and Lamont (2000). At the same time, it is not incompatible with Steensland's (2006) framework, which likewise incorporates Lamont's (2000) insights on boundaries and boundary work.

14 Applied by Steensland (2006) to explain the evolution of welfare policy in the United States, this framework shows how policymakers came to see potential addressees of that policy in terms of different culturally informed categories of welfare recipients: the "deserving poor," the "working poor," and the "welfare poor." These categories were imbued with moral understandings of who is/is not deserving of assistance, which subsequently informed the kinds of material benefits – and degree of social stigmatization – attached to each category of individuals.

15 Other immigration policy scholars have used the discursive institutionalist approach to focus on the role of ideas in policymaking, but in ways that do not quite break with the treatment of ideas as coherent objects of interested action directed at set goals. As Boswell and Hampshire (2017) point out, attention to ideas in policymaking tends to lean towards either instrumentalist or institutionalist traditions. The former sees ideas as "tools strategically deployed by actors to achieve their ends," while the latter sees ideas as structural constraints on policymakers that limit the scope for policy change. In their own collaborative work, these two scholars aim for a middle ground. They argue that immigration policymakers engage in discursive interactions, (re)interpreting existing ideas about what is feasible or legitimate and devising ways to use them to frame issues and mobilize support for a particular course of action. Yet this compromise, like the problem it is meant to solve, lends ideas a coherence and stability that does not fully embrace pragmatist insights about the contingency and malleability of meaning.

16 The term "economic capital" is used throughout to denote material wealth such as income and assets.

17 Social capital refers to the "aggregate of the actual or potential resources which are linked to the possession of a durable network of more or less institutionalized relationships of mutual acquaintance and recognition" (Bourdieu 1986, 248). In other words, this is about one's position in social networks, the prestige of those networks, and what one might reasonably be expected to accomplish on the basis of that position.

18 Cultural capital exists in three forms: embodied, objectified, and institutionalized. The embodied form comprises internalized cultural signals (e.g., attitudes, preferences, knowledge, behaviours) and reflects "external wealth converted into an integral part of the person, into a habitus" (Bourdieu, 1986, 48). The objectified form manifests in material objects and media such as writing and music but acquires its worth only if the individual is in "possession of the means of 'consuming'" those objects in a meaningful way (Bourdieu, 1986, 48). Finally, institutionalized cultural capital refers to academic qualifications, which function as a guarantee of cultural competence.

4 Individual Merit and Multicultural Skilled Workers

1 Some of the empirical analysis presented in this chapter previously appeared in Elrick (2020). It is reused here with permission of the publisher.
2 See also the discussion of the merit clause in chapter 2.
3 First Immigration Manual, version from 18.2.1954. In RG 76, Vol. 933, Binder 4.
4 Canada, Parliament, *House of Commons Debates,* 21st Parl., 6th Sess., Vol. IV (1952), 4270–1.
5 Memorandum from the Acting Deputy Minister to the Minister of Citizenship and Immigration, Re: East Indians. 29.12.1955. In RG 26 Vol. 127, File 3–33–15 Part 2.
6 First Immigration Manual, Amendment from 18.2.1954. In RG 76, Vol. 933, Binder 4.
7 First Immigration Manual, Amendment from 12.7.71. In RG 76, Vol. 937. It is difficult to pinpoint some changes in the First Immigration Manual exactly, since the version on file is an incomplete collection of piecemeal adaptations. There were significant delays in changing the Manual to reflect the 1967 Immigration Regulations. In my reading, 1971 is the year in which an amendment rewrote chapter 17, previously entitled "Admission of Persons of Chinese Race" to be the chapter on "Statutory Declarations."
8 See chapter 2 for an overview of this portrayal of immigration bureaucrats in the standard historiography of postwar immigration policy change.
9 Notes for a speech to be delivered by the Hon. J.W. Pickersgill, M.P., at Victoria, 18 November 1955, "The Purpose of Immigration." In RG 26, Vol. 143, File 3–40–21.
10 Racialization involves the creation of visibility or invisibility in reference to any real or imagined physical characteristics and/or socio-cultural signifiers (Miles 1993; Miles and Brown 2003). While racialization is most often associated with processes of exclusion (Anthias and Yuval-Davis 1992; Banton 1977; Murji and Solomos 2005), I follow Kushner (2005) and others in recognizing the existence of "positive racialization," which is linked to processes of inclusion. Positive racialization occurs when a group is seen as having innate characteristics that are "deemed as potentially to the wider good"; this has been documented in case of Jews, who became positively racialized as possessing "superior intelligence, international power [and] financial acumen" (Kushner 2005, 211). History shows that some immigrant groups that are positively racialized today have, at other points in time, been negatively racialized, including the Irish, Italians, and Jews (see, e.g., Zolberg and Long 1999). Accounting for positive

racialization is important because the boundary work that classifies individuals and groups as admissible or inadmissible is as much about defining the ideal national self as it is about defining those who are to remain outside that national self. Instances of positive racialization in the boundary work conducted by immigration bureaucrats reveal important aspects of how race relates to the evolution of immigrant inclusion and exclusion during the postwar era. Although racialized ideas about group-level admissibility or inadmissibility did not disappear from selection processes, they ceased to be sufficient grounds for including or excluding individuals.

11 Draft – Canadian Post-War Immigration, 1946–1955, Published by Authority of Hon. J.W. Pickersgill, Minister of Citizenship and Immigration. In RG 26, Vol. 143, File 3–40–21.

12 Memorandum from the Director of the Immigration Branch to the Deputy Minister, Re: A Review of Immigration from the British West Indies, 14 January 1955. In RG 26, Vol. 124, File 3–33–6 Part 1.

13 Definition taken from the Merriam-Webster Online Dictionary, accessed 30 January 2016, http://www.merriam-webster.com/dictionary/standard%20of%20living.

14 Both quotations are from: Notes for a speech to be delivered by the Hon. J.W. Pickersgill at Victoria, 18 November 1955, "The Purpose of Immigration" In RG 26, Vol. 143, File 3–40–21.

15 Letter from the Deputy Minister to the Hon. John R. Nicholson, 30 August 1965. In RG 76, Vol. 723, File 551–25–2 Part 1.

16 See the Methodological Appendix for more information on data and methods.

17 All records referenced here are contained in RG 26, Vol. 89, in files disaggregated by year. There were no relevant admissions in these records for the year 1960. The detailed breakdown by year of admissions notwithstanding section 20 referenced here is: 1954 (65); 1955 (632); 1956 (616); 1957 (62); 1958 (50); 1959 (61); 1960 (0); 1961 (245). The majority of admissions are family-related; those cases are examined in chapter 5.

18 In most cases multiple reasons were given to justify the admissibility of an individual.

19 This moral valance is articulated more clearly in the deportation appeals discussed later in the chapter, which contain much more nuanced descriptions of the individuals involved.

20 Memorandum from the Director of Immigration to the Deputy Minister, Re: Canadian-sponsored applications – Canada-India Agreement, 13.7.1955. In RG 26, Vol. 127, File 3–33–15 Part 2.

21 Memorandum from the Deputy Minister to the Director, Re: Canada-India Agreement, 1958 – unsponsored applications, 27.12.1957. In RG 26, Vol. 127, File 3–33–15 Part 2.

22 See these and further examples in records on order-in-council admissions for 1957–1959 in RG 26, Vol. 89.

23 Memorandum from the Deputy Minister to the Minister, 26 June 1961. In RG26, Vol. 128, File 3–33–19 Part 2.

24 The Department of Citizenship and Immigration implemented the Assisted Passage Loan Scheme in 1951 to give financial assistance to European immigrants who were needed to fill labour shortages but who could not afford the cost of travel (Kelley and Trebilcock 2010, 328).

25 First Immigration Manual, Amendment from 18.2.1954. In RG 76, Vol. 933, Binder 4.

26 Immigration Manual, Amendment #1544 from 1.11.1960. In RG 76, Vol. 935, Binder 10.

27 See the occupation-specific records on immigration policy during the 1950s, which include wood workers, restaurant workers, bakers, construction workers, farm workers, general labourers, and agriculturalists. These can be found in RG 26 Vol. 145.

28 Memorandum from the Director of Immigration to the Deputy Minister, 14 January 1955, Re: A Review of Immigration from the British West Indies. In RG 26 Vol. 124, File 3–33–6 Part 1.

29 Memorandum from C.N.G. to the Chief, Admissions Division, Re: Entry of Students – Student Nurses and Student Nurses' Aides, 10 October 1958. In RG 76, Vol. 847, File 553–110 Part 1.

30 Memorandum from the Acting Director of Immigration to the Deputy Minister, Re: Request for continuation of domestic quota and institution of a quota for nurses' aides from British Guiana, 10 April 1959. In RG 76, Vol. 847, File 553–110 Part 2.

31 Memorandum from the Chief, Admissions Division, to the Chief of Operations, Re: West Indian Mental Nurses, 6 March 1961. In RG 76, Vol. 847, File 553–110 Part 2.

32 Appendix "A" To Chapter 3 "Canadian Immigration Policy and Objectives," Immigration Manual. Amend. No. 2494 from 13.5.1963. In RG 76, Vol. 932, Binder 3.

33 Immigration Manual, "Admissibility under Section 31(a) of the Regulations," Amendment #2152 from 13.3.1962. In RG 76, Vol. 933, Binder 4.

34 Ibid.

35 Order-In-Council P.C. 1967–1616 of 16th August, 1967. Schedule A – Norms of Assessment of Independent Applicants.

36 Letter from the Deputy Minister to the Hon. John R. Nicholson, 30 August 1965. In RG 76, Vol. 723, File 551–25–2 Part 1. See also the following on the direct link between "unskilled" immigration from the British West Indies and "racial riots" in the United Kingdom: Memorandum from the Assistant Deputy Minister to the Deputy Minister, Re: Future Immigration

From West Indian Federation and Outside Colonies in the Caribbean
Areas, 15 September 1958. In RG 26, Vol. 124, File 3–33–6 Part 2.

37 Memorandum from the Assistant Deputy Minister to the Deputy Minister,
Re: Future Immigration from West Indian Federation and Outside Colonies
in the Caribbean Areas, 15 September 1958. In RG 26, Vol. 124, File 3–33–6
Part 1.

38 Memorandum from the Director of Immigration to the Deputy Minister,
Re: A Review of Immigration from the British West Indies, 14 January 1955.
In RG 26, Vol. 124, File 3–33–6 Part 1.

39 Letter from the Deputy Minister to the Hon. John R. Nicholson, 30 August
1965. In RG 76, Vol. 723, File 551–25–2 Part 1.

40 Memorandum from the Minister to the Assistant to the Deputy Minister,
24 May 1960. In RG 26, Vol. 133, File 3–35–2 Part 8.

41 Letter from the Deputy Minister to C. Willis George, Ottawa
Representative, Canadian Manufacturers' Association, 18 October 1965. In
RG 26, Vol. 128, File 3–33–19 Part 2. The quotations relating to Japan being
a "well-developed society" with a high "level of education" are taken
from the internal report entitled Immigration from Japan, Immigration
Branch, June 1964, in the same file.

42 Report entitled Immigration from Japan, Immigration Branch, June 1964.
In RG 26, Vol. 128, File 3–33–19 Part 2.

43 See, for example: (1) Letter from the Deputy Minister to the Head of
the Commonwealth Division of the Department of External Affairs,
23 November 1961. In RG 26, Vol. 131, File 3–33–35 Part 3; (2) Notes on
Canadian Immigration Policy, Deputy Minister's Copy, Revised January
1961. In RG 26, Vol. 133, File 3–35–2 Part 8; and (3) Draft memorandum
from the Deputy Minister to the Minister, Re: Immigration White Paper –
Submissions to Cabinet on Sponsorship and Immigration Appeals,
24 August 1965. In RG 76, Vol. 723, File 551–25–2 Part 1.

44 Memorandum from the Assistant Deputy Minister to the Deputy Minister,
Re: Future Immigration from West Indian Federation and Outside Colonies
in the Caribbean Areas, 15 September 1958. In RG 26, Vol. 124, File 3–33–6
Part 2.

45 Definition taken from the Merriam-Webster dictionary (website). Accessed
30 January 2016. http://www.merriam-webster.com/dictionary/caliber.

46 Memorandum from the Officer-in-Charge, New Delhi, India, to the
Director of Overseas, Re: Immigration from India & Area Offices, 19 April
1965. In RG 76, Vol. 823, File 552–1–567 Part 2.

47 Memorandum from the Immigration Attaché, New Delhi, India, to the
Acting Chief of Operations (Administrative Services), Re: Monthly
Operational Report – July 1963, 3 October 1963. In RG 76, Vol. 823,
File 552-1-567 Part 2.

48 Memorandum from the Officer-in-charge, New Delhi, India, to the Director of Overseas, Re: Immigration from India & Area Offices, 19 April 1965. In RG 76, Vol. 823, File 552–1-567 Part 2.

49 Memorandum from the Director of Immigration to the Deputy Minister, Re: Immigration from the West Indies, 12 September 1958. In RG 26, Vol. 124, File 3–33–6 Part 2.

50 Memorandum from the Acting Officer in Charge, Toronto, to the Central District Superintendent, re: Nurses from the British West Indies, 24 February 1956. In RG 76, Vol. 847, File 553–110 Part 1.

51 Ibid.

52 Memorandum from the Director of Immigration Branch to the Deputy Minister, Re: Proposed Admission – Coloured Telephone Operators, 18 December 1956. In RG 26, Vol. 123, File 3–32–24.

53 Memorandum from the Deputy Minister to the Director of Immigration, 29 August 1961. In RG 26, Vol. 124, File 3–33–6 Part 2.

54 See chapter 3 for an overview of this work.

5 Putting the "Class" in "Family Class"

1 As Gaucher (2018, 55) points out, the fact that the polygamous community of Bountiful, BC, existed without legal intervention from the Canadian state for almost fifty years shows that the Canadian state was "relatively lax on the issue of polygamy" until it was turned into an immigration-related issue in the mid-2000s.

2 All quoted terms and passages here are taken from Order-in-Council P.C. 1954–973 of 30 June 1954. In: RG 26, Vol. 98, File 3–15–1, Part 4.

3 First Immigration Manual, Amendment # 3299, 13.5.1966. In RG 76, Vol. 933, Binder 5.

4 First Immigration Manual, Amendment # 328, 20.11.1954. In RG 76, Vol. 933, Binder 4.

5 First Immigration Manual, Section 4.65 Literacy Tests for Immigrants, version from 18.2.1954. In RG76, Vol. 933, Binder 4.

6 On Chinese fiancé(e)s, see the Confidential Memorandum from the Acting Director of Immigration to the Minister, Re: Chinese Immigration, 25 February 1963. In RG 26, Vol. 125, File 3–33–7 Part 3. On Japanese fiancé(e)s, see the Operational Memorandum from the Acting Chief, Operations Division, to the five Canadian District Superintendents and all overseas offices, Re: Admission of Japanese fiancées, 27 March 1957. In RG 26, Vol. 128, File 3–33–19 Part 1.

7 Memorandum from the Chief, Admissions Division, to the Director of Immigration, Re: Chinese and Japanese Fiancées. 17 April 1958. In RG 26, Vol. 128, File 3–33–19 Part 2.

8 Ibid.

9 Operational Memorandum from the Acting Chief, Operations Division, to District Superintendents & Overseas Offices, Re: Admission of Japanese Fiancées, 27 March 1957. In RG 26 Vol. 128, File 3–33–19 Part 1.

10 Memorandum from the Deputy Minister to the Director of Immigration, 3.3.1954. In RG 26, Vol. 120, File 3–26–1 Part 1.

11 The Canadian Welfare Council, Report on Refugee Adoption Program, 27.10.1961. In RG 26, Vol. 120, File 3–26–1 Part 2.

12 Letter from the Deputy Minister to Dr. J.F. McInerney, Fredericton Medical Clinic, 21.8.1961. In RG 26, Vol. 120, File 3–26–1 Part 2.

13 Although Lipsky ([1980] 2010) makes this point in reference to low-level (or "street-level") bureaucrats, I propose that high-level bureaucrats who are also case processors make use of such routines as well.

14 Memorandum from the Director of Immigration to the Deputy Minister, Re: Mr. T. and wife, Vancouver, desire the admission from Japan for adoption in Canada of two children, whose parents are living in Japan, 19 May 1961. In RG 26, Vol. 120, File 3–26–1 Part 2.

15 Memorandum from the Director of Immigration to the Deputy Minister, Re: Proposed admission of "semi-orphan" children for adoption, 29.9.1961. In RG 26, Vol. 120, File 3–26–1 Part 2.

16 Confidential Memorandum from the Acting Deputy Minister to the Minister, Re: Admission of child for adoption by Mr. and Mrs. W., 21.6.1963. In RG 26, Vol. 120, File 3-26-1, Part 3.

17 Letter from the Deputy Minister to the Hon. G.E. Halpenny, M.P., Minister without Portfolio, Ottawa, 28.11.1961. Memorandum from the Deputy Minister to the Minister, Re: Orphan Refugee Children, 22.8.1961. Both in RG 26, Vol. 120, File 3–26–1 Part 2.

18 Memorandum from the Director of Immigration, C.E.S. Smith, to the Deputy Minister of Immigration, Laval Fortier, Re: Application of Mr. and Mrs. P., Victoria, B.C., for the admission of two Chinese children for adoption, 18.12.1959. In RG 26, Vol. 120, File 3–26–1 Part 2.

19 Memorandum from the Deputy Minister to the Minister, 23.11.1960. In RG 26, Vol. 120, File 3–26–1 Part 2.

20 Memorandum from the Director of Immigration to the Minister, Re: [child's name], 24.10.1962. In RG 26, Vol. 120, File 3–26–1 Part 3.

21 Memorandum from the Acting Director of Immigration to the Acting Deputy Minister, Subj: [three children] – Admission for Adoption, 6.6.1963. In RG 26, Vol. 120, 3–26–1 Part 3.

22 Memorandum from the Acting Director of Immigration to the Deputy Minister, Subj: [child], age 9 months, citizen of Korea, being adopted by [adoptive parents], Canadian Missionaries in Korea, 3.2.1960. Memorandum from the Deputy Minister to the Director of Immigration, 3.3.1954. In RG 26 Vol. 120, File 3–26–1 Part 2 and Part 1, respectively.

23 Memorandum from the Deputy Minister to the Minister, Re: Proposed Ministerial Visit to Hong Kong – The Hong Kong Government's approach to the problems of Chinese migration, 2.3.1964. In RG 26, Vol. 126, File 3–33–7 Part 4.

24 Letter from the Deputy Minister to Dr. J.F. McInerney, Fredericton Medical Clinic, 21.8.1961. In RG 26, Vol., 120, File 3–26–1 Part 2.

25 Memorandum from the Director of Immigration to Deputy Minister Fortier, Re: Application of Mr. And Mrs. P., Victoria, B.C. for the admission of two Chinese children for adoption, 19.12.1959, stamped "Approved" on 22.12.1959. In RG 26, Vol. 120, File 3–36–1 Part 3.

26 Memorandum from the Deputy Minister to the Minister, 2 July 1964. In RG 26, Vol. 126, File 3–33–7 Part 4.

27 Memorandum from the Acting Deputy Minister to the Minister, 23.10.1963. In RG 26, Vol. 120, File 3–26–1 Part 3.

28 Confidential memorandum from the Acting Deputy Minister to the Minister, 3.4.1963. In RG 26, Vol. 120, File 3–26–1 Part 3.

29 Memorandum from the Director of Immigration to Deputy Minister Fortier, Re: Application of Mr. And Mrs. P., Victoria, B.C. for the admission of two Chinese children for adoption, 19.12.1959, stamped "Approved" on 22.12.1959. In RG 26, Vol. 120, File 3–36–1 Part 3.

30 Memorandum from the Acting Deputy Minister to the Minister, 4.7.1963. In RG 26, Vol. 120, File 3–26–1 Part 3.

31 Confidential memorandum from the Acting Deputy Minister to the Minister, 3.4.1963. In RG 26, Vol. 120, File 3–26–1 Part 3.

32 Memorandum from the Director of Immigration to the Deputy Minister, Re: Mr. and Mrs. S., Manitoba, desire the admission from Hong Kong of an orphaned niece, aged 8, 21.5.1959. In RG 26, Vol. 120, File 3–26–1 Part 2.

33 First Immigration Manual, Amendment # 1319 from 27.7.1959. In RG 76, Vol. 933, Binder 4.

34 Letter from J.S. Cross, Executive Assistant to A. Fraser, Executive Assistant to the Leader of the Opposition, The Senate, 4.11.1959. In RG 26, Vol. 120, File 3–26–1, Part 2.

35 First Immigration Manual, Amendment # 2190, 6.4.1962, In RG 76, Vol. 933, Binder 5.

36 Ibid.

37 Memorandum from the Acting Director of Immigration to the Deputy Minister, Re: Admission of Orphan Refugee Children, 20 July 1960. In RG 26, Vol. 120, File 3–26–1 Part 2.

38 Ibid.

39 Memorandum from the Director of Immigration to the Deputy Minister Re: Adoption of orphan refugee children, 29.9.1961. In RG 26, Vol. 120 3–26–1 Part 2.

40 Letter from Minister Fairclough to Miss. J. LaMarsh, M.P., House of Commons, 14.11.1961. In RG 26, Vol. 120, File 3-26-1 Part 2.

41 Confidential Memorandum from the Acting Deputy Minister to the Minister, 3.4.1963. In RG 26, Vol. 120, File 3–36–1 Part 3.

42 All references in this paragraph are taken from the Confidential Memorandum from the Acting Deputy Minister to the Minister, 3.4.1963. In RG 26, Vol. 120, File 3–36–1 Part 3.

43 Confidential memorandum from the Acting Deputy Minister to the Minister, 3 April 1963. In RG 26, Vol. 120, File 3–36–1 Part 3.

44 Ibid.

45 P.C. 1967–1616 from 16 August 1967. Canada Gazette No. 1350, FOR/67–434, 13.9.1967.

46 Letter from Harris to the Parliamentary Assistant to the Minister of Veterans Affairs, 28 February 1953. In RG 26, Vol. 120, File 3–26–1 Part 1.

47 Memorandum from the Deputy Minister to the Director of Immigration, 3 March 1954. In RG 26, Vol. 120, File 3–26–1 Part 1.

48 Letter from Executive Assistant Cross to Rev. and Mrs. I., the Canadian Mission, Pusan, Korea, 28.5.1959. In RG 26, Vol. File 3–26–1 Part 2.

49 Memorandum from the Director of Immigration to the Deputy Minister, Re: Mr. and Mrs. S., Manitoba, Re: Desire for the Admission from Hong Kong of an orphaned niece, aged 8, 21 May 1959. Handwritten at the bottom: "Approved 22.5.59 L.F. [Deputy Minister Laval Fortier]. In RG 26, Vol. 120, File 3–26–1 Part 2.

50 Memorandum from the Director of Immigration to the Deputy Minister, Re: Mr. W. and his wife, application for admission of Chinese child for adoption, 24 March 1959. Handwritten at the bottom: "Approved 1 April 1959." In RG 26, Vol. 120, File 3–26–1 Part 2.

51 Memorandum from the Acting Director of Immigration to the Deputy Minister, Re: Admission for adoption, 15 August 1963. Handwritten decision in the margins: "I concur [with the recommendation to approve the application]." In RG 26, Vol. 120, File 3–36–1 Part 3.

52 Memorandum from the Director of Immigration to the Deputy Minister, Re: Increase in Domestic Servant Movement from the West Indies, 19 May 1960. In RG 26, Vol. 124, File 3–33–6 Part 2.

53 Memorandum from the Asian Section to the Chief, Admission Division, Re: Canada-India Agreement, 10 March 1961. In RG 76, Vol. 823, File 552-1-567 Part 2.

54 Confidential Minutes of the Cabinet Committee on Immigration Policy meeting, 25 November 1965.

55 See, for example, Confidential Draft Immigration White Paper, Project No. 2: Sponsorship of Relatives, 17 March 1965. In RG 76, Vol. 723, File 551–25–2 Part 1.

56 Secret Working Paper – Sponsored Immigration to Canada, 19 August 1965. In RG 76, Vol. 723, File 551–25–2 Part 1.

57 See also Iacovetta (1991), Hawkins (1988), and Kelly and Trebilcock (2010) for broad discussions of the issue of sponsored family immigrants from Italy.
58 Memorandum from the Minister to Cabinet, Immigration to Canada 1958, 6 November 1957. In RG 26, Vol. 133, File 3–35–2.
59 See, for example, (1) Confidential Memorandum from the Deputy General Executive Assistant to the Director of Immigration, Re: East Indian Immigration, 17 November 1961; (2) Notes on Immigration Policy, n.d. (approx. 1962). In RG 26, Vol. 133, File 3–35–2 Part 8; and (3) Confidential minutes of the Cabinet Committee on Immigration Policy meeting, 25 November 1965. In RG 76, Vol. 723, File 551–25–2 Part 1.
60 Confidential minutes of the meeting of the Ad Hoc Committee on Immigration, held on 26 October 1965, 9 November 1964. In RG 26, Vol. 164, File 3–18–1 Part 3.
61 Confidential Report from the Acting Director of Immigration to the Acting Deputy Minister, Re: Comments on Inspection Services' Report, 8 February 1963. In RG 26, Vol. 131, File 3–33–35.
62 Operations Directive No. 46 (Rev.), Re: Form 55 Procedure, 28 May 1952. In RG 26, Vol. 104, File 3–22–1.
63 Annexure II – "Volume and Growth Potential of Sponsored Immigration." Confidential Memorandum to Cabinet, "Immigration White Paper – Sponsored Immigration to Canada," Cabinet Document 561–65, 24 November 1965. In RG 76, Vol. 723 File 551–25–2 Part 1.
64 Operations Memorandum from the Acting Chief, Operations Division, to the District Superintendents and all posts abroad, Re: Priorities for sponsored close relatives, 22 July 1957. In RG 26, Vol. 133, File 3–35–2.
65 Confidential memorandum from the Deputy Minister to the Minister, 4 April 1960. In RG 26, Vol. 133, 3–35–2 Part 8.
66 Annexure VI – "Non-Dependents in the Sponsored movement." Confidential memorandum to Cabinet, "Immigration White Paper – Sponsored Immigration to Canada," Cabinet Document 561–65, 24 November 1965. In RG 76, Vol. 723 File 551–25–2 Part 1.
67 See, for example, Secret Working Paper – Sponsored Immigration to Canada, 19 August 1965. In RG 76, Vol. 723, File 551–25–2 Part 1.
68 See, for example, Memorandum for file, J.L. Manion, Re: White Paper, 22 November 1965. In RG 76, Vol. 723, File 551–25–2 Part 1.
69 Draft Immigration White Paper, Project 2: Sponsorship, n.d. In RG 26, Vol. 723, File 551–25–2 Part 1.
70 Ibid.
71 Letter from the Minister to the Hon. Roland Michener, P.C., Q.C., Toronto, 8 February 1963. In RG 26, Vol. 125, file 3–33–7 Part 3.
72 Confidential minutes of the meeting of the Ad Hoc Committee on Immigration on 26 October, dated 9 November 1964. In RG 26, Vol. 164, File 3–18–1 Part 3.

73 Confidential revised draft – Immigration White Paper, Project No. 2 Sponsored Immigration, 18 November 1965. In RG 76, Vol. 723, File 551–25–2 Part 1.

74 Secret working paper No. 2 – Sponsored Immigration to Canada, 20 August 1965. In RG 76, Vol. 723, File 551–25–2 Part 1.

75 Memorandum from Tom Kent to the Assistant Deputy Minister, Canada Immigration Division, "Verbalization" of the proposed new selection process approved by the Minister, 10 March 1967. In RG 26, Vol. 104, File 3–18–2 Part 2

76 Ibid.

77 The 1955 IMM 1000 form had three spaces dedicated to funds: transferred to Canada, in your possession, to be transferred later. See copy in RG 26, Vol. 104, File 3–22–1. Also, the application form for nominated relatives in 1964 had single spaces allotted for noting occupation, yearly income and other sources of income. See memorandum from the Deputy Minister to the Minister Re: Procedures in Hong Kong, 19 March 1964. In RG 26, Vol. 126, File 3–33–7 Part 4.

78 Operations Memorandum to All Holders of Immigration Manual No. 33 (Revised), Re: Processing of sponsored applications, Amend. No. 3233, 21 January 1966. In RG 76, Vol. 723, File 551-25-2 Part 2.

79 Ibid.

80 Income here includes the net income of both spouses (wages, family allowances, other fixed income) plus one-sixtieth of all liquid assets, for example, bank account, stock, bonds, equity in home, car, business, and so on. Operations Memorandum to All Holders of Immigration Manual No. 33 (Revised), Re: Processing of sponsored applications, Amend. No. 3233, 21 January 1966. In RG 76, Vol. 723, File 551-25-2 Part 2.

81 Memorandum from Tom Kent to the Assistant Deputy Minister, Canada Immigration Division, "Verbalization" of the proposed new selection process approved by the Minister, 10 March 1967. In RG 26, Vol. 104, File 3–18–2 Part 2.

82 Immigration Regulations P.C. 1953–859 of 26 May 1953. In RG 26, Vol. 98, File 3–15–1 Part 4.

83 Confidential minutes of the Cabinet Committee on Immigration Policy meeting, 25 November 1965. In RG 76, Vol. 723, File 551–25–2 Part 1.

84 See chapter 2 for details on the nationally defined admissions categories created by P.C. 1956–783.

85 According to Doerr (1982), the practice of issuing white papers became popular under Prime Minister Pearson (1963–8). A white paper is "a document which provides information on what the government is doing or intends to do on a policy matter" (367). They are approved by Cabinet, tabled in the House of Commons, then normally referred to parliamentary

committees for review and engagement with interested groups. The process gives the government the opportunity to define a policy situation in line with its own interests and make the case for its preferred solutions. At the same time, it gives elected representative an opportunity to scrutinize and criticize government policy. Doerr argues that the rise in the use of white papers, especially after the election of the Pierre Trudeau administration in 1968, was due to an increased interest in the "application of rational and systematic planning systems within government [whereby] white papers were considered as integral components of long-range planning exercises directed to improving government decision-making and to facilitating policy reviews" (369).

86 In 1966, Prime Minister Pearson merged the Department of Citizenship and Immigration with the Department of Labour, in a move that Triadafilopoulos (2012, 98) argues signalled intent to manage immigration "in a more technocratic manner."

87 See the discussion in chapter 2 of macro-level and meso-level pressures to universalize Canada's immigration policy.

88 The backlash was also fuelled by public dissatisfaction as expressed in media and submissions from organizations to the Special Joint Committee of the Senate and the House of Commons that was appointed in 1966 to examine the document (Hawkins 1988; Triadafilopoulos 2012).

89 Pressure for this change emerged during consultations on the White Paper as well as from a report by Joseph Sedgwick, a Toronto lawyer who had conducted an inquiry into the Department's discretionary practices (see, e.g., Kelley and Trebilcock 2010, 349–54).

90 See chapter 1 for an overview of this debate.

6 Conclusion

1 Memorandum from the Deputy Minister to the Director of Immigration, 29 August 1961. In RG 26, Vol. 124, File 3–33–6 Part 2.

2 Memorandum from the Minister to the Assistant to the Deputy Minister, 24 May 1960. In RG 26, Vol. 133, File 3–35–2 Part 8.

3 Comparative work by Hawkins (1991) on Canada and Australia shows that Australia's 1958 Migration Act gave similarly vast discretionary powers over admission and deportation to high-level immigration bureaucrats. Additionally, Ellermann (2021) notes that the central role of the executive in policy formulation in Canada is partly a function of its Westminster-style of government. Since Australia shares this system, it could be a particularly useful comparative case.

4 Confidential memorandum to Cabinet, Re: Immigration Policy and Programme, 14 January 1964. In RG 76, Vol. 948, File SF-C-1–1 Part 3.

5 Appendix A "Demand for Unskilled," Confidential Draft Immigration White Paper, Project No. 2 Sponsored Immigration, Revised 18 November 1965. In RG 76, Vol. 723, File 551–25–2 Part 1.

6 Annexure IV. Confidential memorandum to Cabinet, "Immigration White Paper – Sponsored Immigration to Canada," Cabinet Document 561–65, 24 November 1965. In RG 76, Vol. 723 File 551–25–2 Part 1.

7 The category of nominated relatives comprised relations beyond the nuclear family, including siblings, children over the age of twenty-one, parents, grandparents under the age of sixty, nieces and nephews, uncles and aunts, and grandchildren. See chapter 5 for an extended discussion of this category and its emergence.

8 Based on a qualitative content analysis of documents in RG 26, Vol. 89.

9 Citizenship and Immigration Canada, "Determine your eligibility – Federal skilled workers," accessed 1 November 2015, http://www.cic .gc.ca/english/immigrate/skilled/apply-who.asp.

10 The category of sponsored dependents comprised spouses, fiancé(e)s, unmarried children under the age of twenty-one, adopted children, siblings, nieces/nephews, parents and grandparents over the age of sixty (or under the age of sixty if they were incapable of supporting themselves financially or if they were widowed) as well as additional relatives. See chapter 5 for an extended discussion of this category and its emergence.

11 For a general overview and discussion of neoliberalism see Harvey (2005).

12 Memorandum from Tom Kent to the Assistant Deputy Minister, Canada Immigration Division, "Verbalization" of the proposed new selection process approved by the Minister, 10 March 1967. In RG 26, Vol. 104, File 3–18–2 Part 2.

13 Confidential Revised Draft, Immigration White Paper, Project No. 2 – Sponsored Immigration, 18 November 1965. In RG 76, Vol. 76, file 551–25–2 Part 1.

14 Memorandum from Tom Kent to the Assistant Deputy Minister, Canada Immigration Division, "Verbalization" of the proposed new selection process approved by the Minister, 10 March 1967. In RG 26, Vol. 104, File 3–18–2 Part 2.

15 Draft memorandum from the Assistant Deputy Minister (Immigration) to the Deputy Minister, Re: Minor Improvements in White Paper, March 1967. In RG 76, Vol. 76, file 551–25–2 Part 2.

16 Secret Working Paper No. 2 – Sponsored Immigration to Canada, 20 August 1965. In RG 76, Vol. 76, file 551–25–2 Part 1.

17 Ibid.

18 Draft Memorandum from the Assistant Deputy Minister (Immigration) to the Deputy Minister, Re: Minor Improvements in White Paper, March 1967. In RG 76, Vol. 76, file 551–25–2 Part 2.

19 Ibid.

20 Ibid.
21 First Immigration Manual, Chapter 24, "The Immigration Selection System." Amendment #4408, 19.1.1970. In RG 76, Vol. 938, Binder 19.
22 Ibid.
23 Operations Memorandum to All Holders of Immigration Manual, No. 33 (Revised), Re: Processing of sponsored applications, Amend. No. 3233, 21 January 1966. In RG 76, Vol. 723, File 551–25–2 Part 2.
24 See numerous pieces of correspondence between the federal government and the provinces throughout the 1950s, including, for example, Memorandum from Central District Superintendent, Toronto, to the Director of Immigration, Attn: Chief, Settlement Division, Re: Co-operation in exchange of information with Provincial officials, 4 December 1953. In RG 26, Vol. 134, File 3–36–1.
25 Memorandum from the Assistant Deputy Minister (Immigration) to the Canadian Service Directorate, Special Services Directorate, Policy and Planning Directorate, Support Services Directorate, Overseas Service Directorate, Re: Selection Criteria for Unsponsored Immigrants – Regulation 31(a)(ii), 18 March 1966. In RG 76, Vol. 723, File 551–25–2 Part 2.
26 The extent to which entry categories matter, over and above the attributes of individuals within them, is subject to debate. Comparing mainly the Federal Skilled Worker Program (FSWP) and Family Class (FC), Hum and Simpson (2002), Mata and Pendakur (2017), and Warman, Webb, and Worswick (2019) note similar economic outcomes to the ones described here, especially the superior economic performance of workers under the FSWP. Often, this superior performance is attributed to the higher levels of education and other human capital measures possessed by immigrants under that category that result from greater selectivity in the admissions process (see, e.g., Hum and Simpson 2002). Other scholars have argued that being in one entry category or another has an effect that cannot be reduced to human capital attributes (see, e.g., Elrick and Lightman 2016; Banerjee and Phan 2015; Lightman et al. 2021).
27 The study's novelty is that it compares and contrasts a more diverse range of entry categories than are usually included in a single analysis. Some of these categories offer immediate access to permanent resident status, giving immigrants a high degree of legal security as well as access to settlement services (e.g., FSWP, FC). Others make permanent resident status contingent on a period of employment in Canada (e.g., CEC and LIC). Those so-called two-step entry categories place immigrants in a precarious legal position at first and delay access to settlement services until permanent resident status is achieved. Both of those things can impact employment and income. Neither the LIC nor the categories for spouses/partners are usually treated as skilled worker pathways. Their inclusion here reflects the authors' efforts to foreground intersectional

selection effects, as skilled women (racialized skilled women, in the case of the LIC) are over-represented in them. The entry categories examined in the study are the ones that were in place for most of the time period covered. Readers should note that the LIC was replaced in 2014 by the "Caregiver Program," which removed the live-in component. It also placed new caps on the number of caregivers who could gain permanent residency each year (Banerjee et al. 2018). The FSWP and CEC categories came under the umbrella of the Express Entry program in 2015.

28 See also Banerjee et al. (2018) on the long-term economic disadvantages faced by racialized women who have entered as live-in caregivers. Interestingly, Lightman et al. (2021) argue that the strong concentration of Filipina women in the care work sector under the LIC may have knock-on effects for Filipina women who enter under the FSWP. The authors propose that the relatively poor economic returns to Filipina workers under the FSWP, compared to comparably skilled women from other origins, may be due to the stigmatizing effect of Filipinas having become associated with low-paid care work over time.

29 Minutes of the meetings with Provincial representatives – Maritime Provinces, 10 June 1953. In RG 26, Vol. 134, File 3–36–1.

30 Cabinet Document 142–58, 10 May 1958. In RG 2, Vol2741, File C-20–5.

31 First Immigration Manual, Amendment #24–44, 1.3.1971. In RG 26, Vol. 938, Chapter 24, Appendix "B."

32 See Bilodeau et al. (2019) for contradictory evidence. However, the authors admit that "it is difficult to account for the discrepancy between our findings and those of prior research" (6).

33 See Bonjour and Duyvendak (2018) and others for a discussion of this stance on receiving-society values in "civic integration" programs in Europe since the 1990s.

Methodological Appendix

1 Toronto lawyer Joseph Sedgewick was commissioned by the Canadian government to investigate and report on ministerial discretion in the immigration process and other issues in the mid-1960s (see Kelley and Trebilcock 2010, 367–8).

2 Confidential minutes of the Cabinet Committee on Immigration Policy meeting, 25 November 1965. In RG 76, Vol. 723, File 551–25–2 Part 1.

3 Secret Working Paper No. 2 Sponsored Immigration to Canada, 20 August 1965. In RG 76, Vol. 723, File 551–25–2 Part 1.

4 Preface, Instructions for the Guidance of Immigration and Visa Officers. In RG 76, Vol. 932, Binder 1.

5 First Immigration Manual, version from 18.2.1954. In RG 76, Vol. 933, Binder 4.

Bibliography

Abella, Irving, and Harold Troper. 1991. *None Is Too Many: Canada and the Jews of Europe, 1933–1948*. Toronto: Lester Publishing.

Abu-Laban, Yasmeen. 1998a. "Keeping 'Em Out: Gender, Race, and Class Biases in Canadian Immigration Policy." In *Painting the Maple: Essays on Race, Gender, and the Construction of Canada*, edited by Veronica Strong-Boag, Sherrill E. Grace, Joan Anderson, and Avigail Eisenberg, 69–82. Vancouver: UBC Press.

– 1998b. "Welcome/STAY OUT: The Contradiction of Canadian Integration and Immigration Policies at the Millenium." *Canadian Ethnic Studies* 30 (3): 190–213.

Adams, Julia, and Tasleem Padamsee. 2001. "Signs and Regimes: Rereading Feminist Work on Welfare States." *Social Politics* 8 (1): 1–23. https://doi.org/10.1093/sp/8.1.1.

Aiken, Sharryn. 2007. "From Slavery to Expulsion: Racism, Canadian Immigration Law, and the Unfilled Promise of Modern Constitutionalism." In *Interrogating Race and Racism*, edited by Vijay Agnew, 55–111. Toronto: University of Toronto Press.

Alboim, Naomi, and Karen Cohl. 2012. *Shaping the Future: Canada's Rapidly Changing Immigration Policies*. Toronto: The Maytree Foundation. http://maytree.com/wp-content/uploads/2012/10/shaping-the-future.pdf.

Alpes, Maybritt Jill, and Alexis Spire. 2014. "Dealing with Law in Migration Control: The Powers of Street-Level Bureaucrats at French Consulates." *Social & Legal Studies* 23 (2): 261–74. doi: 10.1177/0964663913510927.

Anderson, Benedict. 1991. *Imagined Communities: Reflections on the Origin and Spread of Nationalism*. London: Verso.

Anderson, Bridget. 2013. *Us and Them? The Dangerous Politics of Immigration Control*. Oxford: Oxford University Press.

Anderson, Kay. 1995. *Vancouver's Chinatown: Racial Discourse in Canada, 1975–1980*. Montreal: McGill-Queen's University Press.

Anthias, Floya, and Nira Yuval-Davis. 1992. *Racialized Boundaries: Race, Nation, Gender, Colour, and Class and the Anti-Racist Struggle*. New York: Routledge.

Bail, Christopher A. 2008. "The Configuration of Symbolic Boundaries against Immigrants in Europe." *American Sociological Review* 73: 37–59. doi: 10.1177/000312240807300103.

Bakan, Abigail, and Daiva Stasiulis. 2012. "The Political Economy of Migrant Live-In Caregivers: A Case of Unfree Labour?" In *Legislated Inequality: Temporary Labour Migration in Canada*, edited by Patti Lenard and Christine Straehle, 202–26. Montreal: McGill-Queen's University Press.

Banerjee, Pallavi. 2019. "Subversive Self-Employment: Intersectionality and Self-Employment among Dependent Visas Holders in the United States." *American Behavioral Scientist* 63 (2): 186–207. doi: 10.1177/0002764218793685.

Banerjee, Rupa, and Mai Phan. 2015. "Do Tied Movers Get Tied Down? The Occupational Displacement of Dependent Applicant Immigrants in Canada." *Journal of International Migration and Integration* 16 (2): 333–53. https://link.springer.com/content/pdf/10.1007/s12134-014-0341-9.pdf.

Banerjee, Rupa, Philip Kelly, Ethel Tungohan, Petronila Cleto, Conely de Leon, Mila Garcia, Marco Luciano, Cynthia Palmaria, and Chris Sorio. 2018. "From 'Migrant' to 'Citizen': Labor Market Integration of Former Live-In Caregivers in Canada." *International Labour Review* 71 (4): 908–36. https://doi.org/10.1177/0019793918758301

Banton, Michael. 1977. *The Idea of Race*. London: Tavistock.

Bassel, Leah. 2010. "Intersectional Politics at the Boundaries of the Nation State." *Ethnicities* 10 (2): 155–80. doi: 10.1177/1468796810361818.

Bauder, Harald. 2011. *Immigration Dialectic: Imagining Community, Economy, and Nation*. Toronto: University of Toronto Press.

Baumgartner, Frank. 2014. "Ideas, Paradigms and Confusions." *Journal of European Public Policy* 21: 475–80. doi: 10.1080/13501763.2013.876180.

Beaman, Jean. 2017. *Citizen Outsider: Children of North African Immigrants in France*. Oakland: University of California Press.

Becker, Howard S. 1953. "Becoming a Marihuana User." *American Journal of Sociology* 59 (3): 235–42.

Béland, Daniel. 2009. "Ideas, Institutions, and Policy Change." *Journal of European Public Policy* 16: 701–18. doi: 10.1080/13501760902983382.

Bell, Daniel. 1972. "On Meriocracy and Equality." *The Public Interest* 29: 29–68. https://www.nationalaffairs.com/public_interest/detail/on-meritocracy-and-equality.

Berman, Sheri. 2013. "Ideational Theorizing in the Social Sciences since 'Policy Paradigms, Social Learning and the State." *Governance: An International Journal of Policy, Administration, and Institutions* 26: 217–37. doi: 10.1111/gove.12008.

Bhabha, Jacqueline. 2006. "Border Rights and Rites: Generalizations, Steretypes and Gendered Migration." In *Women and Immigration Law: New Variations on Classical Feminist Themes*, edited by Sarah van Walsum and T. Spijkerboer, 15–34. New York: Routledge-Cavendish.

Bilodeau, Antoine, Stephen White, Luc Turgeon, and Ailsa Henderson. 2019. "Feeling Attached and Feeling Accepted: Implications for Political Inclusion among Visible Minority Immigrants in Canada." *International Migration* Online first: 1–17. doi: 10.1111/imig.12657.

Bleich, Erik. 2003. *Race Politics in Britain and France: Ideas and Policymaking since the 1960s*. Cambridge: Cambridge University Press.

Blinder, Scott. 2015. "Imagined Immigration: The Impact of Different Meanings of 'Immigrants' in Public Opinion and Policy Debates in Britain." *Political Studies* 63: 80–100. doi: 10.1111/1467-9248.12053.

Block, Laura. 2015. "Regulating Membership: Explaining Restriction and Stratification of Family Migration in Europe." *Journal of Family Issues* 36 (11): 1433–52. doi: 10.1177/0192513X14557493.

Bloemraad, Irene. 2006. *Becoming a Citizen: Incorporating Immigrants and Refugees in the United States and Canada*. Oakland: University of California Press.

– 2015. "Re-Imagining the Nation in a World of Migration: Legitimacy, Political Claims-Making and Membership in Comparative Perspective." In *Fear and Anxiety over National Identity*, edited by Nancy Foner and Patrick Simon, 59–82. New York: Russel Sage Foundation.

Bloemraad, Irene, Anna Korteweg, and Gökçe Yurdakul. 2008. "Citizenship and Immigration: Multiculturalism, Assimilation, and Challenges to the Nation-State." *Annual Review of Sociology* 34: 153–79. doi: 10.1146/annurev.soc.34.040507.134608.

Bloemraad, Irene, and Matthew Wright. 2012. "Is There a Trade-Off between Multiculturalism and Socio-Political Integration? Policy Regimes and Immigrant Incroporation in Comparative Perspective." *Perspectives on Politics* 10 (1): 77–95. doi: 10.1017/S1537592711004919.

Blyth, Mark. 2013. "Paradigms and Paradox: The Politics of Economic Ideas in Two Moments of Crisis." *Governance: An International Journal of Policy, Administration, and Institutions* 26: 197–215. doi: 10.1111/gove.12010.

Bonjour, Saskia. 2011. "The Power and Morals of Policy Makers: Reassessing the Control Gap Debate." *International Migration Review* 45 (1): 89–122. doi: 10.1111/j.1747-7379.2010.00840.x.

Bonjour, Saskia, and Betty de Hart. 2013. "A Proper Wife, a Proper Marriage: Constructions of 'Us' and 'Them' in Dutch Family Migration Policy." *European Journal of Women's Studies* 20 (1): 61–76. doi: 10.1177/1350506812456459.

Bonjour, Saskia, and Jan Willem Duyvendak. 2018. "The 'Migrant with Poor Prospects': Racialized Intersections of Class and Culture in Dutch Civic Integration Debates." *Ethnic and Racial Studies* 41 (5): 882–900. doi.org /10.1080/01419870.2017.1339897.

Borjas, George. 1990. *Friends or Strangers: The Impact of Immigrants on the U.S. Economy.* New York: Basic Books.

Borrelli, Lisa Marie. 2021. "The Border Inside: Organizational Socialization of Street-Level Bureaucrats in the European Migration Regime." *Journal of Borderlands Studies* 36 (4): 579–98. doi: 10.1080/08865655.2019.1676815.

Boswell, Christina. 2007. "Theorizing Migration Policy: Is There a Third Way?" *International Migration Review* 41: 75–100. doi: 10.1111/j.1747-7379.2007.00057.x.

– 2009. *The Political Uses of Expert Knowledge: Immigration Policy and Social Research.* Cambridge: Cambridge University Press.

Boswell, Christina, and James Hampshire. 2017. "Ideas and Agency in Immigration Policy: A Discursive Instituionalist Approach." *European Journal of Political Research* 5 (1): 133–50. doi: 10.1111/1475-6765.12170.

Bouchard, Genvieve, and Barbara W. Carroll. 2002. "Policy-Making and Administrative Discretion: The Case of Immigration in Canada." *Canadian Public Administration* 45: 239–57. doi: 10.1111/j.1754-7121.2002.tb01082.x.

Boucher, Anna. 2013. "Bureaucratic Control and Policy Change: A Comparative Venue Shopping Approach to Skilled Immigration Policies in Australia and Canada." *Journal of Comparative Policy Analysis: Research and Practice* 15 (4): 349–67. doi: 10.1080/13876988.2012.749099.

– 2016. *Gender, Migration and the Global Race for Talent.* Manchester: Manchester University Press.

– 2020. "How 'Skill' Definition Affects the Diversity of Skilled Immigration Policies." *Journal of Ethnic and Migration Studies* 46 (12): 2533–50. https://doi .org/10.1080/1369183X.2018.1561063.

Boucher, Anna, and Justin Gest. 2018. *Crossroads: Comparative Immigration Regimes in a World of Demographic Change.* Cambridge: Cambridge University Press.

Bourdieu, Pierre. 1986. "The Forms of Capital." In *Handbook of Theory and Research for the Sociology of Education*, edited by John Richardson, 241–57. New York: Greenwood Press.

– 1994. "Rethinking the State: Genesis and Structure of the Bureaucratic Field." *Sociological Theory* 12 (1): 1–18. doi.org/10.2307/202032.

Boyd, Monica, Gustave Goldmann, and Pamela White. 2000. "Race in the Canadian Census." In *Race and Racism: Canada's Challenge*, edited by Leo Driedger, 33–54. Montreal: McGill-Queen's University Press.

Brubaker, Rogers. 1996. *Nationalism Reframed: Nationhood and the National Question in the New Europe.* New York: Cambridge University Press.

– 2009. "Ethnicity, Race, and Nationalism." *Annual Review of Sociology* 35: 21–42. doi: 10.1146/annurev-soc-070308-115916.

Brubaker, Rogers, and Frederick Cooper. 2000. "Beyond Identity." *Theory and Society* 29: 1–47. doi: 10.1023/A:1007068714468.

Calavita, Kitty. 2010. *Inside the State: The Bracero Program, Immigration, and the I.N.S.* New Orleans: Quid Pro Books.

Calliste, Agnes. 1993. "Women of 'Exceptional Merit': Immigration of Caribbean Nurses to Canada." *Canadian Journal of Women and the Law* 6 (1): 85–102.

Canada, Department of Manpower and Immigration. 1966. White Paper on Immigration. Ottawa.

Carstensen, Martin. 2011. "Ideas Are Not as Stable as Political Scientists Want Them to Be." *Political Studies* 59: 596–615. doi: 10.1111/j.1467-9248.2010.00868.x.

– 2015. "Conceptualizing Ideational Novelty: A Relational Approach." *The British Journal of Politics and International Relations* 17: 284–97. doi: 10.1111/1467-856X.12030.

Cashmore, Ernest. 1978. "The Social Organization of Canadian Immigration Law." *Canadian Journal of Sociology* 3 (4): 409–29. https://doi.org/10.2307/3339774.

CBC. 2014. "Canada Accepting 5,000 Parent, Grandparent Sponsorship Applications." *CBC News*. Last modified 3 January 2014. https://www.cbc.ca/news/politics/canada-accepting-5-000-parent-grandparent-sponsorship-applications-1.2481803.

– 2016. "Canada Will Take in 10,000 Parent, Grandparent Sponsorship Applications this Year." *CBC News*. Last modified 8 January 2016. https://www.cbc.ca/news/politics/canada-will-take-in-10-000-parent-grandparent-sponsorship-applications-this-year-1.3396179.

Chauvin, Sébastien, and Blanca Garcés-Mascareñas. 2014. "Becoming Less Illegal: Deservingness Frames and Undocumented Migrant Incorporation." *Sociology Compass* 8 (4): 422–32. doi: 10.1111/soc4.12145.

Chauvin, Sébastien, Blanca Garcés-Mascareñas, and Albert Kraler. 2013. "Working for Legality: Employment and Migrant Regularization in Europe." *International Migration* 51 (6): 118–31. doi: 10.1111/imig.12109.

Choo, Hae Yeon, and Myra Marx Ferree. 2010. "Practicing Intersectionality in Sociological Research: A Critical Analysis of Inclusions, Interactions, and Institutions in the Study of Inequalities." Sociological Theory 28 (2): 129–49. doi: 10.1111/j.1467-9558.2010.01370.x.

Collins, Patricia Hill. 2015. "Intersectionality's Definitional Dilemmas." *Annual Review of Sociology* 41: 1–20. doi: /10.1146/annurev-soc-073014-112142.

Cooke, Fang Lee. 2007. "'Husband's Career First': Renegotiating Career and Family Commitment among Migrant Chinese Academic Couples in

Britain." *Work, Employment and Society* 21 (1): 47–65. https://doi.org/10.1177
/0950017007073615.

Cook-Martín, David, and David FitzGerald. 2015. "Culling the Masses:
A Rejoinder." *Ethnic and Racial Studies* 38 (8): 1319–27. doi: 10.1080/01419870
.2015.1016076.

Dauvergne, Catherine. 2016. *The New Politics of Immigration and the End of
Settler Societies*. Cambridge: Cambridge University Press.

Delgado, Richard, and Jean Stefancic. 2017. *Critical Race Theory: An
Introduction*. 3rd ed. New York: New York University Press.

Deterding, Nicole, and Mary Waters. 2021. "Flexible Coding of In-Depth
Interviews: A Twenty-First Century Approach." *Sociological Methods &
Research* 50 (2): 708–39. doi: 10.1177/0049124118799377.

Dewey, John. 1988. *Human Nature and Conduct, 1922: The Middle Works of John
Dewey, 1899–1924*. Vol. 14. Carbondale: Southern Illinois University Press.

DiMaggio, Paul. 1997. "Culture and Cognition." *Annual Review of Sociology* 23:
263–87. doi: 10.1146/annurev.soc.23.1.263.

Doerr, Audrey. 1982. "The Role of Coloured Papers." *Canadian Public
Administration/Administration publique du Canada* 25 (3): 366–79. doi: 10.1111
/j.1754-7121.1982.tb02081.x.

Eggebø, Helga. 2013. "A Real Marriage? Applying for Marriage Migration
in Norway." *Journal of Ethnic and Migration Studies* 39 (5): 773–89. doi:
10.1080/1369183X.2013.756678.

Ellermann, Antje. 2006. "Street-Level Democracy: How Immigration
Bureaucrats Manage Public Opinion." *West European Politics* 29 (2): 293–309.
doi: 10.1080/01402380500512627.

– 2009. *States against Migrants: Deportation in Germany and the United States*.
Cambridge: Cambridge University Press.

– 2019. "Human-Capital Citizenship and the Changing Logic of Immigrant
Admissions." *Journal of Ethnic and Migration Studies* 46 (12): 2515–32. doi:
10.1080/1369183X.2018.1561062.

– 2021. *The Comparative Politics of Immigration: Policy Choice in Germany, Canada,
Switzerland, and the United States*. Cambridge: Cambridge University Press.

Elrick, Jennifer. 2017. "Family|Class: Race and Third Order Policy Change in
Post-War Canada." PhD diss., University of Toronto.

– 2020. "Bureaucratic Implementation Practices and the Making of Canada's
Merit-Based Immigration Policy." *Journal of Ethnic and Migration Studies*
Online first. doi: 10.1080/1369183X.2020.1817731.

Elrick, Jennifer, and Naomi Lightman. 2016. "Sorting or Shaping? The
Gendered Economic Outcomes of Immigration Policy in Canada."
International Migration Review 15 (2): 352–84. doi: 10.1111/imre.12110.

Elrick, Jennifer, and Elke Winter. 2018. "Managing the National Status Group:
Immigration Policy in Germany." *International Migration* 56 (4): 19–32. doi:
10.1111/imig.12400.

Emirbayer, Mustafa. 1997. "Manifesto for a Relational Sociology." *American Journal of Sociology* 103: 281–317. https://doi.org/10.1086/231209.

Environics. 2019. "Canadian Public Opinion about Immigration and Refugees." In *Focus Canada – Spring 2019*. Toronto: Environics Institute for Survey Research.

Eule, Tobias G. 2018. "The (Surprising?) Nonchalance of Migration Control Agents." *Journal of Ethnic and Migration Studies* 44 (16): 2780–95. doi: 10.1080/1369183X.2017.1401516.

FitzGerald, David, and David Cook-Martín. 2014. *Culling the Masses: The Democratic Origins of Racist Immigration Policy in the Americas*. Cambridge, MA: Harvard University Press.

FitzGerald, David, David Cook-Martín, Angela Garcia, and Rawan Arar. 2018. "Can You Become One of Us? A Historical Comparison of Legal Selection of 'Assimilable' Immigrants in Europe and the Americas." *Journal of Ethnic and Migration Studies* 44 (1): 27–47. doi: 10.1080/1369183X.2017.1313106.

Fox, Cybelle. 2015. "What Counts as Racist Immigration Policy?" *Ethnic and Racial Studies* 38 (8): 1286–91. doi: 10.1080/01419870.2015.1016069.

Freeman, Gary. 1995. "Modes of Immigration Policies in Liberal Democratic States." *International Migration Review* 24: 881–902. doi: 10.1177/019791839502900401

Friedman, Sara. 2010. "Determining 'Truth' at the Border: Immigration Interviews, Chinese Marital Migrants, and Taiwan's Sovereignty Dilemmas." *Citizenship Studies* 14: 167–83. doi: 10.1080/13621021003594817.

Gabriel, Christina, and Laura MacDonald. 2012. "Debates on Temporary Agricultural Worker Migration in the North American Context." In *Legislated Inequality: Temporary Labour Migration in Canada*, edited by Patti Lenard and Christine Straehle, 95–116. Montreal: McGill-Queen's University Press.

Galabuzi, Grace-Edward. 2006. *Canada's Economic Apartheid: The Social Exclusion of Racialized Groups in the New Century*. Toronto: Canadian Scholars' Press.

Gaucher, Megan. 2018. *A Family Matter: Citizenship, Conjugal Relationships, and Canadian Immigration Policy*. Vancouver: UBC Press.

Gellner, Ernest. 1983. *Nations and Nationalism*. Ithaca, NY: Cornell University Press.

Gilboy, Janet. 1991. "Deciding Who Gets In: Decisionmaking by Immigration Inspectors." *Law and Society Review* 25: 571–600. doi: 10.2307/3053727.

Goldring, Luin, and Patricia Landolt, eds. 2013. *Producing and Negotiating Non-Citizenship: Precarious Legal Status in Canada*. Toronto: Toronto University Press.

Goldstein, Judith, and Robert Keohane. 1993. "Ideas and Foreign Policy: An Analytical Framework." In *Ideas and Foreign Policy: Beliefs, Institutions, and Political Change*, edited by Judith Goldstein and Robert Keohane, 3–30. Ithaca, NY: Cornell University Press.

Gordon, Milton. 1964. *Assimilation in American Life: The Role of Race, Religion, and National Origins*. Oxford: Oxford University Press.

Government of Canada. 2020. "#Immigration Matters: Canada's Immigration Track Record." Last modified 10 August 2020. https://www.canada.ca/en/immigration-refugees-citizenship/campaigns/immigration-matters/track-record.html.

Green, Alan. 1976. *Immigration and the Postwar Canadian Economy*. Toronto: Macmillan Hunter.

Hacking, Ian. 1986. "Making Up People." In *Reconstructing Individualism: Autonomy, Individuality, and the Self in Western Thought*, edited by Thomas Heller, Morton Sosna, and David Wellbery, 222–36. Stanford: Stanford University Press.

Hall, Peter. 1993. "Policy Paradigms, Social Learning, and the State: The Case of Economic Policy Making in Britain." *Comparative Politics* 25: 275–96. doi: 10.2307/422246.

Hall, Peter, and Michèle Lamont. 2013. "Why Social Relations Matter for Politics and Successful Societies." *Annual Review of Political Science* 16: 49–71. doi: 10.1146/annurev-polisci-031710-101143.

Hampshire, James. 2013. *The Politics of Immigration: Contradictions of the Liberal State*. Cambridge: Polity Press.

Hankivsky, Olena, and Julia S. Jordan-Zachery. 2019. "Introduction: Bringing Intersectionality to Public Policy." In *The Palgrave Handbook of Intersectionality in Public Policy*, edited by Olena Hankivsky and Julia S. Jordan-Zachery, 1–28. New York: Palgrave-Macmillan.

Hansen, Randall. 2009. "The Poverty of Postnationalism: Citizenship, Immigration, and the New Europe." *Theory and Society* 38: 1–24. doi: 10.1007/s11186-008-9074-0.

Harvey, David. 2005. *A Brief History of Neoliberalism*. Oxford: Oxford University Press.

Hawkins, Freda. 1988. *Canada and Immigration: Public Policy and Public Concern*. 2nd ed. Montreal: McGill-Queen's University Press.

– 1991. *Critical Years in Immigration: Canada and Australia Compared*. Montreal: McGill-Queen's University Press.

Helbling, Marc, Stephan Simon, and Samuel Schmid. 2020. "Restricting Immigration to Foster Migrant Integration? A Comparative Study across 22 European Countries." *Journal of Ethnic and Migration Studies* 46 (13): 2603–24. doi: 10.1080/1369183X.2020.1727316.

Hollifield, James F. 1992. *Immigrants, Markets, and States*. Cambridge, MA: Harvard University Press.

Hou, Feng, and Garnett Picot. 2020. "The Decline in the Naturalization Rate among Recent Immigrants in Canada: Policy Changes and Other Possible Explanations." *Migration Studies* Online first. doi: 10.1093/migration/mnaa010.

Hum, Derek, and Wayne Simpson. 2002. "Selectivity and Immigration in
   Canada." *Journal of International Migration and Integration* 3(1): 107–27.
   https://link.springer.com/content/pdf/10.1007/s12134-002-1005-8.pdf.
Iacovetta, Franca. 1991. "Ordering in Bulk: Canada's Postwar Immigration
   Policy and the Recruitment of Contract Workers from Italy." *Journal of
   American Ethnic History* 11 (1): 50–80. https://www.jstor.org/stable/27500904.
Immigration, Refugees, and Citizenship Canada (IRCC). 2020. "How Much
   Income Do I Need to Sponsor My Parents and Grandparents?" Last
   modified 30 January 2020. https://www.cic.gc.ca/english/helpcentre
   /answer.asp?qnum=1445&top=14.
Jakubowski, Lisa. 1997. *Immigration and the Legalization of Racism*. Halifax:
   Fernwood Publishing.
Jenkins, Richard. 1994. "Rethinking Ethnicity: Identity, Categorization and
   Power." *Ethnic and Racial Studies* 17: 197–223. doi: 10.1080/01419870.1994
   .9993821.
Joas, Hans. 1996. *The Creativity of Action*. Cambridge: Polity Press.
Joppke, Christian. 1998. "Immigration Challenges the Nation-State." In
   Immigration in Western Europe and the United States, edited by Christian
   Joppke, 5–48. Oxford: Oxford University Press.
– 2005a. "Exclusion and the Liberal State: The Case of Immigration and
   Citizenship Policy." *European Journal of Social Theory* 8: 43–61. doi: 10.1177
   /1368431005049327.
– 2005b. *Selecting by Origin: Ethnic Migration in the Liberal State*. Cambridge,
   MA: Harvard University Press.
Kang, S. Deborah. 2017. *The INS on the Line: Making Immigration Law on the
   US-Mexico Border, 1917–1954*. New York: Oxford University Press.
Kaufman, Herbert. 2001. "Major Players: Bureaucracies in American
   Government." *Public Administration Review* 61 (1): 18–42. doi: 10.1111/0033
   -3352.00003.
Kelley, Ninette, and Michael Trebilcock. 2010. *The Making of the Mosaic:
   A History of Canadian Immigration Policy*. 2nd ed. Toronto: University of
   Toronto Press.
Kent, Tom. 1988. *A Public Purpose: An Experience of Liberal Opposition and
   Canadian Government*. Montreal: McGill-Queen's University Press.
Kertzer, David, and Dominique Arel, eds. 2002. *Census and Identity: The
   Politics of Race, Ethnicity, and Language in National Censuses*. Cambridge:
   Cambridge University Press.
Kilbourn, William. 1968. "The 1950s." In *Part One of the Canadians: 1867–1967*,
   edited by J. Careless and R.C. Brown. Toronto: The Macmillan Company.
Kilic, Sevgi, Switri Saharso, and Birgit Sauer. 2008. "Introduction: The Veil –
   Debating Citizenship, Gender and Religious Diversity." *Social Politics* 15 (4):
   397–410. doi: 10.1093/sp/jxn022.

Kim, Jaeeun. 2011. "Establishing Identity: Documents, Performance, and Biometric Information in Immigration Proceedings." *Law and Social Inquiry* 36: 760–86. doi: 10.1111/j.1747-4469.2011.01249.x.

Knowles, Valerie. 1997. *Strangers at Our Gates: Canadian Immigration and Immigration Policy, 1540–1997.* Toronto: Dundurn Press.

Kofman, Eleonore. 2010. "Family-Related Migration: A Critical Review of European Studies." *Journal of Ethnic and Migration Studies* 30: 243–62. doi: 10.1080/1369183042000200687.

– 2014. "Towards a Gendered Evaluation of (Highly) Skilled Immigration Policies in Europe." *International Migration* 52 (3): 116–28. doi: 10.1111/imig.12121.

Korteweg, Anna. 2003. "Welfare Reform and the Subject of the Working Mother: Get a Job, a Better Job, Then a Career." *Theory and Society* 32: 445–80. doi: 10.1023/A:1025525509540.

Korteweg, Anna, and Jennifer Elrick. 2014. *Citizenship Research Synthesis 2009–2013 – CERIS Research Synthesis Report.* Toronto: Centre of Excellence for Research on Immigration and Settlements.

Korteweg, Anna, and Triadafilos Triadafilopoulos. 2013. "Gender, Religion, and Ethnicity: Intersections and Boundaries in Immigrant Integration Policy Making." *Social Politics* 20 (1): 109–36. doi: 10.1093/sp/jxs027.

Korteweg, Anna, and Gökçe Yurdakul. 2014. *The Headscarf Debates: Conflicts of National Belonging.* Stanford: Stanford University Press.

Kushner, Tony. 2005. "Racialization and 'White European' Immigration to Britain." In *Racialization*, edited by Karim Murji and John Solomos, 207–25. Oxford: Oxford University Press.

Kymlicka, Will. 1995. *Multicultural Citizenship: A Liberal Theory of Minority Rights.* Oxford: Clarendon Press.

– 2017. "Multiculturalism without Citizenship?" In *Multicultural Governance in a Mobile World*, edited by Anna Triandafyllidou, 139–61. Edinburgh: Edinburgh University Press.

Lahav, Gallya, and Virginie Guiraudon. 2006. "Actors and Venues in Immigration Control: Closing the Gap between Political Demands and Policy Outcomes." *West European Politics* 29 (2): 201–23. doi: 10.1080/01402380500512551.

Lamont, Michèle. 1992. *Money, Morals, and Manners: The Culture of the French and American Upper-Middle Class.* Chicago: University of Chicago Press.

– 2000. *The Dignity of Working Men: Morality and the Boundaries of Race, Class, and Immigration.* Cambridge, MA: Russel Sage Foundation Books at Harvard University Press.

Lee, Catherine. 2013. *Fictive Kinship: Family Reunification and the Meaning of Race and Nation in American Immigration.* New York: Russell Sage Foundation.

– 2015. "Family Reunification and the Limits of Immigration Reform: Impact and Legacy of the 1965 Immigration Act." *Sociological Forum* 30 (S1): 528–48. doi: 10.1111/socf.12176.

Lenard, Patti, and Christine Straehle. 2012. "Introduction." In *Legislated Inequality: Temporary Labour Migration in Canada*, edited by Patti Lenard and Christine Straehle, 3–25. Montreal: McGill-Queen's University Press.

Liberal Party of Canada. 2019. *Forward: A Real Plan for the Middle Class*. Ottawa: Liberal Party of Canada.

Lightman, Naomi, and Jennifer Elrick. 2021. "Merit-Based Immigration Policies and Intersectional Inequalities: The Case of Canada, 1980–2016." Unpublished manuscript.

Lightman, Naomi, Rupa Banerjee, Ethel Tungohan, Conely de Leon, and Philip Kelly. 2021. "An Intersectional Pathway Penalty: Filipina Immigrant Women Inside and Outside Canada's Live-In Caregiver Program." *International Migration*. Online first. https://onlinelibrary.wiley.com/doi/full/10.1111/imig.12851.

Lipsky, Michael. (1980) 2010. *Street-Level Bureaucracy: Dilemmas of the Individual in Public Services*. Reprint, New York: Russell Sage Foundation.

Loveman, Mara. 1999. "Is 'Race' Essential?" *American Sociological Review* 64 (6): 891–8. doi: 10.2307/2657409.

– 2014. *National Colors: Racial Classification and the State in Latin America*. New York: Oxford University Press.

Madokoro, Laura. 2012. "'Slotting' Chinese Families and Refugees, 1947–1967." *The Canadian Historical Review* 93 (1): 25–56. doi: 10.3138/chr.93.1.25.

– 2016. *Elusive Refuge: Chinese Migrants in the Cold War*. Cambridge, MA: Harvard University Press.

Marshall, T.H. (1950) 1965. *Class, Citizenship, and Social Development: Essays by T.H. Marshall*. Garden City, NY: Anchor Books.

Mata, Fernando, and Ravi Pendakur. 2017. "Of Intake and Outcomes: Wage Trajectories of Immigrant Classes in Canada." *Journal of International Migration and Integration* 18 (3): 829–44. https://link.springer.com/article/10.1007/s12134-016-0501-1.

McPherson, Miller, Lynn Smith-Lovin, and James M Cook. 2001. "Birds of a Feather: Homophily in Social Networks." *Annual Review of Sociology* 27: 415–44. https://doi.org/10.1146/annurev.soc.27.1.415.

Menjivar, Cecilia. 2006. "Liminal Legality: Salvadoran and Guatemalan Immigrants' Lives in the United States." *American Journal of Sociology* 111 (4): 999–1037. doi: 10.1086/499509.

Meyer, John W., John Boli, George M. Thomas, and Francisco O. Ramirez. 1997. "World Society and the Nation-State." *American Journal of Sociology* 103 (1): 144–81. doi.org/10.1086/231174.

Miles, Robert. 1993. *Racism after "Race Relations."* New York: Routledge.

Miles, Robert, and M. Brown. 2003. *Racism*. London: Routledge.

Mohr, John, Christopher A. Bail, Margaret Frye, Jennifer C. Lena, Omar Lizardo, Terence E. McDonnell, Ann Mische, Iddo Tavory, and Frederick F. Wherry. 2020. *Measuring Culture*. New York: Columbia University Press.

Morgan, Kimberly, and Ann Shola Orloff. 2017. "Introduction: The Many Hands of the State." In *The Many Hands of the State: Theorizing Political Authority and Social Control*, edited by Kimberly Morgan and Ann Shola Orloff, 1–34. New York: Cambridge University Press.

Motomura, Hiroshi. 2014. *Immigration Outside the Law*. New York: Oxford University Press.

– 2015. "Looking for Immigration Law." *Ethnic and Racial Studies* 38 (8): 1305–11. doi: 10.1080/01419870.2015.1016073.

Muegge, Liza, and Sara de Jong. 2013. "Intersectionalizing European Politics: Bridging Gender and Ethnicity." *Politics, Groups, and Identities* 1 (3): 380–9. doi: 10.1080/21565503.2013.816247.

Mullally, Sasha, and David Wright. 2007. "La Grande Séduction? The Immigration of Foreign-Trained Physicians to Canada, c. 1954–76." *Journal of Canadian Studies/Revue d'études canadiennes* 41 (3): 67–89. doi: 10.3138 /jcs.41.3.67.

Murji, Karim, and John Solomos. 2005. "Introduction: Racialization in Theory and Practice." In *Racialization*, edited by Karim Murji and John Solomos, 1–27. Oxford: Oxford University Press.

Myrdahl, Eileen Muller. 2010. "Legislating Love: Norwegian Family Reunification Law as a Racial Project." *Social & Cultural Geography* 11 (2): 103–16. doi: 10.1080/14649360903514368.

Nobles, Melissa. 2000. *Shades of Citizenship: Race and the Census in Modern Politics*. Stanford: Stanford University Press.

OECD. 2019. *Recruiting Immigrant Workers: Canada 2019*. Paris: OECD.

OECD, ILO, IOM, and UNHCR. 2018. "G20 International Migration and Displacement Trends Report 2018." Paris: OECD.

Oreopoulos, Philip. 2011. "Why Do Skilled Immigrants Struggle in the Labor Market? A Field Experiment with Thirteen Thousand Resumes." *American Economic Journal: Economic Policy* 3 (4): 148–71. doi: 10.1257/pol.3.4.148.

Page, Edward C., and Bill Jenkins. 2005. *Policy Bureaucracy: Government with a Cast of Thousands*. Oxford: Oxford University Press.

Palmer, Howard. 1998. "Reluctant Hosts: Anglo-Canadian Views of Multiculturalism in the Twentieth Century." In *Readings in Canadian History: Post-Confederation*, edited by R.S. Francis and D.B. Smith, 125–39. Toronto: Harcourt & Brace Company.

Paquet, Mireille. 2015. "Bureaucrats as Immigration Policy-Makers: The Case of Subnational Immigration Activism in Canada." *Journal of Ethnic and Migration Studies* 41 (11): 1815–35. doi: 10.1080/1369183X.2015.1023185.

– 2019. "Immigration, Bureaucracies and Policy Formulation: The Case of Quebec." *International Migration* 58 (1): 166–81. doi: 10.1111/imig.12555.

Pellander, Saara. 2015. "'An Acceptable Marriage': Marriage Migration and Moral Gatekeeping in Finland." *Journal of Family Issues* 36 (11): 1472–89. doi: 10.1177/0192513X14557492.

– 2019. "Buy Me Love: Entanglements of Citizenship, Income and Emotions in Regulating Marriage Migration." *Journal of Ethnic and Migration Studies* Online first. doi: 10.1080/1369183X.2019.1625141.

Porter, John. (1965) 2015. *The Vertical Mosaic: An Analysis of Social Class and Power in Canada*. 50th Anniversary Edition. Toronto: University of Toronto Press.

Pratt, Anna. 2005. *Securing Borders: Detention and Deportation in Canada*. Vancouver: UBC Press.

Pratt, Anna, and Lorne Sossin. 2009. "A Brief Introduction of the Puzzle of Discretion." *Canadian Journal of Law and Society* 24 (3): 310–12. doi: 10.1017/S082932010001005X.

Preibisch, Kerry, and Jenna Hennebry. 2012. "Buy Local, Hire Glboal: Temporary Migration in Canadian Agriculture." In *Legislated Inequality: Temporary Labour Migration in Canada*, edited by Patti Lenard and Christine Straehle, 48–72. Montreal: McGill-Queen's University Press.

Reitz, Jeffrey. 2012. "The Distinctiveness of Canadian Immigration Experience." *Patterns of Prejudice* 46 (5): 518–38. doi: 10.1080/0031322X.2012.718168.

Reitz, Jeffrey, and Rupa Banerjee. 2007. "Racial Inequality, Social Cohesion and Policy Issues in Canada." In *Belonging? Diversity, Recognition and Shared Citizenship in Canada*, edited by Keith Banting, Thomas Courchene, and Leslie Seidle, 1–57. Montreal: Institute for Research on Public Policy.

Reitz, Jeffrey, Josh Curtis, and Jennifer Elrick. 2014. "Immigrant Skill Utilization: Trends and Policy Issues." *Journal of International Migration and Integration* 15 (1): 1–26. doi: 10.1007/s12134-012-0265-1.

Reitz, Jeffrey, Patrick Simon, and Emily Laxer. 2017. "Muslims' Social Inclusion and Exclusion in France, Québec, and Canada: Does National Context Matter?" *Journal of Ethnic and Migration Studies* 43 (15): 2473–98. doi: 10.1080/1369183X.2017.1313105.

Richmond, Anthony. 1988. "Sociological Theories of International Migration: The Case of Refugees." *Current Sociology* 36 (2): 7–25. doi: 10.1177/001139288036002004.

Ridgeway, Cecilia, and Sandra Nakagawa. 2015. "Status." In *Handbook of the Social Psychology of Inequality*, edited by Jane McLeod, Edward Lawler, and Michael Schwalbe, 3–25. New York: Springer.

Romero, Mary. 2008. "Crossing the Immigration and Race Border: A Critical Race Theory Approach to Immigration Studies." *Contemporary Justice Review* 11 (1): 23–37. https://doi.org/10.1080/10282580701850371.

Roy, Patricia. 2007. *The Triumph of Citizenship: The Japanese and Chinese in Canada, 1941–67*. Vancouver: UBC Press.

Saini, Angela. 2019. *Superior: The Return of Race Science*. Boston: Beacon Press.

Satzewich, Vic. 1989. "Racism and Canadian Immigration Policy: The Government's View of Caribbean Migration, 1962–1966." *Canadian Ethnic Studies* 21 (1): 77–97.

– 2014a. "Canadian Visa Officers and the Social Construction of 'Real' Spousal Relationships." *Canadian Review of Sociology* 51 (1): 1–21. doi: 10.1111/cars.12031.

– 2014b. "Visa Officers as Gatekeepers of a State's Borders: The Social Determinants of Discretion in Spousal Sponsorship Cases in Canada." *Journal of Ethnic and Migration Studies* 40 (9): 1450–69. doi: 10.1080/1369183X.2013.854162.

– 2015. *Points of Entry: How Canada's Immigration Officers Decide Who Gets In*. Vancouver: UBC Press.

Scheel, Stephan, and Miriam Gutekunst. 2019. "Studying Marriage Migration to Europe from Below: Informal Practices of Government, Border Struggles and Multiple Entanglements." *Gender, Place & Culture* 26 (6): 847–67. doi: 10.1080/0966369X.2018.1489375.

Schmidt, Vivien. 2002. *The Futures of European Capitalism*. Oxford: Oxford University Press.

– 2010. "Taking Ideas and Discourse Seriously: Explaining Change through Discursive Institutionalism as the Fourth 'New Institutionalism'." *European Political Science Review* 2: 1–25. doi: 10.1017/S175577390999021X.

Schneiderhan, Erik. 2011. "Pragmatism and Empirical Sociology: The Case of Jane Addams and Hull-House, 1989–1895." *Theory and Society* 40: 589–617. doi: 10.1007/s11186-011-9156-2.

Sciortino, Giuseppe. 2000. "Toward a Political Sociology of Entry Policies: Conceptual Problems and Theoretical Proposals." *Journal of Ethnic and Migration Studies* 26 (2): 213–28. doi: 10.1080/13691830050022776.

Scott, James C. 1998. *Seeing Like a State: How Certain Schemes to Improve the Human Condition Have Failed*. New Haven: Yale University Press.

Sen, Amartya. 2000. "Merit and Justice." In *Meritocracy and Economic Inequality*, edited by Kenneth Arrow, Samuel Bowles, and Steven Durlauf, 5–16. Princeton: Princeton University Press.

Shanahan, Brendan. 2014. "Enforcing the Colorline and Counting White Races: Race and the Census in North America, 1900–1941." *American Review of Canadian Studies* 44 (3): 293–307. doi: 10.1080/02722011.2014.939425.

Sharma, Nandita. 2006. *Home Economics: Nationalism and the Making of "Migrant Workers" in Canada*. Toronto: University of Toronto Press.

Simmons, Alan. 1999. "Immigration Policies: Imagined Futures." In *Immigrant Canada: Demographic, Economic, and Social Challenges*, edited by L. Driedger and S. Halli, 21–50. Toronto: University of Toronto Press.

Simon, Patrick. 2008. "The Choice of Ignorance: The Debate on Ethnic and Racial Statistics in France." *French Politics, Culture & Society* 26 (1): 7–31. doi: 10.3167/fpcs.2008.260102.

Skrentny, John. 2002. *The Minority Rights Revolution*. Cambridge: Belknap Press of Harvard University Press.

– 2006. "Policy-Elite Perceptions and Social Movement Success: Understanding Variations in Group Inclusion in Affirmative Action." *American Journal of Sociology* 111: 1762–815. https://doi.org/10.1086/499910.

Slaven, Mike, and Christina Boswell. 2019. "Why Symbolise Control? Irregular Migration to the UK and Symbolic Policy-Making in the 1960s." *Journal of Ethnic and Migration Studies* 45 (9): 1477–95. doi: 10.1080/1369183X .2018.1459522.

Smith, Anthony. 1998. *Nationalism and Modernism: A Critical Survey of Recent Theories of Nations and Nationalism*. London: Routledge.

Spade, Dean. 2013. "Intersectional Resistance and Law Reform." *Signs: Journal of Women in Culture and Society* 38 (4): 1031–55. doi: 10.1086/669574.

Starr, Paul. 1992. "Social Categories and Claims in the Liberal State." *Social Research* 59 (2): 263–95. https://www.jstor.org/stable/40970693.

Statistics Canada. 2013. "Obtaining Canadian Citizenship: National Household Survey (NHS), 2011 NHS Brief." Catalogue no. 99-010-X2011003. Ottawa: Statistics Canada.

– 2015. "Low Income Lines, 2013–2014." In Income Research Paper Series No. 75F0002M. Ottawa: Statistics Canada.

– 2017a. "The Daily – Distribution of Foreign-Born Population, by Region of Birth, Canada, 1987 to 2036." https://www.statcan.gc.ca/eng/dai/btd /othervisuals/other009.

– 2017b. "The Daily: Immigration and Ethnocultural Diversity – Key Results from the 2016 Census." https://www150.statcan.gc.ca/n1/daily -quotidien/171025/dq171025b-eng.htm.

Staver, Anne. 2015. "Hard Work for Love: The Economic Drift in Norwegian Family Immigration and Integration Policies." *Journal of Family Issues* 36 (11): 1453–71. doi: 10.1177/0192513X14557491.

Steensland, Brian. 2006. "Cultural Categories and the American Welfare State: The Case of Guaranteed Income Policy." *American Journal of Sociology* 111 (5): 1273–326. doi.org/10.1086/499508.

Steinmetz, George. 1999. "Introduction." In *State/Culture: State-Formation after the Cultural Turn*, edited by George Steinmetz, 1–49. Ithaca, NY: Cornell University Press.

Stewart, Emma. 2008. "Exploring the Asylum-Migration Nexus in the Context of Health Professional Migration." *Geoforum* 39: 223–35. doi: 10.1016 /j.geoforum.2007.04.002.

Swidler, Ann. 1986. "Culture in Action: Symbols and Strategies." *American Sociological Review* 51 (2): 273–86. https://www.jstor.org/stable/2095521.

Thompson, Debra. 2016. *The Schematic State: Race, Transnationalism, and the Politics of the Census.* Cambridge: Cambridge University Press.

Tichenor, Daniel. 2002. *Dividing Lines: The Politics of Immigration Control in America.* Princeton: Princeton University Press.

Tichenor, Daniel, and Robin Jacobson. 2020. "Tenuous Belonging: Diversity, Power, and Identity in the U.S. Southwest." *Journal of Ethnic and Migration Studies* 46 (12): 2480–96. doi: 10.1080/1369183X.2018.1561060.

Tilly, Charles. 1999. "Epilogue: Now Where?" In *State/Culture: State-Formation after the Cultural Turn,* edited by George Steinmetz, 407–19. Ithaca, NY: Cornell University Press.

Triadafilopoulos, Triadafilos. 2012. *Becoming Multicultural: Immigration and the Politics of Membership in Canada and Germany.* Vancouber: UBC Press.

Tungohan, Ethel, Rupa Banerjee, Wayne Chu, Petronila Cleto, Conely de Leon, Mila Garcia, Philip Kelly, Marco Luciano, Cynthia Palmaria, and Christopher Sorio. 2015. "After the Live-In Caregiver Program: Filipina Caregivers' Experiences of Graduated and Uneven Citizenship." *Canadian Ethnic Studies* 47 (1): 87–105. doi: 10.1353/ces.2015.0008.

UNESCO. 1950. *The Race Question.* Paris: UNESCO. https://unesdoc.unesco.org/ark:/48223/pf0000128291.

van Walsum, Sarah Katherine. 2009. *The Family and the Nation: Dutch Family Migration Policies in the Context of Changing Family.* Newcastle: Cambridge Scholars.

Walby, Sylvia. 2011. "Is the Knowledge Society Gendered?" *Gender, Work and Organization* 18 (11): 1–29. doi: 10.1111/j.1468-0432.2010.00532.x.

Wallerstein, Immanuel Maurice. 1991. "Social Conflict in Post-Independence Black Africa: The Concepts of Race and Status-Group Reconsidered." In *Race, Nation, Class,* edited by Etienne Balibar and Immanuel Maurice Wallerstein, 187–203. London: Verso.

Warman, Casey, Matthew Webb, and Christopher Worswick. 2019. "Immigrant Category of Admission and the Earnings of Adults and Children: How Far Does the Apple Fall?" *Journal of Population Economics* 32 (1): 53–112. https://link.springer.com/article/10.1007/s00148-018-0700-5.

Weber, Max. 2007a. "Class, Status, Party." In *From Max Weber,* edited by Hans Heinrich Gerth and C. Wright Mills, 180–95. New York: Routledge.

– 2007b. "Politics as a Vocation." In *From Max Weber,* edited by Hans Heinrich Gerth and C. Wright Mills, 77–128. New York: Routledge.

Whitaker, Reg. 1987. *Double Standard: The Secret History of Canadian Immigration.* Toronto: Lester & Orpen Dennys Limited.

Whitford, Josh. 2002. "Pragmatism and the Untenable Dualism of Means and Ends: Why Rational Choice Theory Does Not Deserve Pradigmatic Privilege." *Theory and Society* 31 (3): 325–63. doi: 10.1023/A:1016232404279.

Wilson, James Q. 1980. "The Politics of Regulation." In *The Politics of Regulation*, edited by James Q. Wilson, 357–94. New York: Basic Books.

Wimmer, Andreas. 2008. "The Making and Unmaking of Ethnic Boundaries: A Multilevel Process Theory." *American Journal of Sociology* 113: 970–1022. doi: 10.1086/522803

Winter, Elke. 2014a. *Becoming Canadian: Making Sense of Recent Changes to Citizenship Rules*. IRPP Study No. 44 Montreal: Institute for Research on Public Policy.

– 2014b. "What Can Weberian Sociology Tell Us about Multiculturalism and Religion?" In *Multiculturalism and Religious Identity: Canada and India*, edited by Sonya Sikka and Lori Beaman, 189–208. Montreal: McGill-Queen's University Press.

– 2015. "Rethinking Multiculturalism after its "Retreat": Lessons from Canada." *American Behavioral Scientist* 59 (6): 637–57. doi: 10.1177 /0002764214566495.

– 2021. "Multicultural Citizenship for the Highly Skilled? Naturalization, Human Capital, and the Boundaries of Belonging in Canada's Middle-Class Nation-Building." *Ethnicities* 21 (2): 289–310. doi: 10.1177 /1468796820965784.

Wolgin, Philip. 2013. "Re-Forming the Gates: Postwar Immigration Policy in the United States through the Hart-Celler Act of 1965." In *Wanted and Welcome? Immigrants, Minorities, Politics and Policy*, edited by Triadafilos Triadafilopoulos, 61–81. New York: Springer.

Wolgin, Philip, and Irene Bloemraad. 2010. "'Our Gratitude to Our Soldiers': Military Spouses, Family Re-Unification, and Postwar Immigration Reform." *Journal of Interdisciplinary History* 41 (I): 27–60. doi.org/10.1162 /jinh.2010.41.1.27.

Woodsworth, James S. 1909. *Strangers within Our Gates, or, Coming Canadians*. Toronto: F.C. Stephenson.

Wray, Helena. 2006. "An Ideal Husband? Marriages of Convenience, Moral Gate-Keeping and Immigration to the UK." *European Journal of Migration and Law* 8 (3): 303–20. doi: 10.1163/157181606778882582.

– 2009. "Moulding the Migrant Family." *Legal Studies* 29 (4): 592–618. doi: 10.1111/j.1748-121X.2009.00132.x.

Young, Michael. (1958) 2017. *The Rise of the Meritocracy*. New York: Routledge.

Yuval-Davis, Nira. 1997. *Gender & Nation*. London: Sage.

Yuval-Davis, Nira, Floya Anthias, and Eleonore Kofman. 2005. "Secure Borders and Safe Haven and the Gendered Politics of Belonging: Beyond Social Cohesion." *Ethnic and Racial Studies* 28 (3): 513–35. doi: 10.1080 /0141987042000337867.

Zolberg, Aristide. 1999. "Matters of State: Theorizing Immigration Policy." In *The Handbook of International Migration: The American Experience*, edited by

Charles Hirschman, Philip Kasinitz, and Josh DeWind, 71–93. New York: Russell Sage Foundation.

– 2006. *A Nation by Design: Immigration Policy in the Fashioning of America*. New York: Russell Sage Foundation and Harvard University Press.

Zolberg, Aristide R., and Long Litt Woon. 1999. "Why Islam Is Like Spanish: Cultural Incorporation in Europe and the United States." *Politics and Society* 27 (1): 5–38. doi: 10.1177/0032329299027001002.

Index

Note: Page numbers in *italics* denote figures and numbers in **bold** denote tables.

"Canadian Indians," 78, 90. *See also*
Indigenous peoples (Canada)
Canadian Pacific Railway (CPR), 52
Canadian Welfare Council, 122
Carstensen, Martin, 76–7
case processing. *See* immigration
policy implementation
CBA. *See* Chinese Benevolent
Association (CBA)
CCL. *See* Canadian Congress of
Labour (CCL)
censuses: and discrimination,
173; and nation-building, 55–7,
78, 88
chain migration. *See* seed
immigration model
Chinese Benevolent Association
(CBA), 26–7
Chinese immigrants: admission of,
5–6, 46, 88, 92, 95–6, 103, 122, 141;
adoptions, 124–7; in Canadian
immigration policy, 6, 28, 46, 52,
120, 135; in deportation appeals,
97; group-level perceptions of,
6, 33, 119, 121, 123, 131–2, 137;
lobbying efforts, 34; orphaned
children (Hong Kong), 129–30.
See also Asian; Asian immigrants;
Chinese Benevolent Association
(CBA)
Chinese Immigration Act, 6, 52
citizenship: and border control,
58–9, 169; "citizen outsiders," 173;
citizenship test, 168; and family
sponsorship, 147–8; "human
capital citizenship," 168. *See also*
multiculturalism; naturalization
class. *See* social class
Cold War, influence on immigrant
exclusion, 33–4, 187n16
Commonwealth, and Canadian
immigration policy, 33, 55, 83–4,
108–9

Cook-Martín, David, 4, 32, 33, 35,
38–9, 60
CPR. *See* Canadian Pacific Railway
(CPR)
cultural capital: defined, 190n18; in
immigrant admissions, 17, 79, 80,
153, 184
cultural repertoires: defined,
16, 74–5, 152, 189n13. *See also*
boundary work; cultural sociology
of immigration policy
cultural schemas, relation to cultural
repertoires, 189n13
cultural sociology of immigration
policy: as analytical framework,
13, 16–17, 74–7, 153, 154; applied
to the Canadian case (overview),
17–18, 77–80, 152–3; boundary
work mechanism defined,
16, 75–6; cultural repertoires
mechanism defined, 16, 74–5;
institutionalization mechanism
defined, 16–17, 76; "recasting"
mechanism defined, 16, 76–7, 79

Dauvergne, Catherine, 156–7, 162
decolonialization: and change in
normative context, 4, 53, 54; and
discrediting of discriminatory
policies, 4, 55
Department of Citizenship and
Immigration: Assisted Passage
Loan Scheme, 193n24; Department
of Manpower and Immigration
(re-naming), 20, 40, 184; economic
pressures on, 32; employee
demographics, 21; foreign policy
pressures on, 32–3, 107–10,
152–3; organizational structure
(historical), 21–4; perspective
on immigration management,
39–42; provision of settlement
services (historical), 162–3;

relationship to RCMP, 33; as target of lobbying efforts, 26–7, 34. *See also* deportation appeals; high-level immigration bureaucrats; immigration policy formulation; order-in-council admissions; street-level bureaucrats

Department of Manpower and Immigration. *See* Department of Citizenship and Immigration

dependents, in Canadian immigration policy (contemporary), 159–60, 163–4. *See also* 1967 immigration regulations; family; family immigration; nominated relative (1967 entry category); sponsored dependents (1967 entry category)

deportation appeals: administrative procedure, 47; boundary work in, 70, 73, 75, 78, 98–103, 113; case summaries, 96–8, 188n20; description of archival records, 47–8, 178, 183; as object of study, 181. *See also* Immigration Appeal Board (IAB); immigration policy implementation

Diefenbaker, John, 129, 146, 184

discursive institutionalism, 13, 76, 190n15

Dominion Bureau of Statistics, 56

economic capital, 184; defined, 190n16. *See also* boundary work; cultural capital; social capital; social class

economic immigration: blue-collar immigrants, 157; Canadian Experience Class (CEC), 93, 174, 203n27; Federal Skilled Worker Program (FSWP), 93, 103, 159, 164–5, 174, 203n26, 203n27; independent immigrants (1967

entry category), 30, 106–7, 145; Live-In Caregiver program (LIC), 61, 165, 204n28; Non-Immigrant Employment Authorization Program (NIEAP), 60; nurses, 83, 104, 110–11, 155; Seasonal Agricultural Worker Program (SAWP), 61; skilled workers admissions, 17, 30, 92–6, 104–5, 110–11, 165; skill measurements, 30–1, 143, **144**; Temporary Foreign Worker Program (TFWP), 61; tradespeople, 30, 98, **144**, 158; unskilled immigrants, 78, 107, 135, 137 141, 143, **144**, 146, 147, 158, 180. *See also* 1962 immigration regulations; 1967 immigration regulations; gender; merit; merit-based immigration policy; points system

education, requirements in Canadian immigration policy, 28, 29, 30–1, 32, 40, 59, 93, 105, 106, 142, 143, **144**, 145, 147, 158. *See also* boundary work; cultural capital; economic immigration; human capital; merit; social class

Ellermann, Antje, 33, 66, 72, 73, 168

entry categories (contemporary), 164–6, 174–5, 203n26, 203n27. *See also* admissions; gender; immigration policy; intersectionality

Ethnic Diversity Survey, 172

ethnicity, use as a term, 51, 54, 56, 87

European, Western Hemisphere immigrants, 15, 18, 51, 58, 85–6, 88–90

exceptional merit. *See* merit

Fairclough, Ellen, 146

family: normative definitions in immigration policy, 116, 118, 120,

Holocaust, and discrediting of
discriminatory immigration
policies, 4, 31–2, 53, 54. *See also*
Jewish immigrants, exclusion of
homophily principle, in family
immigration, 134
Hong Kong: admissions from, 92,
96, 125, 126, 127, 132–3, 141; and
Canadian immigration policy, 28,
129–30. *See also* Asian immigrants;
Chinese immigrants
human capital: and gender, 165–6;
"human capital citizenship,"
168; in immigration policy
(Canadian), 19, 30, 32, 84, 112, 168;
in immigration policy (general),
3, 58, 59, 91, 118, 168; and indirect
racial discrimination, 61. *See also*
economic immigration; merit;
merit-based immigration policy

imagined community: and
family, 117; in immigration
policy (Canadian), 169. *See also*
multiculturalism; national identity,
Canadian; nation-building
Immigration and Naturalization
Service (INS), 10, 66
Immigration Appeal Board (IAB),
26, 47, 96, 148. *See also* deportation
appeals
immigration appeals, ministerial
discretion in, 26
immigration bureaucrats. *See* high-
level immigration bureaucrats;
street-level bureaucrats
immigration policy formulation:
defined, 10, 81; cultural factors
in, 13, 40–1; economic factors in,
13, 32, 40, 52, 83, 157–9; foreign
policy and, 4, 32–4; ideas in, 76–7;
immigration bureaucrats and,

10–12, 24, 42–8, 67–71, 73–4, 151–2;
implementation as formulation,
11–12, 42, 58, 70–1, 73–4, 110, 112,
123, 153–4, 180; institutionalist
theories of, 64–5; nation-building
and, 3, 8, 36, 50, 51–2, 62, 88;
normative contexts and, 4, 31–2;
organized interests and, 34;
Parliament and, 154–8; pluralist
theories of, 63–4; and pragmatist
theories of action, 70; state-
centred theories of, 65–7. *See also*
cultural sociology of immigration
policy; deportation appeals;
intersectionality; order-in-council
admissions
immigration policy implementation:
absence from historical analyses,
38–9; archival data on, 14–15,
46–8, 180–2; cultural factors in, 71;
family norms in, 25, 116–18, 120–2,
127, 131, 142; and immigrant
exclusion, 5, 24–5, 35–8, 72–3,
113, 116; and immigrant inclusion,
150, 171; as immigration policy
formulation, 11–12, 42, 58, 70–1,
73–4, 110, 123, 153–4, 180; macro-
level organizational factors in, 66,
71–2; moral assessments in, 12–13,
73, 75, 96; personal attitudes/role
conceptions, 72; routine of practice
in, 123–9. *See also* deportation
appeals; high-level immigration
bureaucrats; intersectionality;
merit; order-in-council
admissions
independent immigrants (1967 entry
category), 30, 106–7, 145. *See also*
1967 immigration regulations;
economic immigration
Indigenous peoples (Canada), 51, 53,
90. *See also* "Canadian Indians"

www.ingramcontent.com/pod-product-compliance
Lightning Source LLC
Chambersburg PA
CBHW030241030426
42336CB00009B/206